OXFORD ENGLISH FOR CAREERS

FINANCE

Richard Clark and David Baker

Student's Book

OXFORD
UNIVERSITY PRESS

Contents

1 Choosing jobs

Countdown

1 Read the profiles of people talking about their jobs in finance. Match the profiles a–h with the jobs 1–8.

1 an equity trader _____a_____

2 a customer advisor in a bank _____

3 an insurance broker _____

4 an accountant _____

5 an investment banker _____

6 an auditor _____

7 a company treasurer _____

8 an analyst _____

2 Work in pairs. Which of the jobs in **1**

- appeals to you the most?
- requires the longest training?
- is the most stressful?
- is the best paid?

3 What are you looking for in a job? Which **four** of these features are most important to you? Rank the features 1–4 (1= most important).

- to work in a local company near my home ☐
- to work in a large international company ☐
- to work long hours, but get a big salary ☐
- to have evenings and weekends free ☐
- to work directly with customers and the public ☐
- to work with statistics and tables ☐
- to work with companies' financial accounts ☐
- to work on the financial markets ☐
- to have a lot of responsibility early in my career ☐

4 Work in groups of three or four. Explain your choices to your partners and decide together which of the jobs in **1** would suit each of you the best.

The world of global finance

a 'I buy and sell shares on the stock market in New York.'
Louise Plotkin, New York

c 'I have to investigate company accounts to check if they are true and accurate.'
Jose Matos de Selva, Barcelona

d 'I manage the daily cash flow of the company.'
Natalia Welter, Munich

f 'I analyse companies and sectors and I forecast trends in the economy.'
Olga Zubkov, Moscow

h 'I advise customers on the best place to find insurance for their car or flat.'
Hiromi Osawa, Osaka

b 'I advise companies about mergers, finance, and raising money from investors.'
Raoul Lopez, São Paulo

e 'In my job I serve customers who come into the branch to withdraw cash or open accounts.'
Laurent Rousselet, Ivory Coast

g 'I help companies to prepare accounts and advise on tax.'
Hussein Ali Habib, Oman

In this unit
- jobs in the finance sector
- skills you need for different jobs
- question types
- why choose a career in finance?
- preparing for an interview and writing a covering letter

Vocabulary

Describing a job

Look at the groups of verbs in **2** that people use to describe their jobs in finance.

1 Work in pairs. Discuss the differences in their meaning. Look at examples of how they are used and which words they are used with in a dictionary like the *Oxford Advanced Learner's Dictionary*.

2 Complete the sentences with the best verb.

In my job I have to ...

advise	answer	serve

1 _____ customers on their choice of financial products

2 _____ customers who need cash or to make payments

3 _____ telephone enquiries

analyse	forecast	set

4 _____ what will happen to consumer demand for the next twelve months

5 _____ the financial results for last year

6 _____ a budget for spending in each department

borrow	issue	lend	raise

7 _____ shares or bonds

8 _____ capital by issuing shares on the financial markets

9 _____ money to customers

10 _____ money from the banks in short-term loans

investigate	manage	prepare

11 _____ the accounts at the end of each quarter

12 _____ the accounts to check for accuracy

13 _____ the cash in our current accounts.

3 Now, using the verbs in the boxes below, complete the two job adverts from an Internet website for financial recruitment.

advise	answer	borrow	investigate
lend	manage	prepare	serve

An exciting opportunity has arisen at one of the UK's largest banks within a lively call centre environment on the inbound / outbound customer service department.

As a customer relationship trainee, you will have to _____ [1] customers who want to carry out transactions, _____ [2] questions, and _____ [3] them on the right products to suit their needs. The work involves making quick decisions about customers who want to _____ [4] money on their credit cards and deciding who to _____ [5] money to by using our credit check systems. NO COLD CALLING INVOLVED!!

Supporting our marketing division, you will have to _____ [6] reports on internal errors and _____ [7] customer complaints plus _____ [8] a database of customer usage.

Previous call centre / sales experience is preferred, but not essential, as full training is provided.

If you are interested in the above role, please call immediately on 0234 326 7635.

---

advise	manage	raise	set

International opportunities for young graduate accountants to train in a multinational accountancy team. Working in São Paulo, Brazil, you will be responsible for advising international companies on their operations in the country. Key tasks include presenting solutions to clients on

how to _____ [9] cash flow more efficiently

how to _____ [10] capital from the banks

how to _____ [11] budgets and implement control systems

how to _____ [12] clients on better tax planning.

Financial markets

If you own **shares** (UK) or **stocks** (USA), you own a part of a company and 'share' in its profits when they pay **dividends**. Traders buy and sell shares on **stock markets** or **equity markets** like Wall Street.

If you own **bonds**, you own a part of a government or company's debt. Bonds usually pay a fixed interest, **the yield**, for example, for ten years.

Which investment is safer? Which do you think gives the best long-term return?

It's my job

1 Look at the list of qualities that could be important to work in financial markets. Mark them VI (very important), QI (quite important), or NI (not important). Then compare your answers in pairs.

1 having a lot of experience in business or finance _____ ☐
2 being able to get on well with your clients _____ ☐
3 being good at working in a team _____ ☐
4 being good at socializing _____ ☐
5 being good at listening to and remembering information _____ ☐
6 being able to think quickly _____ ☐
7 being good at taking risks _____ ☐

2 Now read an interview with Jilly Atkins, a bond trader who works in the debt markets, buying and selling government debt. Tick (✓) the qualities in **1** that she mentions.

3 Read the interview again and write T (true) or F (false).

1 Jilly chose her job mainly because of the salary.
2 Nearly all the trading takes place outside the office.
3 Clients normally prefer to deal with just one bank.
4 Traders need to have an excellent memory.
5 Traders often make a big profit on a single deal.

Webquest

Go on the Internet to find this information.

1 Who are the best international companies to work for in finance? Look for companies who win international awards for 'best places to work' or companies who come out best in international comparisons. Try *www.ft.com* as a starting point.

2 Make a list of the best four companies you have found and their best features. Work together and tell the group the results of your research. Decide together what you need to consider when choosing a company to work for.

Jilly Atkins

Before you got your job, did you study business or finance at college?
No, actually, I didn't. In fact, when I applied for my first job, I really had no experience in finance. I just looked on the Internet to see which finance jobs paid the best. I saw that as a bond trader you could earn £100,000 after only two years in the job. So I decided that was the job for me!

What skills and qualities were they looking for?
I hope I impressed them. You definitely need good personal skills in this job because everything depends on contacts. You have to be good on the telephone so people want to call you with a deal. But it's not only in the office. If you want to make a lot of money, you also have to socialize and network with clients at night. That means lots of eating in restaurants. That's where you hear the best news. You're always competing with other banks for the same business so you have to keep the clients very happy. It's fun, but hard work.

It's a very demanding job. Do you work a long day?
Yes, I do. We start work every day at 7.00 a.m. We have to go to the morning briefing, when the analysts tell us about information in the news that is important for prices. Then the head of the division explains the strategy for the day. We begin to call people at 7.40 and the markets open at 8.00 when we make the first deals. The phone never stops and we have to keep a lot of information in our heads.

How much money are you dealing in?
We are trading in tens of millions and that means you can't make any mistakes. The profit on a deal is so small that we have to trade in very large quantities to make money. So the ability to think fast and decide things quickly is essential.

I think I know what you will say to this question ...
Is your job interesting?
Yes, of course, it's absolutely fascinating.

● Language spot
Question types

1 Look at these questions the interviewer asks Jilly. Which ones can she answer *yes* or *no*?

1 Before you got your job, did you study business or finance at college?
2 What skills and qualities were they looking for?
3 Do you work a long day?
4 How much money are you dealing in?
5 Is your job interesting?

How are *yes* / *no* questions different from information questions?

>> Go to **Language reference** p.119

2 Make these statements into *yes* / *no* questions.

1 You can earn a lot.

_____

2 An insurance broker works with insurance policies.

_____

3 They work for Paribas.

_____

4 She is an analyst.

_____

5 I have to socialize with clients.

_____

6 The share price could rise considerably.

_____

3 Ask information questions to get the answers below.

1 Q:_____
 A: They sell a range of insurance products.
2 Q:_____
 A: She earns £50,000 a year.
3 Q:_____
 A: We have ten branches in Spain.
4 Q:_____
 A: It takes two years to train as a broker.
5 Q:_____
 A: I decided to become an accountant because I love working with numbers.

4 Work in pairs.

Student A, choose a finance job, but don't tell your partner what your job is. Answer your partner's questions with only 'yes' or 'no'.

Student B, guess what Student A's job is by asking them *yes* / *no* questions. This means you can only ask them questions like *Do you work in a bank?* and NOT ~~*Where do you work?*~~.

When you have finished, do it again, but this time Student A has to guess what Student B's job is. The person who guesses their partner's job with the fewest questions wins.

Pronunciation
Intonation in questions

1 🎧 Listen to these questions.

1 Is your office in London?
2 Where do you work?
3 Can you earn a lot?
4 How much can you earn?
5 Do you work for Paribas?
6 Who do you work for?

● The intonation at the end of questions 1, 3, and 5 goes **up** because they are closed (*yes* / *no*) questions.

● The intonation at the end of questions 2, 4, and 6 goes **down** because they are open (*Wh-*) information questions.

2 Decide what kind of questions these are: closed or open. Then say them to your partner.

1 What did you study at university?
2 Do you work at weekends?
3 Is your job well paid?
4 Does your job involve a lot of travel?
5 Why did you decide to work in finance?
6 How many people work in your company?

3 🎧 Listen and check. Practise saying them again, using the right intonation for each question type.

comparative analysis (*n*) a study of the financial figures of a company in relation to similar companies in the same sector. Often shortened to 'a comp' in investment banking.

loan application (*n*) a request by a company to borrow money from a bank

merger (*n*) the act of joining two or more businesses or organizations into one

spreadsheet (*n*) a computer program that is used, for example, when doing financial or project planning

Reading

What can you expect from a career in banking?

You are going to read two reports from a university magazine on careers in banking. Helen works in the corporate finance department of an investment bank and Angus is a customer service advisor in a retail bank.

1 Discuss these questions in pairs.

1 What do you think each job involves?

2 What skills do you think each job needs?

2 Work in pairs and complete the questions below.

1 Who _____ work for?

2 When (start) _____ in the morning?

3 What sort of skills _____ need?

4 What tasks _____ in the office?

5 What kind of reports _____?

6 How many customers _____ each day?

7 How much _____ earn?

8 How often _____ meetings?

9 How many hours _____ in a day?

10 How long (take) _____ get home?

3 Student A, go to p.108 and read the text about Angus. Student B, read the text about Helen opposite. Find the answers to the reporter's questions in **2**.

4 Student A, you are the reporter. Interview Helen and ask her about her job.

Student B, you are Helen. Answer your partner's questions and tell them about your job.

Now change roles: Student A, you are Angus. Student B, you are the reporter.

5 Now work together and find the words in the two texts to match the definitions.

Someone who ...

1 has finished university is a _____.

2 is starting in a company is _____.

3 works well with customers has _____.

4 doesn't make mistakes is _____.

5 works well with other colleagues is a _____.

6 is enthusiastic about their job is _____.

Helen Marshall (2003–06)
Analyst, Morgan Straits

If you join an investment bank as a graduate trainee, you can expect to work long hours. It's part of the culture.

My day starts at about 8.00 a.m. when I check my email and voicemail to see who wants information immediately. It can continue until about 1.00 in the morning if we are working on a big merger. Fortunately, I live only twenty minutes from the bank. I usually get my main work from my boss at the daily team meeting at 10 o'clock, which can be a comparative analysis of companies or completing a report on a loan application for a big company.

As an analyst, you need to be good at statistics because you spend a lot of the day working at the computer on tables or spreadsheets. It's also important to be well organized and a good team player because you depend on your colleagues to meet deadlines.

It is a very exciting job because you learn very quickly and they are good at giving you training – I have already done courses on how to value companies and on accountancy. But there is not much chance of meeting with customers, so you can feel isolated at times. After a year, I still love the excitement of the job and the salary is great, £40,000. But if you are thinking of joining an investment bank, make sure you are well motivated and good at computer skills before you start.

The biggest investment banks, the 'bulge bracket', are mainly based in New York – banks like Morgan Stanley, JP Morgan Chase, Goldman Sachs, Merrill Lynch. But which is the best to work in? Goldman Sachs is usually top in M&A advisory work, but who is the best in bond trading? For profiles of the companies, try *Hoovers Online*.

Listening

Reasons for going into finance

1 🎧 Listen to three people talk about why they chose to go into finance. Match the people with their jobs 1–3 and their main motivations a–c.

Toshi

Daniella

Abdullah

Person	Job	Motivation
Toshi	1 investment banker	a to help their country
Daniella	2 accountant	b to work mainly on figures
Abdullah	3 bank manager	c to be independent

2 🎧 Listen again and write T (true) or F (false).

Toshi

1 became an accountant after he left university
2 didn't like his first job
3 is motivated by the reaction of his clients
4 works from home rather than going to the office.

Daniella

5 came to UK because she spoke good English
6 had one interview that lasted twenty minutes
7 works long hours so she doesn't like the training
8 is no longer stressed by giving presentations.

Abdullah

9 was a hard-working student at university
10 was influenced to study finance by his friends
11 was frightened of going to the UK to study
12 wants to make money by starting a business.

3 The three people describe what motivated them to choose a career in finance. Work in pairs. Make a list of other motivations people might have.

● Language spot

Present Simple v Present Continuous

1 Look at these sentences.

*I **am** well organized.*
*I **start** work at 9.00 a.m.*
*I **work** for an insurance company.*
*This week, I **am preparing** a report for my manager.*
*In my country, the markets **close** at 5.00 p.m.*
*We **are not receiving** any mail due to the current postal strike.*

Complete the rules with *Present Simple* or *Present Continuous*.

1 We use the _____ to talk about our skills and abilities.
2 We use the _____ to talk about daily routines.
3 We use the _____ to talk about what we are doing 'now' or what is happening 'now'.
4 We use the _____ to talk about facts.
5 We use the _____ to talk about temporary situations and arrangements.

2 Jilly Atkins, the bond trader, receives a call from another broker. Complete the dialogue using the correct form of the verbs in brackets.

Ed Hi, Jilly. *Are you having* [1] (you / have) a busy day?

Jilly Of course. You know this job, Ed. There's always something going on. This morning the markets _____ [2] (go up), but I _____ [3] (lose) money on a dollar trade.

Ed What do you normally do for lunch? _____ [4] (you / have) it in the canteen?

Jilly Oh, I usually _____ [5] (go) to a restaurant, but today I _____ [6] (not do) anything special.

Ed _____ [7] (you / want) to meet up for lunch? I _____ [8] (have) a few ideas I want to talk about. I've heard the Japanese government _____ [9] (think) about changing its policy on currency reserves. Usually, they _____ [10] (buy) dollars, but now they _____ [11] (begin) to move into euros. It could be interesting.

» Go to **Language reference** p.119

Preparing for an interview

Candidates often fail an interview because they haven't done their preparation. So, use a mind map to help you.

- In the centre of a piece of paper, write the word *interviewer*.
- Think of six questions they may ask you. Put each in a circle around the interviewer.
- Draw a line from each circle and note down how you will answer the question.
- Draw a box under the notes and write one example from your experience.

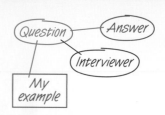

Writing

A covering letter

When you apply for a job, you normally send a **CV** and a **covering letter**.

1 Complete the covering letter by choosing the correct verbs. (Use the explanations in *Language spot* on p.9.)

> Ms M Wilson
> JBD Bank
> 56 Cheapside
> LONDON EC4Y 2WD
> 23 June 20—
>
> Dear Ms Wilson,
>
> I *write / am writing*[1] to apply for the job of customer advisor, as advertised on your website on 13 June (reference WRF/236).
>
> I *am / am being*[2] numerate, I *have / am having*[3] good personal skills, and I am very interested in banking. I *like / am liking*[4] contact with customers and I am good at communicating with people.
>
> As you can see from my CV, I studied economics at school and I *now study / am now studying*[5] for a diploma in business studies. I *think / am thinking*[6] this gives me a good background for the job.
>
> I *currently work / am currently working*[7] part-time in a bookshop, so I *have / am having*[8] experience of dealing with customers and handling money. Every day I *prepare / am preparing*[9] the cash balance when we close the shop. Presently, during the holiday period, I *also help / am also helping*[10] my uncle with his accounts on the computer.
>
> I would be very pleased to have the opportunity to discuss this application further. You can contact me by email at: jsmith@meganet.com.
>
> I look forward to hearing from you.
>
> Yours sincerely,
>
> *James Smith*
>
> James Smith

2 Choose your favourite job from *Webquest* or the unit and write a covering letter to apply for it.

Professional skills

First impressions

Read the article and answer the questions.

1 Would you dress differently for an interview with a bank or a call centre?
2 What other ways can you make a good impression in the first minute?
3 What is the most interesting thing you like people to know about you?

When you are first interviewed for a job, make sure that in the first minute you make the right start: you have dressed correctly, arrived on time, shaken hands confidently, and made good eye contact.

In the first minute, people will judge you and it is important that there is no reason to have a negative feeling. 'I never give a job to someone who has made no effort to look clean and tidy,' says Jacqueline King, a recruitment manager in the private banking sector.

It is also very important that you prepare as much as possible before the interview by doing research on the company. 'I always ask a couple of general questions about my firm and the competition during an interview just to find out if the candidate is really interested in us,' remarks Robert Pitt, a partner with one of the big four accountancy firms.

Of course you are not the only person going for the position, so you should also try to do or say something that is a little different and which will help people remember you later. Make sure the conversation is not one-way. If you can smile from time to time, that is a good thing too!

The people who get the jobs are enthusiastic, honest, well presented, and lucky. So if you don't get the first job you apply for, keep on trying.

Speaking

Presenting your skills to an employer

In a job interview, you have to explain why you want to do a job and why you would be good at it.

Work in groups of three or four.

1 Choose your favourite job from the unit. Prepare to explain to the others why you want the job. Use the *Useful language* below to help you think of ideas. Tell the others just the name of the job you have chosen.

2 Prepare at least six questions to ask the other members of your group about their job choices. Use the *Useful topics* below and different types of question from *Language spot* on p.7. **Three** questions must be information / open *Wh-* questions and **three** must be *yes / no* questions.

3 One student presents their choice to the others, explaining why they want the job. The others are the interview panel who ask questions to see if the person is suitable. Take turns so that everyone presents.

Useful topics
- your education
- skills
- experience (with examples)
- motivation
- understanding of the job's needs
- what you can offer to an employer

Useful language
- I would like to be a ... because I want to ...
- In this job you need to ...
- I like / enjoy / am good at
  - analysing figures and data
  - selling things
  - working on computers
  - solving problems
  - working with people in a team.
- At the moment I am studying ...
- For me, the most important thing is ...
- I think this job will help me to ...
- I think a ... needs to be ...

Checklist

Assess your progress in this unit. Tick (✓) the statements which are true.

- [ ] I can talk about what a person does in their job
- [ ] I can talk about where and how they work
- [ ] I can ask a range of different questions about jobs in finance
- [ ] I can discuss what skills and qualities are needed for jobs in finance
- [ ] I can prepare for an interview and write a covering letter

Key words

Adjectives
accurate
numerate

Nouns
candidate
career
covering letter
deadline
equity trader
graduate
job application
motivation
skill
team player
training
trend

Verbs
advise
analyse
apply (for)
borrow
deal with
forecast
investigate
lend
serve

Look back through this unit. Find five more words or expressions that you think are useful.

2 Personal finance

Countdown

1 Look at the pictures. Match the services 1–7 with the photos a–g.

1 a cash machine
2 a high street bank
3 an online account
4 an insurance policy
5 a credit / debit card
6 a rental contract
7 a mortgage

2 How many ways can you

a borrow money?
b save money?
c pay for something in a store?
d pay your telephone bill?
e protect the things you own?

Vocabulary

What can you do with these services?

1 Make sentences from the three columns.

EXAMPLE

You can use *a cash machine to take out money from your account.*

You can use ...

a a cash machine	1 to borrow	A things in a store.
b a credit card	2 to save	B all your accounts at home.
c a home insurance policy	3 to buy	C money from your account.
d direct debit	4 to manage	D your bills automatically.
e a bank loan	5 to pay	E money and earn interest on it.
f an online account	6 to protect	F more than you have in your account.
g an overdraft facility	7 to spend	G money to buy a car.
h a deposit account	8 to take out	H your house against accidents.

2 How many of the services in **1** have you or your family used? Tell your partner about them.

3 Read the advertisement from SBA bank about their services. Complete the text with the prepositions *from*, *in*, *for*, *on*, or *into*.

SBA Bank

If you need to borrow money _____ [1] a bank, save money _____ [2] a deposit account, or even invest _____ [3] shares, why not try SBA?

Our accounts are simple to use and we are easy to find in any High Street. You can pay money _____ [4] a current account or withdraw money _____ [5] your account simply by visiting a branch or even online.

If you find you have spent too much _____ [6] shopping or you owe too much _____ [7] your credit card, you can always apply _____ [8] an overdraft.

So call into your local branch and join us.

It's my job

1 Discuss the questions in pairs or small groups.

1 What do you think are the advantages and disadvantages of working at night? Would you like to do it?
2 What kind of person do you think would want to work at night? Why?

2 Now read about Dave and compare what he says with your answers.

Dave Sweetman

Only a few years ago banks closed every day at 3.30 and there were no cash machines. In today's world, we expect to access our banks 24 hours a day. But who are the people who make this possible? Our reporter visits the 24-hour call centre of a British bank and talks to Dave Sweetman about the life of a night worker.

Why do you choose to work at night?
Well, my wife and I have just had our first child. Because I work at night, I can see my son during the day. It's much better.

How many people work the night shift?
There are twenty of us at night. It's a huge office and a lot of people work here during the day, but at night it's a bit empty.

How is working at night different from working normal hours?
The volume of calls at night is far lower than during the day. But because the team is small, you have more responsibility and people make friends more easily. Plus, of course, you earn more and get a bigger bonus.

And why do people call at night?
We take a lot of calls from overseas customers based in different time zones, as well as from people on holiday who have lost their credit cards or need money quickly.

What is the best part of the job?
It is the customers that make the job. At night, somehow people are more relaxed and there is more time to develop a conversation. It's surprising what customers start talking about. The latest football scores or the news in UK if they are on holiday. Sometimes they forget the real reason for the call.

Finally, what's the most unusual problem you've had to deal with?
Some of the stories are extraordinary. Last week, for example, I had a call from a guy who had just got married. He had bought drinks for all his guests all evening and the hotel had now refused his credit card so he couldn't pay. He was really embarrassed. But we solved it and had a laugh.

The UK banking sector contributes significantly to the UK and its economy.

- Banking employs about half a million people. The wider financial industry employs over 1.1 million and, together with related activities (accountancy, business, computer and legal services, etc.), some 3 million people rely on the financial industry for their jobs.

- Banks and financial services contribute £70 bn to the UK's national output (6.8% of GDP).

- The main retail banks handle over 125m accounts, clear 7bn transactions a year and facilitate 2.3bn cash withdrawals per year from a network of over 30,000 free ATMs.

Audited figures from 2006, © British Bankers' Association, 2010.

Listening

Which services do you use?

A bank customer, Kevin Browne, is having a 'financial check-up' interview with a bank employee.

1 🎧 Listen to Part 1 of the interview and tick (✓) the Southern Star Bank products and services Kevin uses.

2 🎧 Now listen to the customer advisor's suggestions in Part 2. Make notes in the 'Advice' column.

Southern Star Bank plc

Customer review interview

Category	Southern Star product / service used	Customer name *Kevin Browne*	Advice for customers
1 Spending	Cash withdrawal at branch counter	☐	
	Cash machines	☐	
	Debit card	☐	
	Credit card	☐	
	Cheque book	☐	
2 Paying bills	Standing order	☐	
	Direct debit	☐	
	Bank transfer	☐	
3 Saving	Deposit account	☐	
	Online savings account	☐	
4 Borrowing	Overdraft	☐	
	Mortgage	☐	
	Other loans	☐	

● Language spot
Suggestions and advice

1  Listen again to Part 2 of *Listening* and complete the suggestions.

   1 _____ use the cash machines more?

   2 Also, _____ using your debit card more and your cheque book less?

   3 And _____ applying for the bank's credit card as well?

   4 _____ use our card as a second card if you want to keep your existing card.

   5 _____ to open an online account.

   6 Also, _____ setting up a small overdraft?

Here are some ways of making suggestions and giving advice in English.

STRONG ADVICE	*I think you should ...*
	The best thing to do is ...
	Why don't you ...?
	How about ...?
	Have you thought about / considered ...?
POSSIBLE SUGGESTION	*Perhaps / Possibly you could ...*

The form of the verb that follows these expressions varies, depending on which expression you use.

2 Choose the correct verb to complete the sentences. Use your answers to **1** to help you decide.

   1 I think you should *open / to open* an online account.

   2 The best thing to do is *paying / to pay* your bills by standing order.

   3 Why don't you *borrow / to borrow* money to buy a car?

   4 How about *invest / investing* your money in shares?

   5 Have you thought about *protect / protecting* your house with insurance?

   6 Perhaps you could *save / to save* your money in a deposit account?

3 Work in pairs. Choose one of the problems below and take turns to ask for and give advice.

EXAMPLE

A *I want to ... What can I do?*

B *Why don't you get an overdraft? / Perhaps you could use a credit card.*

I want to ...

   1 go out tonight, but I don't have any cash.

   2 change some foreign currency.

   3 insure my flat against accidents.

   4 buy a new television, but I don't get paid until the end of the month.

   5 borrow the money to buy a flat.

   6 send some money to my parents in Poland.

   7 go on holiday, but I don't want to take a lot of cash.

   8 pay the rent on my flat every month.

>> Go to **Language reference** p.120

Speaking
Financial check-up

Work in pairs.

Student A, you are a bank customer. Go to p.108.

Student B, you work for Southern Star Bank. Go to p.115.

Store cards are another form of credit card offered to customers by big shops and department stores. They were developed as a form of promotion to encourage customers to spend more in the shop by offering incentive discounts or big credit limits.

Reading

Who is better at managing money: men or women?

1 Discuss these comments in pairs. Which of them do you think are true?

1 Women are more careful about managing money and bank accounts.
2 Men usually have more debt than women.
3 Women use store cards more than men because they love buying new clothes.
4 Young women have more financial responsibilities for children than men.
5 Women save more money than men.

2 Now read the article about a survey of debt among young people and find out if the author thinks the statements in **1** are true or false. Write T (true) or F (false) next to each statement.

3 Read the article again and answer the questions.

1 Who borrows more on their credit cards: men or women?
2 Why do women have more problems with paying debts on their credit cards? Find two reasons.
3 Why don't women use banks to borrow money?
4 Which of these comments best summarizes the writer's purpose in the article?
  a to show that young women earn less than men
  b to show that men are better at managing money
  c to show that our popular opinions about women and money are wrong
  d to show that men and women are not equal
5 Do the facts in the survey match your own experience with managing money? Why / Why not?

Who's more in debt: men or women?

A recent study by the Debt Foundation shows that it is young men who have the biggest debts on their credit cards, but it is young women who have the biggest problems with paying that debt. Why the difference?

Stereotypes!

Many people still think that women are just bad at managing money. They cannot stop buying new shoes, handbags, or clothes when they see them, and so they borrow money on store cards that you can get from big shops. But the results of the survey show this is simply not true. Young men, it seems, use store cards just as much as women. Sometimes, they are worse. Also, they save less money than women from their salaries. They open fewer savings accounts than women and take bigger risks with their finance, investing in things like shares. Young men are also less likely to have insurance on their homes and possessions.

What about equality?

No, the real reason women can't pay is that women usually have debts on basic things for the home like rent and services simply because they are poorer and often have to support children or older parents on low incomes. The study shows that today at the age of 24 most women earn 15% less than men and have more responsibilities with family and children. These are the real causes of debt problems. So much for equality!

But the worst news from the survey is that, because of their poverty, women often cannot go to big banks to borrow money. They have to use other service companies that charge the highest rates of interest. So, they suffer more and pay more in interest because their family needs are more desperate. The result is that there are more women who have their gas or electricity turned off for non payment.

Vocabulary

Talking about customer service

1 Look at the adjectives below which describe customer services. Match the positive adjectives 1–6 with the negative ones a–f.

1	cheap / affordable	a	inefficient
2	polite	b	expensive
3	secure	c	risky
4	efficient	d	rude
5	fast	e	ill-informed
6	well-informed	f	slow

2 Which of the adjectives do we use to describe

1 the staff? _____

2 the service? _____

3 the price? _____

3 Read the newspaper article below and complete the text with words from **1**.

Rip-off Britain

The Daily Recorder investigates consumer banking. National Bank came bottom in our latest survey on UK banking. Here are our good reasons why you should leave National Bank.

- With interest rates as high as 20%, an overdraft at National Bank is very _____[1].
  We recommend moving to banks like Halibank where the new rate of only 7% is really _____[2].
- Our survey showed that staff at National Bank lacked basic customer training. They were often _____[3] to customers and very _____[4], making frequent mistakes in simple bank transactions.
  At SB Bank, by contrast, we found staff were well-trained and _____[5] about the accounts they offered. Our experience at SB was very positive, and the bank staff were always _____[6] to customers and very _____[7] at dealing with complaints.
- When testing National Bank at lunchtime, we found long queues so service was very _____[8]. Other banks have learnt from customer complaints and offer a _____[9] service with plenty of staff at the counter.
- Finally, low levels of e-protection makes Internet banking at National Bank very _____[10]. Other banks have invested heavily in technology to stop e-crime and make their services _____[11] from hackers.

Pronunciation

-s endings

- After these unvoiced consonant sounds /p/, /f/, /t/, /k/, and /θ/, the final s is pronounced /s/.
  groups, products, stocks

- After these voiced consonant sounds /b/, /d/, /g/, /v/, /ð/, /l/, /m/, /n/, or /ŋ/, the final s is pronounced /z/.
  teams, rules, standards

- After these other consonant sounds /s/, /z/, /ʃ/, /tʃ/, /ʒ/, or /dʒ/, the final s is pronounced /ɪz/.
  expenses, percentages

1 Look at these plural nouns and say them aloud. Tick (✓) the correct column.

	/ɪz/	/s/	/z/
1 debts			
2 services			
3 shops			
4 problems			
5 offices			
6 banks			
7 savings			
8 houses			
9 bills			
10 risks			
11 branches			
12 cards			

2 🎧 Listen and check.

3 Work in pairs. Find three more plural words for each column. Your words should be either in this unit or connected with finance.

Writing

Handling customer complaints

1 You are a trainee customer relationship manager in a bank. You have just received this email from a customer complaining about the service. Read the email and <u>underline</u> the key facts that you think need checking and responding to.

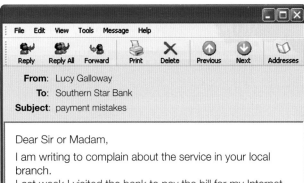

From: Lucy Galloway
To: Southern Star Bank
Subject: payment mistakes

Dear Sir or Madam,

I am writing to complain about the service in your local branch.
Last week I visited the bank to pay the bill for my Internet account. As usual I had to wait fifteen minutes just to get some service from your counter staff. They all seemed more interested in discussing their weekend plans than serving customers.
I arranged to transfer £126 to the Internet company's account by direct transfer. However, this morning I received a letter from the company telling me that the bill had still not been paid. As a result, they will stop my services unless I pay the bill plus £30 penalty charges.
I would like to know what you propose to do to correct the mistake made by your assistant. As a minimum, I think you should pay me for the charges I must now pay the Internet company because of your mistake.
I look forward to hearing from you.
Yours faithfully,

Lucy Galloway

2 You discover that the customer is right and the payment was not made. The mistake was due to an error in the bank's reference code caused by a recent upgrade of your software. You correct the mistake and now have to respond to the customer.

Look at the extract opposite from the bank's training manual. Below it are some mixed-up sentences from an email that deals with a similar issue. Match the points in the training manual to the sentences in the email to identify a good structure for your reply.

Bank Training Manual for Staff

Responding to a complaint usually takes this form:

1 use the subject box to say why you are writing
2 acknowledge the customer's letter
3 apologize for the mistake / error
4 explain how it happened
5 tell them what you doing to correct the situation
6 explain how you have corrected the problem and offer some compensation
7 make a second apology
8 close the mail formally

a The problem was due to a computer mistake in recording the date of the salary payments.

b Re: current account payments.

c Once again, please accept my apologies on behalf of the bank.

d The money has now been returned to your account and we would like to offer you £30 as a compensation for the mistake and the inconvenience you have suffered.

e We would like to apologize for the error.

f Yours sincerely,

g Thank you for your email regarding the overcharging on your current account.

h We have now taken steps to correct the software system to make sure it cannot happen again.

3 Now decide what compensation you will offer the client and use the training manual to write your response to Ms Galloway's complaint.

Webquest

Most UK banks have agreed to a code that promises certain service levels to customers. Find out about the **British Bankers' Association** and the **Banking Code**.

1 Which services does the Code cover?
2 What do they advise you to do first if you have financial difficulties, like debts?
3 If you make a complaint to a bank, what promises do they make about solving the problem?

Professional skills

Customer relationship management

Read the text below and then discuss the questions.

1 Do you think banks are right to think of their customers as 'customers for life'?

2 What do you think are the 'changing financial needs of a customer through their life'? Make a list in pairs or small groups, then discuss as a class.

To a valued customer

'"A happy customer is a customer for life." That's the main thing I learned from my training,' says Dereck Jacobs, a customer relationship manager with one of the biggest Swiss banks. 'If we make a mistake, we have to put it right immediately. Companies who just focus on the profit from one sale or one transaction are missing the point.'

'Today, the game is not about winning new customers, but keeping our existing customers throughout their life. It's about selling them new services to meet their changing needs as their life develops: from their first job, to starting a family, buying a house or preparing for their retirement. It costs a fortune in marketing and communication to win a new customer; if we lose them, we are throwing away all our investment. What kind of financial strategy is that? It's crazy.'

'This means: acknowledge your mistakes and respond positively. Try to meet, or even exceed, the customer's expectations by showing how much you care. A great sales team knows that a complaining customer is actually not just an opportunity to put things right, but it's also a way of demonstrating the company's commitment to them. That way, the best companies turn their complaining customers into fans and build loyalty for life. The short-term cost is nothing compared with the long-term gain.'

Checklist

Assess your progress in this unit. Tick (✓) the statements which are true.

- I can explain what different financial products and services are used for
- I can give suggestions and advice
- I can talk about the problem of personal debt
- I can talk about what makes good customer service
- I can write an email to deal with a complaint

Key words

Nouns

cash machine / ATM
compensation
complaint
current account
debt
deposit account
direct debit
inconvenience
loyalty
mortgage
overdraft
standing order
transaction

Verbs

acknowledge
apologize (for)
charge
earn
respond
save
transfer
withdraw

Adjective

secure

Look back through this unit. Find five more words or expressions that you think are useful.

3 Company financial services

Countdown

1 Some of the biggest companies in the world today are supermarkets. Think about all the things they do: buying and transporting goods, making payments, managing stores and staff. What kind of financial services do you think they need to support their activities?

2 Look at the financial service providers a–f used by one of the biggest supermarket groups in the UK. Which of these companies

1 provides protection against risks?
2 manages the cash accounts and payments?
3 checks the company accounts for the shareholders?
4 gives advice on raising money from the capital markets?
5 manages the pension funds?
6 advises on tax and investment planning?

a Tax advisor: *KPMG*
b Investment bank: *Goldman Sachs*
c Commercial bank: *RBS*
d Insurer: *AXA commercial insurance*
e Pension fund manager: *Merrill Lynch*
f Company auditor: *PricewaterhouseCoopers*

Listening

Scheduling appointments

1 🎧 Dave Carter, the finance director of a supermarket chain, is talking to his assistant, Helen, about his schedule for next week. Listen to their conversation and using the notes below, fill in the time and contacts for his appointments in the first column.

4.00 p.m.	9.00 a.m.	10.00 a.m.
3.00 p.m.	2.00 p.m.	

RBS commercial division
John Kerry at Goldman Sachs
fund management division at Merrill Lynch
AXA commercial insurance
Russell at KPMG

Meeting		Reason for meeting
Monday 24 May		
Time		
Meeting with		
Tuesday 25 May		
Time		
Meeting with		
Wednesday 26 May		
Time		
Meeting with		
Thursday 27 May		
Time		
Meeting with		
Friday 28 May		
Time		
Meeting with		

2 🎧 Now listen again and complete the second column of the diary with the purpose of each meeting.

In this unit
- financial services a company needs
- making requests and offers
- advantages and disadvantages of outsourcing services
- solving a business problem with expense accounts
- modals of obligation and permission
- writing a memo to staff

● Language spot

Requests and offers

1 ⊙ In his conversation with Helen, Dave uses a number of requests to ask Helen to do things. Listen to the conversation again and complete the sentences.

1 I'll be away tomorrow so ___*can we*___ go through appointments for next week?

2 _____ contact Russell at KPMG and arrange a meeting for Monday?

3 _____ set up a meeting for Tuesday afternoon. Say about 2.00 p.m.?

4 _____ contact Phil and ask him to talk to AXA Commercial Insurance.

5 _____ set up something for the morning?

6 _____ phoning Pete for me and get him to put together some figures for us?

7 And I'll need to be at Merrill Lynch at 4.00 p.m., so please _____ organize a taxi for me.

The way in which we make requests and offers depends on who we are talking to.

>> Go to **Language reference** p.120

2 ⊙ Listen again and complete the table below by writing down the expressions Helen uses to

1 agree   2 offer other help.

3 Helen uses a mixture of formal and informal expressions in her replies and offers of help. Mark the expressions you have noted down **F** (formal) or **I** (informal).

4 Match the requests in A with the responses in B. Check your answers by working in pairs and taking turns to make the requests and responses, completing each sentence with an appropriate phrase.

A	B
1 _*Can you*_ arrange a taxi to pick me up at the airport?	a _____ show you where the photocopier is as well?
2 _____ look after my laptop while I'm at lunch?	b _____ lock it in the cabinet?
3 _____ show me where the stationery is?	c _____ prepare name cards for the guests, too?
4 _____ send out a memo about the new expense forms?	d _____ also send people a copy of the form?
5 _____ organize some food for the reception?	e _*Shall I*_ organize a hotel, too?
6 _____ help me fill in this application form?	f _____ check your CV as well?

Request	Agree	F / I?	Offer other help	F / I?
... contact Russell at KPMG and arrange a meeting for Monday?	1 _____		2 _____ make that for 9.00 a.m.?	
... set up a meeting for Tuesday afternoon?	3 _____		4 _____ ask Bill along, too?	
We could do that on Wednesday at 3.00.	5 _____			
... so what about 10.00?	6 _____		7 _____ book a meeting room, too?	
... and get him to put together some figures for us on the new company pension plan?	8 _____		9 _____ for figures for last year as well?	

Pronunciation

Intonation in requests

1 🎧 Listen to the way Dave makes requests.

1 Could you contact Russell at KPMG?

2 Would you set up a meeting on Tuesday, please?

3 Would you mind phoning Pete for me?

2 🎧 Listen again and repeat.

3 🎧 Listen to these requests and mark them P if they sound polite and R if they sound rude.

1 Can you call me a taxi for three o'clock?
2 Could you check these figures for me again?
3 Can we meet at four tomorrow afternoon?
4 Would you mind working late this evening?
5 Do you think you could explain the expenses system to me?
6 Can I speak to the head of department, please?

4 🎧 Listen again. When the intonation sounds polite, agree to the request. When it is rude, don't reply.

Speaking

Making requests

Work in pairs. Student A, go to p.112. Student B, read the notes below.

1 You are the manager and Student A is your assistant. Ask your assistant to do the tasks on your list. Use expressions from *Language spot* p.21 to help you and make sure your requests sound polite (see *Pronunciation*).

1 Find out the grants available for building new factories.
2 Phone the human resources department for figures on pension costs.
3 Ask the bank to convert £200,000 into US dollars.

2 Now change roles. Student A is now your manager. Listen to his / her requests, agree to help, and offer other help with one of the suggestions below.

1 check the other customer accounts at the same time?
2 get quotes from different companies?
3 ask about borrowing or issuing shares?

Vocabulary

Phrasal verbs for office tasks

We use many phrasal verbs (verbs with a preposition attached that changes their meaning) in finance work. These phrasal verbs often have a single-word equivalent that is more formal.

1 Match the phrasal verbs in A with their formal equivalent in B.

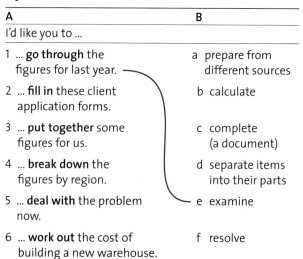

A	B
I'd like you to …	
1 … **go through** the figures for last year.	a prepare from different sources
2 … **fill in** these client application forms.	b calculate
3 … **put together** some figures for us.	c complete (a document)
4 … **break down** the figures by region.	d separate items into their parts
5 … **deal with** the problem now.	e examine
6 … **work out** the cost of building a new warehouse.	f resolve

2 Use the phrasal verbs from **1** to complete the email from Dave to his assistant.

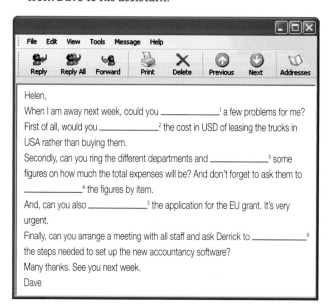

Helen,

When I am away next week, could you _____¹ a few problems for me?

First of all, would you _____² the cost in USD of leasing the trucks in USA rather than buying them.

Secondly, can you ring the different departments and _____³ some figures on how much the total expenses will be? And don't forget to ask them to _____⁴ the figures by item.

And, can you also _____⁵ the application for the EU grant. It's very urgent.

Finally, can you arrange a meeting with all staff and ask Derrick to _____⁶ the steps needed to set up the new accountancy software?

Many thanks. See you next week.

Dave

Listening

A finance department and its service providers

1 🎧 Dave Carter, the finance director, is talking to a journalist who is preparing a profile of the company. Dave is explaining the financial services the company uses. Listen and complete the table.

Financial services used	Provider of the service	Company/ department name
a cash management	commercial bank	_____ 1
b _____ 2	_____ 3	Goldman Sachs
c controlling budgets	in-house department	_____ 4
d insurance	commercial insurers	_____ 5
e _____ 6	auditors	_____ 7

2 🎧 Now listen again and answer these questions.
1 What is the main advantage of the RBS pooled account?
2 Why does he go to the investment bank for special advice on funding?
3 What three ways can the company raise money?
4 What does a master budget contain?
5 What kind of protection does business continuity insurance provide?

It's my job

1 If you decide on a career in finance, you may have to choose between working in banking and working in the finance department of a big company in industry. How do you think the two careers are different?

2 Lucille has tried both careers, but which did she prefer? Read the text and find three things she likes about her career in industry.

3 Which of these careers would you prefer?

Lucille Lagrange

Job Risk investment manager for an international oil company
Location Houston, Texas
Studied Business Administration, specializing in Finance
Started present job March 2010

Why did you decide to work for an international oil company?
Three words – global, exciting, challenging.
After university, my first job was with a large investment bank. I worked in a dealing room but I quickly decided that it wasn't the career I wanted. After a year, I decided to resign and to find a job where I could use my knowledge of finance directly in industry. So far, I am very happy with my choice.

What do you most enjoy about your job?
I love the challenges of the big projects I work on here and the diversity of the people in the company. Last month I worked in a team of eight people from every continent. I also love the part of my job that involves managing risk. Building refineries, for example, creates wealth and jobs in poorer countries but also involves managing huge risks of pollution or potential accidents. Even the choice of equipment we use affects the global environment and global warming. So your decisions have a direct impact on people's lives. Solving these problems is one of the most difficult parts of the job, but it's also the most rewarding.

What are your future career plans?
I'm not sure what and where my next job will be. To work as a controller would probably be the next obvious step. But working here I know the company will help me to develop into what I want to become – a financial manager whose job has a real effect on people's lives.

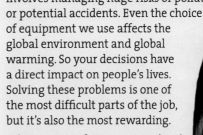

global village (*n*) the whole world, looked at as a single community that is connected by electronic communication systems

Reading

Outsourcing financial services

1 Look at these headlines. What do you understand by 'outsourcing'? Check the meaning by looking at the dictionary definitions below.

> **JP Morgan Chase to hire 4500 graduates in India: plan to shift 30% of back-office staff**

> **Union campaigns against HSBC's jobs outsourcing: 4500 back-office jobs lost in UK**

> **Deutsche Bank uses Russian IT company for 27 different projects**

> **outsourcing** *noun* [U] the process of arranging for sb outside a company to produce goods or provide services for that company
> **in-house** *adj* existing or happening within a company
> **back office** *noun* the part of a business which does not deal directly with the public

2 Now read the article *'Who pays your salary?'* and answer the questions.

1 Find four examples of financial services that companies outsource today.
2 What are the main advantages of outsourcing?
3 How do workers usually react to outsourcing?

3 Work in small groups. Choose two or three of these questions, discuss them, and report back to the class.

1 How would you feel if your salary was paid by an outsourced company? Would you be worried? Why?
2 Many people say outsourcing is 'bad for workers but good for consumers'. Do you agree? Why?
3 Why do you think an outsourcing company can provide a cheaper service?
4 What sort of cultural problems can a company have if it outsources services to a foreign country?
5 Have you used any outsourcing services like Internet help lines or telephone banking? If so, what did you think of the service?

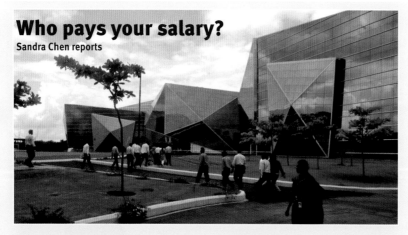

Who pays your salary?
Sandra Chen reports

Who pays your salary every month? Who owns the office or factory in which you work? Who organizes all your business travel arrangements for you? Who manages the company's pension funds?

If you work for a big European company today, your salary is probably paid and managed by another company – an outsourcer – and not by your employer. Maybe it's in India or South Africa. Your office is probably owned by a financial property company who rents the building to your company. Your pension may be managed by an investment bank or fund manager for a fee. And if you have to travel for business, all the expenses you claim are often paid by a travel expense specialist.

The fact is that, in a global world, it is no longer a good idea to manage all the financial services in the company. Instead, it is much better to give the work to a specialist provider. Then, your managers can spend their time on the really important business areas where the company makes its money. This means it can often cut costs, improve the quality of its service, and free its top managers from administration and office work. It is a win-win situation. Maybe we need to change many of our old ideas about what a company's finance department should do.

Welcome to the world of outsourcing. But what does it mean for staff?

When you ask people about outsourcing, many employees are frightened. They talk of job losses and of insecurity – 'it could be my job next'. But the fact is that many don't really see any change. What's more, they go home and use the same services in their private life. Paying bills, talking to their telephone bank or insurance provider, or booking their holidays, many of these jobs are already done in foreign countries. It seems that, in the global village, we depend on service providers in countries or places we have never seen.

■

According to a report by *Deloitte Touche Tohmatsu*, the financial services industry will move 20% of its costs base offshore by the end of 2010, compared to the current average of 3.5%. *Citigroup*, *Morgan Stanley*, and *JPMorgan Chase* have all established outsourcing and offshoring operations.

In a separate report, Indian officials claim India will gain about eight million outsourcing jobs over the next decade. Bangalore is India's most famous offshore location, but the city of Hyderabad is also one of the country's outsourcing hotspots.

Webquest

Find out more about how the big banks are using outsourcing. Choose one of these banks: *HSBC*, *Lloyds TSB*, *Bank of America*, *Deutsche Bank*. Go on the Internet and search for '*Deutsche Bank + outsourcing*'.

- What kind of services are they choosing to outsource?
- Where are they moving the work?
- What are the benefits?
- What do customers think of the service?

Compare your results with your partner. Are the banks right to outsource? Decide together.

Speaking

Controlling business expenses

When you travel on a business trip for your company, you can usually claim travel expenses when you return. But different companies have different rules for expenses.

1 What kind of things do you think you are allowed to (and not allowed to) claim for? Make a list with your partner.

2 *Sergo* is a fast-growing company which specializes in lighting for domestic security and gardens. Last year they expanded into southern Europe. However, with the fast growth, the finance department neglected cost control. Travel expenses are at least 30% over budget. As a result, the finance director is considering outsourcing all the expenses claims to control the problem.

Your company, a specialist outsourcer, has just received this email from Jean Martin, the CFO of Sergo, explaining their problem. Read the email and, using the comment boxes, make a note of the questions you need to ask Sergo about their expenses policy.

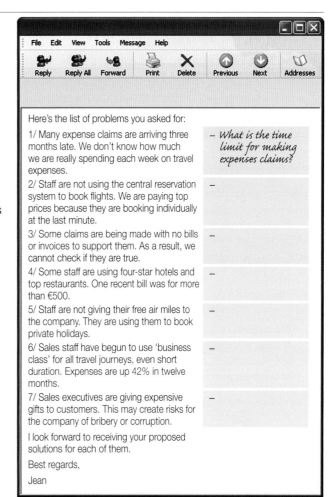

| File   Edit   View   Tools   Message   Help |

Here's the list of problems you asked for:

1/ Many expense claims are arriving three months late. We don't know how much we are really spending each week on travel expenses.

– What is the time limit for making expenses claims?

2/ Staff are not using the central reservation system to book flights. We are paying top prices because they are booking individually at the last minute.

–

3/ Some claims are being made with no bills or invoices to support them. As a result, we cannot check if they are true.

–

4/ Some staff are using four-star hotels and top restaurants. One recent bill was for more than €500.

–

5/ Staff are not giving their free air miles to the company. They are using them to book private holidays.

–

6/ Sales staff have begun to use 'business class' for all travel journeys, even short duration. Expenses are up 42% in twelve months.

–

7/ Sales executives are giving expensive gifts to customers. This may create risks for the company of bribery or corruption.

–

I look forward to receiving your proposed solutions for each of them.

Best regards,

Jean

3 Work in pairs. Student A, you work for Sergo. Student B, you work for the outsourcing company. Have a meeting to work out a policy on travel expenses. Using the list of points in the email above as an agenda, decide together what the company policy should be.

Make notes on the decisions you make in the action plan below. The first one is done for you.

1 time limit on submitting expenses claims   *submit within four weeks*
2 booking travel
3 receipts
4 accommodation / meals
5 policy on air miles
6 flights: business / economy class
7 gifts

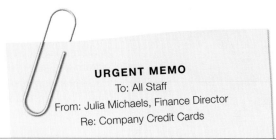

URGENT MEMO
To: All Staff
From: Julia Michaels, Finance Director
Re: Company Credit Cards

● Language spot

Modals of obligation and permission

When managers or companies give instructions or explain rules to staff they often use modal verbs.

Remember that some modal verbs like *have to* need an auxiliary verb like *do / don't* in questions and negatives.

Need has two forms in the negative: a modal form: *you needn't* and a regular form *you don't need to*.

1 Look at the list of modal verbs and other phrases used to express permission and obligation. Match phrases 1–10 with the four definitions below.

1 you can	6 you may
2 you don't have to	7 you don't need to
3 you must	8 it is not allowed (to)
4 you needn't	9 you must not
5 you are allowed to	10 it is compulsory to

It's necessary: _____
It's not necessary: _____
It's permitted: _____
It's not permitted: _____

2 Complete these instructions from an airline company on rules for passengers. Choose the correct form.

1 If you register online, you *don't need / needn't* check in at the airport.
2 You *mustn't / don't have to* carry liquids or sharp objects in your hand luggage. These *must / need* be carried in your baggage in the hold.
3 You *must / may* show your passport or identity card before boarding.
4 You *are not allowed to / don't have to* use mobile phones during the take-off. All mobiles *are not allowed to / must be* switched off before.
5 Your hand luggage *must not / needn't* exceed 20 kg.
6 Smoking *is not compulsory / is not permitted* in any part of the terminal building.

>> Go to **Language reference** p.121

Writing

A memo

One task you will probably need to do in the office is to give information to colleagues using a memo.

A good memo

- makes it clear who is meant to read it
- has a short subject heading that makes it clear what the memo is about
- presents information as briefly and clearly as possible using a numbered list or bullet points
- is normally written in a formal style. This means the writer avoids using the personal pronouns *I*, *you*, and *we*.

1 Look back at the notes you made in *Speaking* about travel expenses at Sergo and complete the memo on the next page, using modals from *Language spot*. Then add two extra rules about expenses of your own.

2 Your boss has asked you to send a memo to all staff reminding them about company rules for using email and the Internet. She thinks people are spending too much time on personal emails. The company also recently suffered a virus attack caused by a member of staff downloading games onto his computer. Work in pairs and decide together

1 What rules should be included in the memo? Look back at the structures in *Language spot* to help you to decide which rules you want to include.
2 What is a good subject title?
3 How will you introduce the memo and explain the recent problem?

Use the *Sergo* model opposite to help you write your memo.

SergoCo

From: Jean Martin

Memo to: all sales staff

SUBJECT: New guidelines for business travel expenses ⟶ Subject title

Following our investigation into business travel expenses, we are introducing the following new guidelines for business travel expenses: ⟶ Introduction (explaining purpose of memo)

1   All staff _____ claims within _____ days.

    Staff _____ use the travel expense form.

2   Individual booking of flights _____

    The only exception is _____

3   Staff _____ invoices to support all expense claims.

    If not, _____

4   In future, staff _____ to reserve four-star hotels.

    Staff _____ observe the new limit for daily expenses of €_____

5   Management _____ use business class when _____

    For short European flights, staff _____

6   Sales staff _____ keep air miles for private use.

7   Company employees _____ accept or give gifts of more than €_____

    Any other gifts _____

8   [your rule]

    _____

9   [your rule]

    _____

⟶ Listed items (numbered or with bullet points)

Thank you in advance for your co-operation. ⟶ Concluding note (for thanking, offering to answer queries, etc.)

Jean Martin

Finance Director ⟶ Name and job title of person issuing memo

Key words

Verbs	Other words
arrange	accommodation
be allowed to	appointment
book	budget
mind	cost control
outsource	expenses
	grant
Phrasal verbs	guideline
break down	in-house
fill in	offshore
go through	provider
put together	wealth
set up	
work out	

Look back through this unit. Find five more words or expressions that you think are useful.

4 Economic indicators

Countdown

1 What facts do you know about the economy in your country? Work in pairs and make notes of your answers.

  1 How many people live in your country?
  2 What is happening to prices in the shops?
  3 How many people have no job?
  4 What is the exchange rate of your country's currency to the US dollar?
  5 Is your country's economy growing or declining?
  6 How much interest do you pay on bank loans?

Report back your answers to the class.

2 When we talk about these facts, we are talking about 'economic indicators'. The pictures below represent key economic indicators. How many of them can you name?

CURRENCY		BELI BUYING	JUAL SELLING
UNITED STATES	USDB	9615	9645
UNITED STATES KECIL	USDK	9565	9620
UNITED STATES $1	USD$1	9075	9575
USD TRAVEL CHECK	USDTC	9400	
EURO	EUR	13000	13059
AUSTRALIAN DOLLAR	AUD	6999	7000
SINGAPORE DOLLAR	SGD	6560	6585
JAPANESE YEN	JPY	9350	9450
HONGKONG DOLLAR	HKD	1235	1240

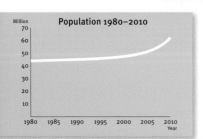

Population 1980–2010

Reading

Interpreting data

1 What can you learn about an economy from its economic indicators? Look at the table for these two developing economies: Turkey and Poland. Match the indicators a–h with the definitions 1–8.

  1 the movement of prices in the economy   *f*
  2 the cost of borrowing money from a bank   _____
  3 the relation between imports and exports   _____
  4 the value of a country's money compared with other currencies, such as the US dollar   _____
  5 the number of people who live in a country   _____
  6 the number of people with no job   _____
  7 the total size of an economy   _____
  8 the rate of expansion in the economy   _____

Economic indicators	Turkey	Poland
a Population	76.8m	
b Gross domestic product		US$ 686.2bn
c Growth rate	-5.8%	
d Interest rates		5.0%
e Unemployment rate	14.6%	
f Inflation		3.4%
g Exchange rate	US$ 1 = YTL* 1.55 * Turkish New Lira	
h Balance of trade		US$ -3.585

2 Student A, go to p.113. Student B, look at the table above. Work together and find the missing statistics in your table. Take turns to ask for and give the missing figures. Then read back the statistics you have written to your partner and check if they are right.

3 What can you learn from this data about the two countries? Discuss in pairs or small groups.

  1 Which country has the bigger economy?
  2 Which country has the higher growth rate?
  3 Which has the worse inflation rate?
  4 Which has the better interest rates for borrowers?
  5 Do you see any dangers for the economy in any of the indicators?

In this unit
● economic indicators
● describing trends and graphs
● making a mini presentation with visuals
● explaining causes
● writing a report

Vocabulary
Describing trends 1

1 Look at the news stories. Underline the **verbs** that tell you how the indicators moved: up or down. Mark them with an arrow showing the direction up (↑) or down (↓).

a
German unemployment rate <u>falls</u> slightly as the economy continues to create new jobs. Exports, especially of machinery, rise dramatically as world demand remains strong.

b
Bank of England warns as inflation increases sharply to 3.4%. House owners suffer more pain as mortgage rates go up by 0.5% from 4.5% to 5%.

c
Oil prices decrease as demand from China goes down sharply.

d
US house prices continue to fall steadily as the number of new homes constructed drops steeply and firms lay off workers.

2 Now complete the table with the verbs you underlined.

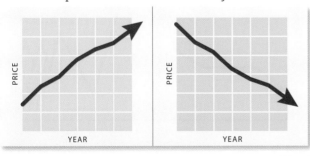

to increase	to decrease

3 When we describe a change, we can be more precise by putting an adverb after the verb. Find these adverbs in the headlines: *slightly*, *steadily*, *sharply*, *steeply*, *dramatically*. Which of the adverbs describe
a a big change?
b a small change?
c a continuous change over time?

Professional skills
Tips for presentations

1 What do you think makes a good presentation? Think about examples you have heard.

2 What typical mistakes do people make? Look at the 'golden rules' below.

Here are some golden rules to make a positive impact with a presentation:
• First, note down all the points you want to make.
• Plan your structure with a clear **introduction**, two or three paragraphs and a **conclusion.**
• Check the stress and pronunciation of any difficult words.
• Don't read out your text. Try and learn it in advance and use only notes.
• Make sure you look directly at your audience and make eye contact.
• Practise with friends and colleagues beforehand.
• When you start, check that the audience can hear you.
• Above all, speak slowly and clearly.

3 Can you think of any other advice for giving presentations?

Newspapers often use abbreviations or technical terms for economic indicators.

Base rates: interest rates set by the Central Bank

Mortgage rates: the interest rate you pay on a loan for a house or flat

GDP: gross domestic product

RPI/CPI: retail / consumer price index = the inflation rate

Forex: foreign exchange

A balance of trade is in **surplus** when exports are larger than imports.

A balance of trade is in **deficit** when exports are lower than imports.

Listening

Presenting figures

You are going to hear a presentation by a financial analyst on the UK economy.

1 🎧 First, listen and write the number you hear next to the year or month in the table below.

Unemployment		Interest rates		Inflation	
2000		2000		January	1.8%
2002		2003		March	
2003	5.5%	2007		May	
2006		2008		July	
2008		2009	0.75%	August	2.4%
2010				October	

2 🎧 Now listen to the presentation again and complete the three graphs.

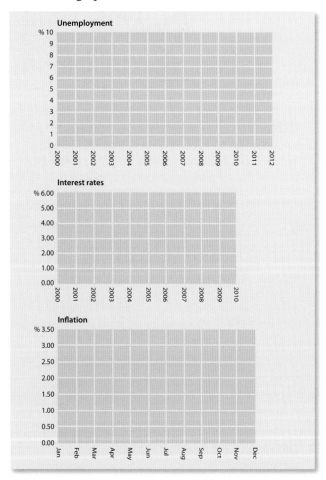

Vocabulary

Describing trends 2

1 The text below continues the article about oil prices in *Vocabulary* on p.29. Read it and underline the verbs and phrases that describe key trends. There are **eight** verbs and phrases in all.

Over the last month oil prices have fluctuated wildly between $95 and $123. Prices rocketed at the beginning of the month and they reached a new peak of $123. But, with fears of an economic slowdown, the price subsequently plunged and hit a low of $95 last Thursday. They levelled off at the beginning of this week at $108 and have now recovered to $115. But oil analysts expect they will surge to new highs over the next 2 months.

2 Now put the verbs and phrases you found in 1 into the graph below, which shows changes in the price of gold.

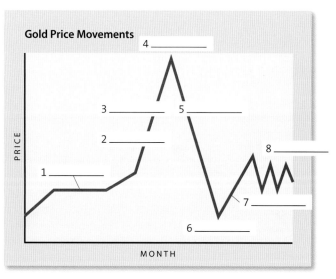

Speaking

Presenting data

You are going to give a presentation to your partner. Student A, go to p.109. Student B, go to p.117.

Reading

Life in modern Britain

1 Economic indicators can give us a picture of the historical development of a country. Think back to the life of your parents' generation. What do you think people spent their money on 50 years ago?

Now read the text and find out about life in the UK 50 years ago.

What can economic indicators tell us about life in modern Britain?

In 1957, the UK government began a survey of the spending of a typical English family called the Family Spending Survey.

In this year, three items made up nearly 50% of all family expenditure: food, fuel, and rent. If you include clothing and travel, these basics made up nearly 70% of all family spending. The main luxuries for the ordinary family were tobacco and alcohol, which represented just under 10% of spending. The next biggest luxury item was meals eaten out in restaurants, representing 3% of spending.

When the government did the same survey fifty years later in 2007, the figures were very different.

2 Discuss in pairs. What do you think are the largest items of family spending today?

3 Put these items in order of importance (1 = biggest item; 5 = smallest item):

food	_____	clothing	_____
housing	_____	leisure	_____
transport	_____		

4 Now read the conclusions of the 2007 report and write the correct percentage against each item. Were you right?

Over the last fifty years, UK family income has doubled in real terms, but the pattern of family spending has changed dramatically. Basic necessities, including food, now account for only 15% of our family budget, compared with 33% in 1957. And half of that food budget now consists of meals and takeaways – a new category introduced in the 1970s.

But the cost of housing, including mortgage interest payments or rent, has more than doubled since 1957 from 9% to 19%.

However, the biggest change is in the growth of leisure, including everything from holidays, DVD rentals and sports clubs. This now represents 7% of spending, while clothing is only 5%.

Motoring and travel costs have increased sharply from 8% of spending in 1957 to 16% in 2006, mostly because of rising car ownership, with three in four families owning at least one car.

Surprisingly, spending on alcoholic drinks accounts for the same proportion of spending as it did 50 years ago at 3% – although in absolute terms it is much higher.

But, in contrast, the proportion of the average budget spent on tobacco has fallen sharply from 6% in 1957 to just 1% in 2006.

5 Discuss in pairs.
1 Why do you think spending on food has fallen so sharply?
2 Why has transport spending increased so dramatically?
3 Family income has doubled over fifty years, but does higher income create happiness? What kind of problems could it bring?

● Language spot

Describing change and cause

past	present

To talk about a period of time that is finished and not connected to the present, we use the Past Simple.
In 1957, three items **made up** *nearly 50% of all house-hold expenditure.*
Last year family income **increased** *by 3.4%.*

To talk about a situation in the past that continues into the present, we use the Present Perfect (*has / have* + past participle).

past	present

Family income **has doubled** *over the last fifty years.*

Since 1957, spending on cars **has risen** *from 8% to 16%.*

Note how the time expressions (*over the last fifty years, Since 1957*) show if a speaker considers the situation or action is finished or not finished.

1 Mark these time expressions **F** (finished), **NF** (not finished), or **B** (both).

1 since 1957	6 for two years
2 over / in the last fifty years	7 until 1980
3 in 2001	8 last year
4 recently	9 so far this year
5 at the end of the war	

2 Now complete these sentences using the verbs in brackets in the correct form.

1 Spending on leisure _____ (increase) sharply since the 1970s.
2 The market for music CDs _____ (grow) steadily until 2001.
3 Tobacco consumption _____ (decrease) dramatically from 1957 to 2006.
4 Spending on electronic goods _____ (go up) by 12% so far this year and economists expect it to rise further by Christmas.
5 Over the last fifty years, spending on transport _____ (rise) dramatically.
6 Oil prices _____ (fall) sharply when the peace talks were announced.
7 We _____ (see) a big increase in obesity problems among children recently.

Causes

To find out why things have changed, we use cause questions:

EXAMPLES
What's behind	
What the reason for	*the increase in petrol costs?*
How do you explain	

and to answer:
This is	*due to*	*the crisis in the Gulf.*
	the result of	*new demand from China.*
	because of	*speculation.*

>> Go to **Language reference** p.122

Speaking

Explaining trends and their causes

Student A, go to p.109. Student B, go to p.117.

Reading

An analyst's report: Kazakhstan

You are an analyst working for an investment fund ABS. Your team has asked you to prepare some background on Kazakhstan and wants you to provide data on economic indicators in order to understand the risks of investing in the country. They have sent you some questions to answer.

1 First, look at the questions and the table and make notes of your answers.

> Can you give us some background on Kazakhstan?
> 1 What has happened to GDP since 2003?
> 2 What is happening to the inflation rate?
> 3 What was the exchange rate to the USD in 2009?

	2003	2005	2007	2009
Population (m)	15.0	15.2	15.5	15.4
GDP (US$ bn)	30.8	57.1	101.2	107
Consumer price inflation (av. %)	6.5	7.6	8.8	7.3
Exchange rate (US$)	149.6	132.9	122.7	147.8

2 Now read the text below about recent developments in Kazakhstan and make notes of your answers.

1 How much oil are they now producing?
2 How much oil will they produce in ten years' time?
3 What are the three biggest risks of investing there?
4 What reforms have they made in the last few years?
5 Is the economy state controlled or private?
6 Who controls the banking sector?
7 How does the banking sector compare with Russia?

Kazakhstan: economic background

During the past few years, the economy in Kazakhstan has grown at an average rate of about 7%, one of the fastest rates in the world. Income per capita is now 65% higher than in 2000. Foreign investment has increased sharply in the last 10 years and will reach $28bn this year, 80% of it in the oil sector. So, the immediate future looks good.

According to the minister of economy, the size of the economy – currently $37.6bn – is expected to triple by 2015 as a result of increased oil production.

At the moment, Kazakhstan is producing 1m barrels of oil a day and planning to triple this output in the next 10 years. However, Kazakhstan is at risk from a sharp increase in the local currency fed by revenues from natural resources, making the economy uncompetitive.

Kazakhstan is already showing some signs of growing too fast. The boom in consumer spending cannot be satisfied by the local economy and it has created a sharp increase in imports and levels of debt.

An even bigger danger is the risk of the government wasting revenues from natural resources by spending them on prestigious projects rather than on health, education and infrastructure.

So far, Kazakhstan has not made any significant mistakes.

In the past decade, the country has restructured its economy and created a free market. In fact, it has overtaken Russia in many of its reforms.

It has built a stable banking system, introduced a private pension plan, and privatized its electricity sector. Unlike Russia, where banking is still dominated by the state-controlled Sberbank, Kazakhstan has privatized all its banks and the private sector is enjoying healthy competition.

Most important of all, it now has a private sector that is driving economic activity: three-quarters of all investments in the country are made by the private sector.

Writing

A report

When writing a financial report it is important to organize the information in clear sections with a heading, sub headings, and numbered paragraphs. A good rule is to think of matching one main idea to one paragraph.

In financial reports, people want to know what is fact and what is opinion and interpretation. So judgements (for example, explanations of what figures mean, predictions of what will happen in the future, and recommendations for what to do) should be separated from the facts.

If you are making a personal judgement, you can use expressions like:

I think / believe that inflation will increase by 5%.
My recommendation is / I would recommend that we invest cautiously in this market.

If you are reporting other people's opinions, you can quote them directly. Or, if you don't want to say whose opinion it is, you can use the passive:

*The IMF **expects** inflation to increase by 5%.*
*The consultants **have recommended that** we invest cautiously in this market.*
*Inflation **is expected** to increase by 5%.*
*Cautious investment in this market **has been recommended**.*

1 An analyst's report usually contains these five main sections. Match the headings 1–5 with the definitions a–e.

1 Title (of the report)
2 Executive summary
3 Objectives
4 Findings
5 Recommendations

a The purpose of the report and who it is written for
b A brief summary in a few sentences of what the report contains
c What action should be taken based on the results of the report
d The information found in all the research, organized by paragraph with subheadings
e What the report is to be called and who wrote it

2 Using your notes from your research on Kazakhstan in *Reading*, complete the report on p.112.

Webquest

You have US $500,000 to invest for your fund in emerging markets. Choose one of the countries below which are also emerging economies.

| Vietnam | China | Ukraine | Chile |
| Slovakia | Morocco | Romania | Indonesia |

1 Look on the Internet to find the key data about its economy. A good place to start looking is *www.economist.com* and look up country reports.

Country	1	2	3
Growth			
Inflation			
Interest rates			
Key sectors			
Main exports			
Risks			
Opportunities			

2 Work with two partners. Ask them questions to get the key data about the country they have researched. Put the data in your table.

3 Work together to decide which is the best place for your fund to invest and why.

It's my job

1 One job that requires a lot of financial research is that of a financial journalist. What else do you think the job involves? Read the interview below and find out.

2 Do you prefer to read the news online or in a newspaper? Why?

Amy Golding

Job title Financial journalist at an online daily newspaper

What does your job involve?
Researching news stories and features for the website and keeping up to date with developments in the financial world.

You worked as a financial journalist on a newspaper before. How is online journalism different?
Readers of websites expect you to react more quickly to events. This means you have to constantly monitor what is happening. At the same time, you have to be accurate: that means checking financial data and economic statistics to illustrate what you are writing about. Also, there are so many websites and so much information already available to the public that you have to work much harder to get a story.

And which do you think is better: websites or newspapers?
Websites, definitely. We can link to background material, show graphs and charts in interesting ways, and we can follow a story as it develops, whereas a newspaper is always slightly out of date. This is especially important for a fast-moving field like finance.

But are there any disadvantages?
Well, we sometimes have technical problems with our software. And there is also the problem of getting people to pay for content, when they are used to getting a lot of material on the web free of charge.

Checklist

Assess your progress in this unit. Tick (✓) the statements which are true.

- [ ] I can identify the key economic indicators for a country
- [ ] I can describe economic and financial trends on a graph
- [ ] I can give a mini presentation
- [ ] I can analyse and explain causes of economic change
- [ ] I can write a short report analysing a country's economy

Key words

Verbs of change
decrease
fall
fluctuate
increase
level off
plunge
reach a peak
rise
rocket
surge

Adverbs of change
dramatically
sharply
slightly
steadily

Economic indicators
balance of trade
exchange rate
gross domestic
    product (GDP)
inflation
interest rates
unemployment rate

Other words
private sector
privatize

Look back through this unit. Find five more words or expressions that you think are useful.

5 Economic cycles

Countdown

1 Look at the graph showing the typical cycles of an economy.

1 How long does a normal economic cycle last? Circle the correct answer.
   a about three months   c about five years
   b about a year   d about ten years
2 Why do economies move in cycles?

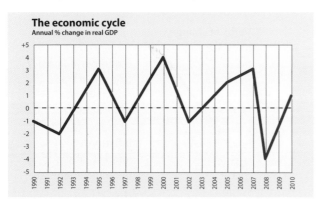

The economic cycle
Annual % change in real GDP

2 How does your spending in the shops affect this cycle? Complete the sentences.

1 When people reduce their spending, the economy experiences a r_____.
2 When they increase their spending, the economy experiences a r_____.

3 Look at the words below which are commonly used to describe economic cycles.

1 Which words describe positive growth and which are negative? Mark them **+** or **−**.
2 Which words describe a short-term phase (three months) and which are medium-term (six months and more)? Mark them **S**, **M** or both.
3 Which words describe extreme conditions of the cycle? Mark them **!**.

	+ / −	S / M	!
a slump			
b upturn			
c recession			
d boom			
e downturn			
f recovery			

Speaking

Recession and recovery

1 Look at the pictures. Say which photos show
   1 a recovery   2 a recession.

2 Work in pairs. Look at the sentences below. Decide which of these things usually happen
   a in a recovery   **b** in a recession.

1 People lose their jobs. ☐
2 Companies create jobs. ☐
3 Companies produce fewer goods. ☐
4 Companies invest to increase production. ☐
5 Interest rates begin to fall. ☐
6 Governments start to increase interest rates. ☐
7 Prices begin to rise and inflation increases. ☐
8 Prices fall and profits decrease. ☐
9 Many companies go bankrupt. ☐
10 People often start up new businesses. ☐

In this unit
- describing economic cycles
- recession and recovery
- the role of the World Bank and the IMF
- writing a report on an industrial market
- discussing and exchanging ideas in a meeting

3 Work in pairs. Student A, go to p.113. Student B, match these effects of a recovery 1–5 with the explanations a–e. Make notes using this structure.

In a recovery ... fall(s) / rise(s), because ...

In a recovery ...

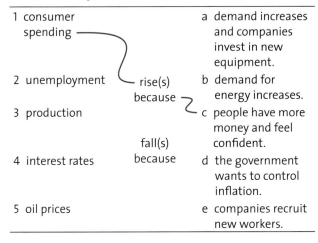

1 consumer spending	a demand increases and companies invest in new equipment.
2 unemployment	b demand for energy increases.
3 production	c people have more money and feel confident.
4 interest rates	d the government wants to control inflation.
5 oil prices	e companies recruit new workers.

rise(s) because

fall(s) because

4 Now ask each other questions. Student B, ask Student A about recessions, using points 1–5.

EXAMPLE

*What usually happens to **consumer spending** in a recession?*

Student A, use your notes to explain the effects of recessions to Student B.

EXAMPLE

*In a recession consumer spending **falls** because people have less money and fear the future.*

5 Then reverse roles so that Student A asks Student B about what happens during a recovery.

Check that you agree with your partner's explanations. Make a note of anything you disagree about and discuss with the whole class.

● Language spot
Predictions: probability

When we make a forecast about the future, we need to say how sure we are of our predictions. We can use **modal verbs** (*will, should, could, may, might*) and **probability adverbs** (*certainly, probably, possibly*).

1 Look at the forecasts below for the world economy. Mark each of them **C, L, P,** or **I** according to how certain the writer is.

CERTAIN (C)	100%
LIKELY (L)	↓
	50%
PERHAPS (P)	↓
IMPOSSIBLE (I)	0%

What will happen to the global economy in the next few years?

1 The Indian software sector <u>should become</u> a major competitor to the USA. ____

2 Emerging markets <u>won't recover</u> in the short term. ____

3 America <u>could lose</u> its dominant position in the world economy. ____

4 Water <u>might possibly become</u> one of the most expensive commodities. ____

5 The Asia-Pacific Rim <u>will certainly become</u> the most important region in the global economy this century. ____

6 The Gulf States <u>will become</u> a major transport centre for the Middle East. ____

7 China <u>will probably become</u> a major centre for car production. ____

8 Oil prices <u>might not increase</u> in the short term. ____

2 What do you think will happen to these sectors of the economy in the next few years? Write some sentences using the expressions in **1**. Then compare your predictions with your partner.

- solar power
- Internet banking
- air travel and tourism
- farming
- the newspaper industry
- TV advertising
- the car industry

>> Go to **Language reference** p.122

The Great Depression in the USA (1929–32)

- 13 million people lose their jobs
- Industrial production falls by 45%
- Home-building drops by 80%
- 5,000 regional banks go bankrupt
- President Roosevelt begins 'the New Deal'

The Credit Crunch (2007–9)

- US stock market falls by 45%
- US unemployment reaches 7%
- $700bn rescue of the banking system
- House prices fall by 25%
- Interest rates fall to 0.25%
- Barack Obama is elected President

Listening

The 'Great Depression'

1 Before you listen, discuss the questions.

What do you know about the Wall Street Crash of 1929? What happened? What caused it?

2 🎧 Listen to an interview about the biggest recession of the twentieth century – the 'Great Depression' of the 1930s. Number the events (1–5).

a the banks stopped lending ☐
b prices of food products fell sharply ☐
c investment in new industries like radio ☐
d global unemployment reached 30% ☐
e the Wall Street crash ☐

3 🎧 Listen again. Write true (T) or false (F).

1 The 1920s were a period of recession because of the First World War.
2 Businesses invested in new industries like the car industry and radio.
3 In 1929, the stock market fell by 16%.
4 After the crash, prices of food and goods increased dramatically.
5 Companies and farmers profited from the crash.
6 Industrial production in the USA and Germany fell by 53% between 1929 and 1932.
7 Unemployment reached 30% by 1932.

4 What examples do you know of recent recessions? How does the 'credit crunch' of 2008 compare with the Great Depression?

Reading

Managing the world economy

Read the article and answer the questions.

1 Why were the IMF and the World Bank founded?
2 What is the difference between them?
3 Which of them could help with a big infrastructure project like a hospital or school?
4 Which of them could help a country if it has a crisis with its foreign exchange rate?
5 Why are they now being criticized?

The IMF and the World Bank

The IMF and the World Bank were set up at the Bretton Woods conference in the USA in 1944. The 45 governments at the conference decided to build a system of economic cooperation among countries to avoid the mistakes that caused the Great Depression of the 1930s.

The IMF is based in Washington, DC, USA and is governed by the 185 countries that are members. However, the IMF is not a bank. Its job is to maintain stability in the world economy and help countries which are experiencing financial difficulties, perhaps with repaying debt on loans or when the value of their currency has collapsed. But the IMF cannot tell a government what to do: it can only advise.

The World Bank has the different task of lending money to developing countries to help long-term construction and to support social programmes to reduce poverty or disease. Many of its programmes in developing countries support big long-term infrastructure projects like dams, water systems, or road systems, which governments do not have the money to build.

Charged with failure

Both institutions face a lot of criticism today. The Fund is often criticized for ignoring local conditions of poverty in developing countries and imposing single 'western' solutions onto weak economies. By advising governments, for example, to cut government spending in order to reduce inflation, they can create unemployment in poor countries. The Bank is criticized for concentrating too much on big infrastructure projects like dams and motorways. Critics say these projects ignore the real needs of poor people to grow food, get water, or set up small businesses. Environmental protesters also say that big projects can destroy local environments for farmers by changing the ecosystem.

Both institutions reject such criticism, and they are making big efforts to reform by talking more with local people and focusing more on small micro projects using local expertise.

Both institutions believe that one of the most important reforms is to have a new emphasis on consulting with national governments, local experts, and aid organizations, before developing any policies.

Pronunciation

Abbreviations and acronyms

An **abbreviation** is where the first letters of a name are used instead of saying the whole name. So, an Annual General Meeting (the shareholders' meeting held by a company every year) becomes an AGM. Each letter is pronounced separately: 'an A-G-M'.

An **acronym** is a word formed from the first letters of the words that make up the name of something. So, the FTSE (Financial Times Stock Exchange) share index is pronounced 'the Footsie' (not the F-T-S-E).

1 Here are some sentences containing abbreviations and acronyms. What do you think the letters stand for?

1 The finance minister is meeting the IMF representative later today.

IMF = _____

2 The CEO is giving a talk for all employees at two o'clock.

CEO = _____

3 The EU has announced new measures to control financial services.

EU = _____

4 My country's debt is equivalent to 56% of its GNP.

GNP = _____

5 OPEC members are meeting to discuss an increase in production.

OPEC = _____

6 The RPI figures show that there has been a fall in inflation this month.

RPI = _____

7 The VIP visitors are being met at the airport.

VIP = _____

8 The bank is holding an EGM to discuss the new share issue.

EGM = _____

2 Now say the sentences aloud.

3 🎧 Listen and check your answers.

Webquest

1 Work in two groups.

Group A, go to the website of the *World Bank*. Find the information and make notes.

1 What do these institutions in the bank do: *IBRD* and *IDA*? Where do they get their finance from?

2 Find an example of a development project the bank is funding in agriculture or water. Find out what its objectives are and how much it will cost.

3 Visit the news section and choose a video on another development project. Make notes to tell the class.

Group B, go to the website of the *IMF*. Find the information and make notes.

1 When can a country borrow from the IMF? Find some examples of countries that have borrowed.

2 What does the IMF do in its 'surveillance' activity?

2 Discuss your results with the other group.

It's my job

The faces behind the IMF

1 Before you listen, discuss the following question in pairs or small groups.

Why do you think people choose to work for international organizations like the IMF or the World Bank rather than in the private sector?

2 🎧 Listen to the interview with Eric Gautier, Resident Representative in the Lao Republic.

3 Discuss in pairs or small groups. Would a job like this interest you? Why / Why not?

Microfinance is the system of providing very small loans to some of the poorest people in the world. The loans are to help them to start businesses so that they can feed their families and villages. It was founded by a young economics professor, **Muhammad Yunus**, in Bangladesh in 1976. Yunus originally lent less than one dollar each to families. In 2006, he won the Nobel Peace Prize for his work.

Vocabulary

The economic cycle

Every year the IMF produces a report on the performance of the world economy, country by country. This report advises countries and governments on better management of their economies.

1 Look at the three examples below which illustrate the type of information contained in these reports (*growth*, *the economic cycle*, *supply and demand*). Find the **opposites** of these economic words in the examples. (The first one is done for you.)

1 to grow   →   *to decline*
2 to suffer   →   _____
3 an upturn →   _____
4 a recovery →   _____
5 sluggish   →   _____
6 to stimulate → _____

1 Growth

The world economy **grew**	by 3% p.a.
The steel sector **declined / contracted**	by 4% p.a.

2 The economic cycle

The Japanese economy **experienced / enjoyed**	**an upturn** (= a short-term change).
	a recovery (= a medium-term change).
	a boom (= an extreme change).
The Spanish economy **experienced / suffered**	**a downturn** (= a short-term change).
	a recession (= a medium-term change).
	a slump (= an extreme change).

3 Supply and demand

Consumer demand was **strong / buoyant**.
Consumer demand was **weak / sluggish**.
The government had to **stimulate** demand.
The government had to **cool** demand.

2 Complete the survey below by underlining the correct words. Use the vocabulary in **1** to help you.

World growth slows, as US enters a downturn

USA

Last year was a good year in the USA and the economy *grew / declined*[1] by 3.4%. The *slump / growth*[2] was caused by consumer spending and borrowing. However, sales in the shops are now falling and the economy is experiencing a slight *downturn / boom*[3]. The fear is that if the government does not act, this may become a long *boom / recession*[4].

Last year, the housing market began to slow down and now *decline / demand*[5] for new houses is *strong / weak*[6] and prices of new homes are falling. The main concern is that the *buoyant / sluggish*[7] demand for housing may result in a fall in consumer spending.

Japan

In Japan, growth has now stopped. The size of the economy has *contracted / expanded*[8] in the last two quarters of the year. The risk is that the economy will now move into a *recession / recovery*[9]. Domestic demand is *strong / sluggish*[10] and the construction industry is *expanding / experiencing*[11] a recession. On the positive side, exports remain strong fed by world *supply / demand*[12] for consumer goods and cars, but the fear is that companies will suffer from *buoyant / sluggish*[13] conditions.

Eurozone

The Eurozone economy last year enjoyed one of its best years for a decade and *contracted / grew*[14] by 3.4%. In Germany, the engineering sector *experienced / suffered*[15] a strong recovery with *buoyant / weak*[16] demand for machinery and cars. After many bad years, consumer demand has turned positive and is now experiencing a *slump / recovery*[17] and the European Central Bank is trying to *cool / stimulate*[18] demand by increasing interest rates.

Mediterranean countries performed less well. With families facing higher fuel and food costs, consumer demand in Italy was *strong / sluggish*[19]. The fear is that, if this continues, the economy will fall into a *boom / recession*[20] next year unless there is a change in government policy. Government efforts so far to *decline / stimulate*[21] demand have not had much success.

Writing

An internal report

You work as an economist for a large European steel maker with global production. Every quarter you produce a report on the conditions in the world economy to circulate to all sales and marketing divisions in the group.

To prepare your report, you have just downloaded the latest data on the world economy.

Look at the table and complete the executive summary of the report. Your summary should present a factual overview of the current conditions in the world economy.

You will need to use different kinds of language in the report. For help, refer to the *Language reference* sections on p.122 about
● Describing change and cause
● Predictions: probability.

Title: Quarterly update on conditions in the world economy

Executive summary

This quarter, the global economy is growing at 3.7%. Most economies are experiencing an upturn led by the recovery in the USA. Demand for commodities is strong. This is partly due to rises in living standards and mainly because of investment in manufacturing. We believe interest rates should fall over the next quarter.

Currently, the USA _____ at 0.5%. The economy _____

Eurozone _____
Japan _____
Emerging markets _____
Commodities: steel _____

	Growth this quarter	Economic cycle	Supply and demand	Causes	Forecast probabilities
GLOBAL ECONOMY	+3.7%	upturn	demand for commodities (very positive)	rises in living standards and investment in new factories	interest rate cuts (probable)
USA	+0.5%	recovery	consumer demand (positive)	large tax cuts and government spending	fall in the dollar (possible)
EUROZONE	-0.4%	downturn	factory closures to reduce capacity	rise in energy prices and high level of the euro	more public sector investment (probable)
JAPAN	-0.7%	recession	domestic demand (poor)	weak consumer spending + fall in exports	slump (possible)
EMERGING ECONOMIES	+6.25%	boom	factories investing to increase capacity	exports of cheap manufactured products and commodities	strong growth next year (certain)
STEEL	+4%	upturn	demand from housing and manufacturing sectors (very positive)	upturn in USA and recovery in housing markets	steel prices increase sharply (strong probability)

Reading

Who controls the economy today?

1 Work in pairs. Discuss these questions about managing the economy. Who do you think

1 is responsible for deciding interest rates?
2 decides which sectors of an economy to invest in?
3 decides the level of taxes in the economy?
4 regulates banks and financial markets?
5 is responsible for controlling inflation?
6 creates jobs in the economy?

Choose from

a the government
b the financial markets
c the central bank
d multinational companies
e bankers.

2 Read the online forum and match each speaker with one of the five possible answers a–e above. Write the speaker's name next to the matching answer, e.g.
The government – Sophie

Speaking

Expressing and responding to opinions

1 Look back at *Reading* 2 and answer the questions.

1 Underline the ten expressions the people use to express their opinion and to agree or disagree.
2 Match each of the expressions you have underlined with one of these categories.
a 'soft' opinions   d agreement
b normal opinions   e qualified agreement
c strong opinions   f disagreement

EXAMPLE
It seems to me ... a

2 You are going to have a meeting to discuss who really controls the economy. Work in groups of three or four. Each person in the group chooses **one** of the roles from the online discussion in *Reading* 2 and prepare to present your argument for who you think controls the economy.

- the government
- the financial markets
- the central bank
- multinational companies
- bankers

3 Choose a chairperson. The chairperson should ask each participant to present their case in one minute. Then open the discussion. Use some of the 'opinion' expressions from 1. Finally, the chairperson should call a vote and you decide together who really controls the economy.

Who really controls the economy?

Carla
It seems to me that the Central Bank is responsible for managing the economy. They set interest rates in order to keep prices stable and make sure the economy grows to create jobs. I'm convinced you can't trust politicians to manage an economy. They are only concerned with the next election.

Raoul
I'm afraid I don't agree with you, Carla. We can't blame the central banks for everything. No, I think that it is financial markets and speculators who really control the economy today. They decide which sectors of the economy to invest in and they can move millions of dollars around just sitting at a computer.

Mika
Raoul, I agree with you. I think you are right that financial markets are very important. But, in my view, it is the multinationals which have the real power. They decide where and when to build new factories. People forget that without them there would not be any jobs or any goods to export and import.

Sophie
I'm afraid I can't accept that, Mika. I'm sure it is the government that has caused the crisis. Look at the money they have borrowed in the last few years and the taxes they have raised. But where has it gone? I think the government failed to set up a good regulator to control the banks and everything went out of control.

Jeff
Sophie, I take your point, but in my view people are forgetting that it is banks, not governments, who lend money to people. If you don't have a strong banking system in an economy, nothing can happen. Businesses can't borrow money to invest and people can't get mortgages.

Professional skills

How to behave in meetings

The way in which people behave in meetings can vary, depending on the nationality of the people taking part, the culture of the company, and the working relationship of the people involved.

1 Do you agree or disagree with these statements? Change the sentences you disagree with so that you agree with them.

- Always arrive at least ten minutes before the scheduled time.
- Don't waste time on small talk before meetings.
- If you want to create a friendly atmosphere, it's best to use people's first names.
- It's polite to shake everyone's hand at the start of the meeting.
- You can take phone calls during meetings but always apologize and explain that it is an important call.
- Never interrupt someone in a meeting.
- You should only speak at a meeting when someone / the chairperson invites you to speak.
- You should never use your hands or make gestures even if you are angry.
- Make sure you know the names of everyone at the meeting and their job.
- It's not a good idea to socialize after meetings: personal and social life must be kept separate.

2 Can you think of any other things you should or shouldn't do during a meeting in your country? Make a list.

Checklist

Assess your progress in this unit. Tick (✓) the statements which are true.

- ☐ I can talk about the effects of a recession and a recovery
- ☐ I can make predictions about the economy
- ☐ I can describe what happened in the 'Great Depression'
- ☐ I can explain the role of the World Bank and the IMF
- ☐ I can write an internal report on economic conditions
- ☐ I can present my views and agree / disagree in a discussion

Key words

Nouns
boom
capacity
crash
depression
downturn
infrastructure
recession
recovery
slump
upturn

Verbs
contract
cool
decline
experience
go bankrupt
grow
recruit
slow down
stimulate
suffer

Adjectives
buoyant
sluggish

Look back through this unit. Find five more words or expressions that you think are useful.

6 Economic sectors

Countdown

1 Where do most people in your country work? Is it in agriculture, in industry, or in services?

2 A modern economy is made up of three different sectors: the **primary sector**, the **secondary sector**, and the **service sector**. Match the sectors with their definitions.

   1 The _____ manufactures finished products.

   2 The _____ provides the raw materials and natural resources for industry.

   3 The _____ provides support activities for customers or other industries.

3 Which sector do you think is the biggest in a developed economy like the USA? Which sectors are biggest in your country? Which are growing and which are declining?

4 Which sector do these international companies belong to: *BP, Nike, McDonalds, Ford, Citigroup, Google, Nestlé, Hilton Hotels, Rio Tinto*?

Vocabulary

Industries and sectors

1 The photographs below show different industries. How many of them can you name? Complete the captions. Then write which sector they belong to. (The first one has been done for you.) Use a dictionary to check your answers.

2 Now compare your answers with a partner and fill in any gaps.

3 How many of these industries do you have in your country?

s _t_ _e_ _e_ _l_ production
Sector: *Secondary*

t _ _ _ _ _ _ _ _
and logistics
Sector: _____

a _ _ _ _ _ _ _ _ _ _ _
Sector: _____

textiles and
c _ _ _ _ _ _ _
Sector: _____

f _ _ _ processing
Sector: _____

m _ _ _ _ _
Sector: _____

a _ _ _ _ _ _ _ _ _ _
Sector: _____

o _ _ exploration
Sector: _____

r _ _ _ _ _ _ _ _ _
Sector: _____

c _ _ manufacturing
Sector: _____

In this unit
- economic sectors and industries
- comparing and contrasting information
- strengths and weaknesses: comparing two economies
- choosing an investment location
- writing a report comparing options
- presenting and reacting to proposals

4 Look at the report below from an investment bank on the structure of the Turkish economy. Complete the report with words from **1**.

The Turkish economy: background

In Turkey, the primary sector is made up of _____[1] which produces basic foods, like fruits, vegetables, and wheat, and the exploration industries like _____ _____[2] which provide our basic energy and gas, or _____[3] which extracts minerals and material for building.

The secondary sector consists of manufacturing industries, like the _____[4] industry. Also there are the processing industries, for example _____ _____[5].

The manufacturing sector is divided into heavy industries which need great power and big investment in machinery, for example _____[6], and light assembly industries, like _____[7], which produce goods for the fashion industry and need little investment.

The service sector includes many different activities which support both businesses and private customers. Businesses need services like _____[8] to move or store goods and other marketing services, like _____[9] to tell customers about their products.

But the biggest part of the private service sector is made up of consumer services, like the _____[10] sector, which contains shops where we buy things, the finance sector, including banks and insurance, and the fast-growing tourism sector for the international travel market.

5 Work in pairs. Discuss how the Turkish economy compares with the economy in your country.

Pronunciation

Syllable stress in nouns and adjectives

It is often difficult to know which syllable to stress in a word. There are some patterns you can learn to help you, but there are a lot of exceptions, so you need to learn the correct stress for words you use regularly. Here are some examples of syllable stress patterns:

1 For nouns with more than three syllables, the stress is often on the third syllable from the end.

machinery	ma-	**chi-**	ne-	ry
manufacturing	ma-	nu-	**fac-**	tu-	ring

2 The syllable stress in a noun can sometimes change because of its ending (suffix). For example, the syllable immediately before -tion is normally stressed whatever the number of syllables in the word. For example: *production*, *exploration*, *pronunciation*.

3 When nouns become adjectives, the syllable which is stressed often changes.

technology	tech-	**no-**	lo-	gy
technological	tech-	no-	**lo-**	gi-	cal

1 Underline the stressed syllable in the word. If you are not sure, check your answer in a dictionary, such as the *Oxford Advanced Learner's Dictionary*. The stress symbol ' in the phonetic transcription shows which syllable is stressed.

EXAMPLE
product /ˈprɒdʌkt/
production /prəˈdʌkʃn/

1	transportation	6	competition
2	purchasing	7	competitive
3	industry	8	advertising
4	industrial	9	agriculture
5	industrialization	10	agricultural

Now practise pronouncing these words.

2 Two of the words in the list do not follow either of the patterns described above. Which ones?

3 ⌂ Now listen and check your answers.

China overtakes Germany

According to the IMF, China overtook Germany to become the third largest economy in the world in 2007. According to the survey, GDP is:

1 USA $13,807bn   2 Japan $4,382bn
3 China $3,382bn   4 Germany $3,321bn

Reading

Competing in the global economy

Most business strategists now believe that a country, like a company, must build on its key strengths – the sectors and industries which give it a competitive advantage over other countries, such as low labour costs, technology, and natural resources.

1 Before you read, discuss what you think are the key strengths of an emerging economy like China.

2 Work in pairs. You are going to compare the key strengths of an emerging economy, China, and a developed economy, the UK. Student A, go to p.110. Student B, read the report on the UK economy and make notes on the strengths and weaknesses of each sector. In order to do this, you will need to

1 find the examples given for each sector
2 find the strengths mentioned
3 find the weaknesses mentioned
4 add the information in note form.

There is an example of how to do this in the first paragraph of the table. When you have looked at this, read the rest of the report and complete the table in the same way.

THE UK ECONOMY

In the UK, the primary sector is made up of farming and energy-related activities. Farming is very mechanized and uses a lot of machinery, producing about 60% of food needs although it employs only 1% of the workforce. But many small farms are no longer profitable on global markets with low-cost world producers. Primary energy accounts for about 10% of GDP, one of the highest figures for a developed economy. The UK also has important reserves of oil, gas, and coal. However, this sector is now declining and oil and gas production will fall sharply in the next ten years, making the economy dependent on foreign imports of energy.

The secondary sector has continued to suffer from the decline of old heavy industries, like steel, and the closing of mass manufacturing like the car industry. This has created big job losses especially in the north. In the last few years, these old industries have been replaced by new specialist engineering companies with high added-value products and niche markets. However, despite government support, the sector has decreased from 20% to 15% of GDP over the past twenty years.

By contrast, the service sector is booming, benefiting from its highly qualified workforce and the concentration of expertise in the south east. It now represents over 70% of the total economy with financial services, computing and marketing contributing 30% to GDP. But the success is very dependent on financial markets, and the recent growth has put great pressure on road and rail infrastructure in the south east. All this means that future growth will be limited in the short to medium-term.

UK	Examples	Strengths	Weaknesses
Primary sector	• Farming	Mechanized Produces 60% of food needs	Employs only 1% of workforce Not profitable on global markets
	• Energy-related activities	Accounts for 10% of GDP High reserves of oil, gas, and coal	Sector declining Production will fall in next 10 years
Secondary sector	• _____ a		Decline of _____ f industries
	• _____ b		Closure of _____ g Big _____ h losses
	• _____ c	• Higher _____ d products • _____ e markets	
Service sector	• _____ i • _____ j • _____ k	_____ l workforce concentration of _____ m	Dependent on _____ n Infrastructure problems, e.g. _____ o

The **Economist Intelligence Unit** forecasts that China will outstrip the US by 2017 in terms of purchasing power. But in spite of rapid growth, Chinese people remain relatively poor. According to the World Bank, in GDP per capita (per person), China ranks 122 behind Egypt, El Salvador, and Armenia.

3 Now complete the table below on the Chinese economy, by asking Student A questions.

EXAMPLES

What are the key industries in the Chinese primary sector?
What are the weaknesses of the Chinese service sector?

4 Work in small groups or as a class. Compare the economies of China and the UK. Which sectors do you think each country should concentrate on? Why? Use the information in the tables to help you.

CHINA	Examples	Strengths	Weaknesses
Primary sector	• Agriculture	New specializations following move to private / village farms Farming more intensive and more productive than US Significant food exports of _____ a, _____ b, and _____ c	Human labour used Lack of _____ d and investment capital Pollution and _____ e problems
Secondary sector	• Electronics • _____ f • _____ g	Modernization caused by: _____ h Low-cost workforce Cheap _____ i	Still investing in old _____ j Poor _____ k Bureaucracy Shortages of _____ l and _____ m
Service sector	• Marketing • _____ n • _____ o	Demand for services dramatically increased because of _____ p and _____ q Private companies use _____ r for investment, making them more flexible and independent	Businesses lack _____ s and _____ t knowledge

● **Language spot**

Contrasting information

Look at these sentences.

*The farming sector produces about 60% of UK food needs, **although** it employs only 1% of the workforce.*

***Despite** government support, the manufacturing sector continues to decline from about 20% of GDP in 1990 to only 15% today.*

*Manufacturers enjoy the benefit of a low-cost workforce and relatively cheap land. **However,** a lot of the country's capital is invested in old state sector industries.*

When we make a contrast between two statements or ideas in the same sentence that seem to contradict each other, we can use linking words to contrast the ideas. We can do this in different ways, using words like *although*, *despite*, and *however*.

1 Complete the rules with *although*, *despite*, or *however*.

1 _____ is followed by a noun (not a complete clause with a verb).

2 _____ is followed by a clause / sentence with a subject and a verb.

3 _____ can be used when the contrast is expressed in a new sentence.

2 Complete these sentences with *although*, *despite*, or *however*.

1 _____ agriculture employs only 1% of the workforce, it produces 60% of UK food.

2 _____ high productivity, manufacturing in the region continues to decline.

3 _____ the service sector contributes 40% of GDP, it suffers from poor infrastructure.

4 The service sector is very developed. _____, it is very dependent on financial markets.

>> Go to **Language reference** p.123

Listening

Investment decisions

1 Which factors are the most important in choosing which country to locate a factory in? Choose three and then rank them in order 1 to 3 (1 = most important).

- wage costs
- government support and grants
- recruiting trained workers
- transport costs
- suppliers
- language and culture
- taxes
- cost of land

Now compare your answers with your partner.

2 🎧 Listen to a discussion from an investment meeting at a UK manufacturing company about the decision to build a new plant in China or the UK. As you listen, tick (✓) the factors in 1 that are mentioned during the discussion.

3 🎧 Listen again and complete the table summarizing the key points discussed in the meeting.

Key issues	China	UK
Labour costs	$_____ per hour	$_____ per hour
Cost of land	$_____	$_____
Suppliers	delivery time: _____ ($_____ saved)	delivery time: _____
Recruitment	lack of _____ workers	new workers can be trained with existing staff
Quality levels	defect levels of _____ per _____	defect levels of _____ per _____
New product development	no communication with research department in the UK, limiting ability to _____ new products and to _____ successfully	research department located here, so _____ contact with production teams

When you have finished, compare your results with a partner and correct any mistakes.

4 🎧 In the meeting, the different managers make their case for an investment. Listen to some extracts from the dialogue and complete the sentences with the expressions used to present an option.

1 'Having looked at this from a financial perspective, _____ certainly to locate in China. There are _____ for this. First of all, ...'

2 'So, overall, I'm _____ China.'

3 'I'm afraid I don't agree with John on this issue. I'm not _____ China. Although he is right about wage costs in China, I'd _____ a number of other key points.'

4 '... what you seem to be saying is this. _____, locating in China will be cheaper and allow us to get closer to suppliers. _____, there is a risk that we will have problems finding workers.'

5 'Is _____ summary?'

Writing

Reports: comparing options

The plant location decision has now been passed to the investment board for a decision. As the assistant to the chairperson you have been asked to prepare a report comparing the two options: the UK or China.

When we make a direct comparison between two ideas or statements, we can use several linking words, including *while* and *whereas*.
*In China, we will have problems with finding experienced business managers **while** / **whereas** in the UK we can use our existing management.*

We can also use *by contrast* when the comparison is expressed in a new sentence.
*In China, few workers have high levels of education. **By contrast**, in the UK, we can recruit graduates easily.*

Look back at the notes you made in *Listening* and complete the report.

Title: _____

1 Objectives:

The purpose of this report is to …

evaluate the options for the location of the new production plant. — General objective

We were asked to compare two options: China and the UK,

and make a recommendation. — Specific objectives

List findings by category. —

2 Findings:

Example

Labour costs: A production worker in the UK can cost up to $30 per

hour, whereas a production worker in China costs only $2 per hour. — In this report, compare China and the UK for each category. Use some of the comparing or contrasting expressions in the *Language spot* on p47.

a labour costs: _____

b land costs: _____

c suppliers: _____

d recruitment: _____

e quality levels: _____

f new product development: _____

State conclusion. —

3 Recommendations:

Having considered the different options, we have

concluded that we are in favour of _____

This is because _____ — Give reason(s) for your conclusion (Use *although*, *despite*, or *however*).

Webquest

1 Go on the Internet to find out about the work of regional development agencies in your country or region. Make notes on these points.

1 How do they promote the benefits of your country / region?
2 What special incentives do they offer companies?
3 What kind of investors do you think they are targeting?

2 Now choose another country or region and compare the results. Do they have any better ideas your country could use?

3 Work in pairs. Using your notes, prepare a simple web page promoting the benefits of investment in your region. Think about the layout: you need a good banner heading, features / benefits in bullet points, and any links to other web pages or websites. Explain your page to the class.

Why choose Frankfurt Rhine-Main region?

- at the crossroads of Europe
- excellent infrastructure
- highly qualified workforce
- the centre for European finance
- home of the ECB and many international banks
- rich cultural life
- world-class universities and schools

It's my job

1 Before you read, discuss the questions in pairs.

How do you think regions or states can attract international investors to come and set up businesses in their area?

Can you think of any areas in your country (or elsewhere) that have attempted to attract foreign investors? What did they do? Were they successful?

2 Now read the interview with Matthias Wolff. What strategies did they use to attract investors to Frankfurt?

3 Work in pairs. Discuss the questions.

1 Do you think governments should spend money on attracting companies to locate in a region? What benefits could they bring?

2 What do you think an international company is looking for when they decide to build a new plant in a country?

3 How would you promote your region or city to international companies? What features would you try and sell?

Speaking

The road to development

1 Which developing countries do you think have been most successful in recent years? Why?

2 Look at the list of different options below. Which are the three best strategies for a developing country to follow? Rank them by importance (1 = the best option). Are there any strategies you think are wrong? (Mark them 'no'.)

a to invest in education and training
b to open the country to global competition
c to protect domestic industries, like agriculture
d to encourage international companies to invest in the country
e to borrow money from the financial markets or institutions like the World Bank
f to develop export industries
g to build infrastructure (road, rail, telecom)
h to privatize state companies
i to cut taxes

Matthias Wolff

Job Regional development officer
Location Frankfurt, Germany

What exactly does a regional development officer do?
People often think that a regional development office just promotes tourism, but in fact our task is to attract international companies to locate in the Frankfurt region. That means creating jobs and income for people in the state.

How do you sell a region for investment?
Well, a lot of the work is basic to any sales job: following up leads, making contacts, building relationships with companies. But then we have to put together a package of incentives to attract investors. This may mean offering special grants or loans to buy land, special tax rates, or more importantly working with local training organizations to provide clients with special courses to train their workers. Training is a key selling point for us.

Why do companies come to Frankfurt? I thought Germany was a very expensive place to do business.
Yes, you're right. Land, office space, and wages are expensive here. But on the other hand, Frankfurt is the German centre for financial services: the stock market is based here and many of the world's biggest banks have operations in the city. So by coming here, companies can connect with a network of businesses with specializations they can't find elsewhere.

3 Look at the different expressions for presenting and reacting to proposals in a meeting. Match the expressions with the language functions in the table below.

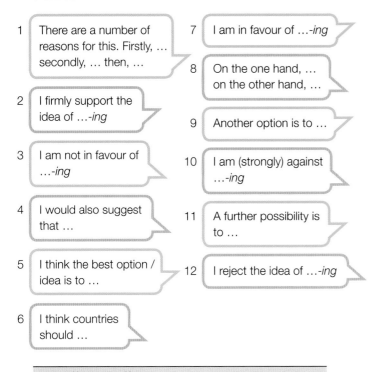

1 There are a number of reasons for this. Firstly, … secondly, … then, …

2 I firmly support the idea of …-*ing*

3 I am not in favour of …-*ing*

4 I would also suggest that …

5 I think the best option / idea is to …

6 I think countries should …

7 I am in favour of …-*ing*

8 On the one hand, … on the other hand, …

9 Another option is to …

10 I am (strongly) against …-*ing*

11 A further possibility is to …

12 I reject the idea of …-*ing*

presenting an option
giving reasons to support your argument
adding a second option
rejecting a proposal
approving a proposal
presenting the positive and negative side of an option

4 Work in groups of three or four. Hold a meeting to discuss the best way for a developing country to build its economy.

Each student should present their three options for development. Use some of the language above to help you.

Discuss the proposals together and try to reach an agreement on the best three options for the group.

Key words

Nouns

agriculture	retailing
demand	secondary sector
developed economy	service sector
emerging economy	shortage
heavy industry	strength
light industry	weakness
logistics	workforce
manufacturing	
mining	**Verbs**
natural resources	account (for)
primary sector	evaluate
raw materials	locate

Look back through this unit. Find five more words or expressions that you think are useful.

Reading bank

Reading bank tips

Most of the questions in this *Reading bank* are in a similar format to ones in the *Test of Reading* in the *Cambridge International Certificate of Financial English (ICFE)*.

More generally, the different types of question in this *Reading bank* can help you to develop the reading and vocabulary skills you will need for your career in finance.

The two things that you most need to do to develop these skills are:

1 **Read as much as possible from real articles and websites about finance** so that you can build up your vocabulary and your general knowledge of the subject. The *Webquest* activities in this book show you different ways of finding interesting authentic material on the Internet.

2 **Keep a careful record of all the new vocabulary you learn**, especially in those areas of finance you are especially interested in. Organize it by theme, learn words with their opposites, and remember to look out for word partnerships, not just individual words. The *Vocabulary* activities in this book show different techniques for learning and practising vocabulary.

Here are some specific tips for answering the different kinds of exam-type question in this *Reading bank*. They should be useful, even if you aren't preparing for an exam.

Multiple choice gap-filling [Text 1 (Question 2); Text 2; and Text 3]

This is similar to Part 1 of the ICFE Test of Reading.

In this type of question, you have to choose the best word or phrase to fill a gap in the text from a choice of four options (A, B, C, or D). When answering:

● **Check that the word or phrase you've chosen has the right meaning.**
Sometimes words can have similar meanings, but they do not mean exactly the same. If you aren't sure, use a dictionary, but see if you can get the right answer without help first.

● **Check that your answer fits grammatically.**
Look at the text immediately before and after the gap. Decide what kind of word fits the gap: is it a noun, verb, adjective, adverb, conjunction, or preposition? Is the answer you've chosen in the right grammatical category?

● **Check that your answer fits in with the text as a whole.**
Make sure that you have read the whole text first. Does the answer you've chosen seem to fit in with the general meaning of the text?

● **Check all the answers twice.**
When you think you've found the right answer, you need to look at all the other possible answers again. Are all the answers you haven't chosen definitely wrong?

Matching summaries to paragraphs [Text 1 (Question 1); Text 4]

This is similar to Part 4 of the ICFE Test of Reading.

In this type of question, you match statements or paragraph headers to each of the individual paragraphs in the text. When answering:

● **Highlight the key words in the text that help you to decide on the right answer.**
This will help you to develop the skill of focusing on the particular information you need to find in a text.

● **Don't choose answers just because they contain words and phrases that also appear in one of the paragraphs.**
You need to think about the overall meaning of the text, rather than just matching words.

Comprehension [Text 5; Text 6]

This is similar to Part 6 of the ICFE Test of Reading.

In this type of question, you have to choose the best answer from a choice of four options (A, B, C, or D). The questions often ask you to decide between a set of opinions and statements: you have to decide which one matches what the writer of the text means to say.

The questions appear in the same order as the text. To answer some of the questions, you will only need to look at one specific paragraph in the text; but to answer others, you will need to have read and understood the whole text. When answering:

● **Read the whole text before you look at the questions.**
You need to have a general idea of what the author's opinion is before you answer the questions.

● **Eliminate the incorrect answers first.**
When you have read the text, look at each of the four options in turn and decide which ones are definitely wrong, and which could be right.

● **Make sure that you read the text very closely; don't just match individual words.**
Sometimes the incorrect answers contain words and expressions used in the text. So, you shouldn't just try to match individual words and phrases in the question options and the text. Instead, you need to be sure that the meaning of the answer you've chosen matches what you think the writer is saying, explaining, or arguing.

1 Retail banking

1 Read the text about the future of retail banking. Match the paragraphs A–E with the headings 1–5 below.

1 A focus on cost reduction and consolidation
2 Only the biggest will survive
3 Why banking will make big profits again
4 The new entrants
5 Our world will continue to need banks

2 Choose the best word or phrase to fill each gap from a, b, c, or d.

1 a of   c in
  b on   d for

2 a too   c lot of
  b much   d plenty of

3 a so important as
  b important that
  c as important as
  d too important than

4 a not enough   c such
  b so   d too

5 a Despite   c Ever
  b Although   d In spite

6 a lot   c already
  b far   d ever

7 a like to   c same
  b so   d such as

8 a although   c neither
  b either   d both

9 a up to date   c up on
  b so far   d on date

10 a not be able to   c unable to
   b able to   d inable to

11 a like   c other
   b such   d others

12 a by   c for
   b with   d in

The future of retail banking

A _____

What is the future of banking? Will banking be profitable again? Every day I am asked this question. And the answer will vary depending _____[1] what kind of banking you are talking about, and what country you are in. But we can see general principles, and _____[2] opportunities for profitable banking in the future.

B _____

As we have seen in the current crisis, banking is vital to a nation's future. Banks are _____[3] hospitals, schools, roads, and railways. Sometimes, like Citigroup, or RBS, they are _____[4] big to fail. Without banks, business and personal life quickly grind to a halt in developed nations where finance and credit needs to flow quickly and easily.

C _____

Many countries in developed nations are 'over-banked'. _____[5] some bank closures, there are still _____[6] too many small banks – especially in countries like America. That means extra costs. There are too many retail outlets – bricks-and-mortar bank branches are expensive to maintain, and increasingly unnecessary for retail banking. Many banks have been re-inventing local branches as specialist advisory centres for financial services products _____[7] pensions, life insurance, larger mortgages, and home loans. But even so, expect consolidation – _____[8] bank mergers, or branch mergers of the same bank.

D _____

Technology is a huge cost for banking and here again we can expect pressures to save cost through mergers. For example, it is a massive task to keep _____[9] with all the latest options for online banking, using mobile devices and so on. Smaller banks can easily get left behind, and are also _____[10] invest in next-generation call centres or customer management systems.

E _____

So we can expect retail banking to continue a relentless shift from face to face to online. At the same time, expect non-banking competition to grow, as companies like Walmart, Tesco, Carrefour, and _____[11] try to grab market share by encouraging their existing customers to bank with them. We will see these companies provide most services online, and deposits and withdrawals provided in local stores at very low cost.
So, retail banking will employ fewer people, charge more for services, and see more non-banking competitors, attracted _____[12] the profits that retail banks are making.

2 The credit crisis

Read the following extract from an article about the credit crunch. Choose the best word to fill each gap from a, b, c, or d.

1. a takeover   c form
   b marry   d merge
2. a bankrupt   c delinquency
   b fail   d collapse
3. a overtaken   c taken over
   b resolved   d taken up
4. a borrowed   c owed
   b loaned   d indebted
5. a afford   c buy
   b save   d spend
6. a provide   c borrow
   b pay   d calculate
7. a decreasing   c fall
   b surge   d declines
8. a crisis   c problem
   b difficulty   d situation
9. a losses   c costs
   b payments   d income
10. a customer   c consumer
    b economy   d industry
11. a redundant   c fired
    b unemployment   d losses
12. a deposit   c safe
    b spend   d borrow

HBOS merger talks close historic week

By Nick Louth

September 17 2008

Financial history is being made this week. Not since the 1929 Wall Street Crash has the global banking system seen anything like it.

In the UK, the decision of HBOS, Britain's biggest mortgage bank, to _____[1] with Lloyds TSB will create Britain's biggest domestic bank. It follows the US government's $85 billion decision earlier this week to rescue AIG, one of the world's largest insurance groups, and the financial _____[2] on Monday of Lehman Brothers, one of the biggest investment banks on Wall Street. In recent months, three giant Wall Street investment banking firms, Bear Stearns, Merrill Lynch, and Lehman, have either collapsed, been rescued, or been _____[3] by other banks.

And it was all caused by the sub-prime loan crisis, namely US banks which over the last few years _____[4] money to people who couldn't _____[5] the mortgage payments on houses that were themselves over-priced. These bad loans were packaged into very complex asset-backed securities, a type of debt whose value was then hard to _____[6]. Since then, the markets have been full of speculation that more banks will collapse. This has led to a complete collapse in market confidence and a big _____[7] in share prices.

To try to stop the _____[8], the US Government has begun a kind of nationalization of parts of the financial system. On Tuesday, it took an 80% stake in AIG Insurance, and through the Federal Reserve loaned it $85 billion, to avoid the collapse of the company and the consequent spread of _____[9] of $128 billion to other parts of the banking system.

Less than two weeks ago, US Treasury Secretary Hank Paulson also took Fannie Mae and Freddie Mac into state control, which between them guarantee more than $5 trillion of American mortgages. The hard-pressed US _____[10], already suffering from higher debts, falling house prices, and higher fuel prices, may not be happy about this extra burden, but can do little about it.

The hundreds of thousands who work for banks or in the City will be fearful of losing their jobs, just like the 5,000 that Lehman employed in London who were made _____[11] earlier this week. It will do nothing to encourage the consumer to spend in the shops or help the British economy grow. Trust in financial institutions, something needed by all banks because we _____[12] our money with them in current accounts and savings accounts, will need a generation to recover.

3 Auditing

Read the article about the auditor's report. Choose the best word to fill each gap from a, b, c, or d.

1   a said   c inspected
    b required   d needed

2   a written   c allow
    b instructing   d appointed

3   a benefits   c accuracy
    b profits   d publishing

4   a auditor's website
    b press report
    c company
    d letter

5   a outlines   c is
    b tells   d follows

6   a like   c according to
    b for example   d between

7   a paid   c driven
    b published   d conducted

8   a exposures   c revelations
    b informations d disclosures

9   a true and fair
    b true and final
    c long and short
    d right and wrong

10 a failure   c previous
    b professional d qualified

The auditor's report

All large companies are _____1 by law to have their accounts audited by an external auditor every year. The auditors are _____2 by the shareholders of the company to examine the company's books and to form an opinion about the _____3 of the accounts. The auditor's report is then published in the _____4 and distributed to shareholders. An auditor's report usually follows a very standard format and all auditors use almost the same language to present their opinion. But the report always contains three main sections:

Respective responsibilities of directors and auditors

This statement _____5 the responsibilities of the company's directors for preparing the accounts _____6 accepted accounting standards and the responsibilities of the auditor.

Basis of audit opinion

This explains the auditing standards used and the methods by which the audit was _____7. It usually contains standard statements like: 'An audit includes examination, on a test basis, of evidence relevant to the amounts and _____8 in the financial statements. It also includes an assessment of the significant estimates and judgements made by the directors in preparation of the financial statements.'

Opinion

The opinion is normally a statement of the fact that 'in our opinion, the financial statements give a _____9 view of the state of affairs of the company'. In the rare case of a _____10 report, this will highlight any special areas of concern which will warn shareholders about significant risks in the company.

4 Mergers and acquisitions

Read the text below about mergers and acquisitions. Which paragraph A–F does each of the statements below 1–6 refer to?

1 The motivation for mergers can be negatively influenced by strong management personalities. _____

2 Data shows that a lot of mergers will not achieve the planned savings. _____

3 A typical reason for failure can be the difference between the working practices of the two companies. _____

4 Sometimes mergers can be motivated by a fear of being taken over by another competitor. _____

5 If managers are realistic, mergers can achieve greater efficiencies. _____

6 Mergers can appear an attractive way to achieve efficiencies, but they don't always work out successfully. _____

Mergers and acquisitions: why they can fail

A

It is no secret that plenty of mergers do not work. Those who advocate mergers will explain that the merger will cut costs or boost revenues by more than enough to justify the price. It can sound so simple: just combine the computer systems in the two companies, merge a few departments, use your size to reduce the price you pay for materials, and the merged giant should be more efficient than its parts. In theory, it sounds great, but, in practice, things can go wrong.

B

Historical trends show that roughly two thirds of big mergers will fail to achieve their objectives. That means they will lose value on the stock market. The motivations that drive mergers can be flawed and efficiencies from economies of scale may not be realized.

C

A merger may often have more to do with the ambitions of top executives than good business strategy. The executive ego, driven by a competitive instinct to win, is a major force in M&A, especially when combined with the influences from the bankers, lawyers, and other advisors who can earn big fees from clients engaged in mergers.

D

In other cases mergers may be driven by uncertainty and a generalized fear of the future. The arrival of new technological developments, globalization, or a fast-changing economic landscape are all factors that can create a strong incentive for defensive mergers. Sometimes, the management team feels they have no choice and must acquire a rival in order to prevent their own company from being acquired. The idea is that only big players will survive in a more competitive world.

E

The chances for success are further reduced if the corporate cultures of the companies are very different. When a company is acquired, the decision is typically based on product or market synergies, but cultural differences are often ignored. It's a mistake to assume that personnel issues are easily overcome.

F

But remember, not all mergers fail. Size and global reach can be an advantage and strong managers can often squeeze greater profits out of badly run companies. The success of mergers depends on how realistic the deal makers are and how well they can merge the two companies while maintaining day-to-day operations.

5 Cash flow

Read the explanation of cash flow. Choose the best answer for each question from a, b, c, or d.

1 According to paragraph 1, cash flow is most affected by
   a sales
   b investment
   c credit
   d profits.

2 Which is true?
   a Cash-flow problems happen when the inflow of cash is greater than the outflow.
   b Cash flow can become a problem if companies do not manage their credit terms with customers.
   c Cash-flow problems happen when a company has a lot of large customers.
   d Cash-flow problems are caused by a liquidity crisis.

3 When a company makes a sale,
   a it usually receives cash
   b it has to wait if it wants cash
   c it usually grants a credit period
   d it makes sure it has enough cash to pay suppliers.

4 According to paragraph 2, customers who place large orders
   a never pay on time
   b benefit from better terms of credit
   c have a good record of payment
   d have a good credit history.

5 The best way for a company to improve cash flow is to
   a stop lending to customers
   b offer incentives or discounts for fast payment
   c increase credit periods for customers
   d offer incentives for quick sales.

Cash flow

The cash flow of a company is a simple record of the real movement of money into, and out of, the company's accounts. These transactions can come from one of three sources: operating activities, investing activities, or financing activities. It is important to realize that cash flow is not the same as sales or profit because cash flow shows only the real movement of money. However, when a company makes a sale, it usually offers the client a period of credit in which to pay (typically, 28 days). So, the company does not receive actual cash immediately. This means the finance department must make sure that the real inflow of cash covers the outflow of cash necessary, to pay its suppliers. Failure to manage this actual movement of money can create a liquidity crisis in which a successful company with a lot of sales does not have enough cash to pay its creditors, resulting in insolvency.

Cash-flow problems typically arise from over-extended credit. When a company grants credit to a customer, it is effectively lending money to the customer. The length of the credit period will vary depending on the credit history of the customer. Generally speaking, this will be longer for customers who place large orders or who have a good record of payment. But if a large customer does not pay promptly, this can generate a cash-flow crisis since the company may not have sufficient funds to pay other creditors. Because of this, many companies offer customers discounts or incentives to pay quickly.

"Oh goodness, did I put it back the wrong way?"
PROFITS

6 Fund management

Read the article about mutual funds. Choose the best answer from a, b, c, or d.

1 According to paragraph 1,
   a mutual funds give you a secure investment over the long term
   b mutual funds are safer than bonds
   c the value of mutual funds moves in relation to the price of the shares they own
   d mutual funds are safer because they are managed professionally.

2 'Stellar performances' are
   a disastrous   b outstanding
   c secure   d risky.

3 According to paragraph 2,
   a overdiversification is a good way to reduce risks
   b diversification means that your money is invested in different stocks
   c overdiversification happens because people buy a lot of different funds
   d it is important to invest in only one sector, like the energy sector.

4 To pool money is
   a to invest the money in mutual funds
   b to ask investors for money
   c to withdraw money from a fund
   d to collect together the money from different investors in one fund.

Disadvantages of mutual funds

Like many investments, mutual funds offer advantages and disadvantages, which are important for you to consider and understand before you decide to buy. Here we explore some of the drawbacks of mutual funds.

1 **Fluctuating returns**   Mutual funds are like many other investments without a guaranteed return: there is always the possibility that the value of your mutual fund will decline. Unlike fixed-income products, such as bonds and Treasury bills, mutual funds experience price fluctuations along with the stocks that make up the fund. When deciding on a particular fund to buy, you need to research the risks involved – just because a professional manager is looking after the fund, that doesn't mean the performance will be stellar. Another important thing to know is that mutual funds are not guaranteed by the US government, so in the case of dissolution, you will not get anything back.

2 **Diversification or overdiversification?**   Although diversification is one of the keys to successful investing, many mutual fund investors tend to overdiversify. The idea of diversification is to reduce the risks associated with holding a single security; overdiversification occurs when investors acquire many funds that are closely related, for example by all being in one sector, like the energy sector. As a result, they don't get the risk reducing benefits of diversification.

3 **Cash, cash, and more cash**   It is important to remember that mutual funds pool money from thousands of investors, so every day, investors are putting money into the fund as well as withdrawing investments. In order to maintain liquidity and the capacity to manage withdrawals, funds typically have to keep a large portion of their portfolios in cash. Having a lot of cash is great for liquidity, but money sitting around as cash is not working for you, and thus is not very advantageous.

4 **Cost warnings**   Mutual funds provide investors with professional management, but it comes at a cost. Funds will typically have a range of different fees that reduce the overall payout. Furthermore, advertisements, rankings, and ratings issued by fund companies only describe past performance. Always note that mutual fund advertisements always include the tagline 'past results are not indicative of future returns'. Be sure not to pick funds only because they have performed well in the past – yesterday's big winners may be today's big losers.

5 **Conclusion**   When you buy any investment, it's important to understand both the good and bad points. If the advantages that the investment offers outweigh its disadvantages, it's quite possible that mutual funds are something to consider. Whether you decide in favour of or against mutual funds, the probability of a successful portfolio increases dramatically when you do your homework.

Reading bank key

5 According to paragraph 3, which of these statements is not true?
a Funds make better returns to investors because they have good liquidity.
b Mutual funds keep a lot of money in cash.
c Money kept in cash does not earn good returns.
d Cash is necessary because investors buy and sell the funds every day.

6 According to paragraph 4,
a professional management improves the returns in mutual funds
b high levels of fees will mean better returns for investors
c the historical information in performance tables is a good guide for investment
d investors should pay close attention to the warnings about performance.

7 According to paragraph 5,
a mutual funds have more advantages than disadvantages
b you should definitely consider investing in mutual funds
c investors must do research and make up their own mind
d investment returns will increase dramatically in a mutual fund.

1 Retail banking

1 Paragraph A: 3
Paragraph B: 5
Paragraph C: 1
Paragraph D: 2
Paragraph E: 4

2 1 b   2 d   3 c   4 d   5 a
6 b   7 d   8 b   9 a   10 c
11 d   12 a

2 The credit crisis

1 d   2 d   3 c   4 b   5 a   6 d
7 c   8 a   9 a   10 c   11 a   12 a

3 Auditing

1 b   2 d   3 c   4 c   5 a   6 c
7 d   8 d   9 b   10 d

4 Mergers and acquisitions

Paragraph A: 6
Paragraph B: 2
Paragraph C: 1
Paragraph D: 4
Paragraph E: 3
Paragraph F: 5

5 Cash flow

1 c   2 b   3 c   4 d   5 b

6 Fund management

1 c   2 b   3 b   4 d   5 a
6 d   7 c

7 Banking

Countdown

1 Where are these banks based? Match the banks with the flags. One of the flags goes with two banks.

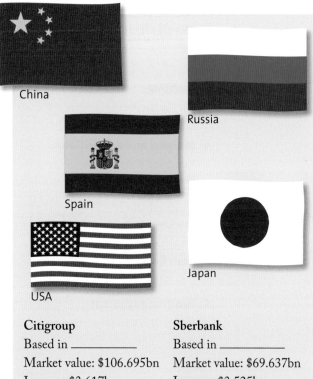

China

Russia

Spain

Japan

USA

Citigroup
Based in _____
Market value: $106.695bn
Income: $3.617bn

ICBC
Based in _____
Market value: $277.235bn
Income: $11.617bn

Banco Santander
Based in _____
Market value: $125.065bn
Income: $14.319bn

Sberbank
Based in _____
Market value: $69.637bn
Income: $3.525bn

Goldman Sachs
Based in _____
Market value: $82.106bn
Income: $11.590bn

Mitsubishi UFJ Financial Group
Based in _____
Market value: $93.846bn
Income: $8.835bn

2 Answer the questions.

1 Look at the profiles of each bank. How many do you know? What do you know about them?
2 Which of the banks was the biggest when the survey was done? Is size important for a bank? Why / Why not?

3 Which of these opinions do you think are true about banks after the credit crisis?

a 'There are parts of the banking system that are a socially useless activity', Lord Turner, chairman of the Financial Services Authority (FSA), UK in 2009.
b 'Banks have to offer big bonuses in order to keep their best performing staff.'
c 'A global bank is much more secure than a regional local bank.'
d 'The state has no place in the banking sector.'

Listening

Types of bank in the UK

Karl Horst is visiting London as part of a delegation from German regional banks to build relationships between European banks. Marion Dempster, a UK bank executive, is explaining the British system to him.

1 🎧 Listen to the conversation and find the customer group each bank serves. Tick (✓) the correct boxes in Marion's presentation slide.

THE UK BANKING SYSTEM

Type of bank	Type of customer / client		
	Individual customers	Small / medium companies	International companies
1 Retail bank			
2 Commercial bank			
3 Investment bank			
4 Building society			
5 Supermarket bank			
6 Internet bank			

2 🎧 Listen again and answer these questions.

1 What is the difference between a mutual and a public listed company?
2 Why have the supermarkets entered financial services?
3 Why do Internet banks have an advantage over older retail banks?

Speaking

Checking, clarifying, reformulating

When someone explains something, you often have to check if you understood correctly or ask for clarification.

1 🎧 Listen to some extracts from the conversation in *Listening* and complete the expressions.

1 ... RBS or Barclays also offer commercial banking, so they provide both services.

_____

2 OK. So if I _____,
the same bank can be both a commercial and a retail bank? Is that right?

3 But they also have large M&A departments,
_____, mergers and acquisitions, ...

4 Sorry, _____ about fees. Could you _____?

5 Sure, _____ was that investment banks don't actually lend money to companies.

6 So, you _____ the customers are really the owners of the building society. Is that right?

7 OK, so if I have _____, there are about six different types of banks in the UK.

2 Now transfer the expressions you have written in **1** to the *Useful language* table below.

3 Work in pairs. Take turns to ask about and explain each of the six types of bank in *Listening*.

A Ask your partner to explain.
What exactly is a 'retail bank'?
B Give your explanation and check they understand.
A Ask for more details.
B Give more details or examples.
A Ask them to repeat.
B Repeat the information and reformulate.
A Explain you didn't understand.
B Summarize the main points.

Webquest

Go on the Internet to find the biggest retail / commercial bank in your country. Find this information about the bank and make notes.

- Where is its HQ?
- Number of staff
- Number of customers
- Organization structure
- Types of products / services / brands it offers
- Its turnover or its profit for last year
- Overseas operations

Useful language	Asking people to give more details or repeat
Checking other people understand you	Could you be more specific?
Is _____¹?	Could you give me / us more details?
OK?	I'm afraid I didn't catch that.
Are you with me?	Sorry, I _____⁵ / follow that.
Checking you have understood	Could you _____⁶ / run through it again?
So, you mean that...	Could you repeat that, please?
So, you _____² ... Is that right?	**Reformulating**
So, if I _____³, ... Is that right?	In other words, ...
So, if I have _____⁴, ...	Sure, the point I _____⁷ was that ...
	That is to say ...

Reading

An organization chart for a bank

1 A bank can organize all its activities in two ways:

a) by functional departments – human resources, marketing, accounting, etc.

b) by product lines focused on particular customer groups.

Look at the organization chart for a UK bank, STR. Which organization structure does the bank use?

2 Look at the five divisions in the second row of the organization chart below. What do you think these different divisions in the bank do?

3 Read the text opposite and, using the STR organigram below, complete 2–6 in the text with the names of the divisions.

4 Now complete the organization chart with the name of the target clients for each division and the typical products they offer.

5 Work in pairs and decide which division of the bank these clients would call for services.

1 A small business that wants to lease some machinery
2 A student who wants to open an Internet savings account
3 Someone who wants to manage a big portfolio of shares
4 A family business that wants to take out a loan
5 A family man who is seeking advice about mortgages in order to buy a flat
6 A rich sports star who is looking for ways to invest his money

Group structure

1 The STR banking group, with its headquarters in London, is made up of five main operating divisions.

2 _____

We provide a complete range of banking services to individuals and families and offer a choice of ways to do business – in branch, by phone, or online. Our product range includes leading brands in current accounts, savings, and investments, plus unsecured personal loans, mortgages, and award-winning insurance.

3 _____

We offer banking and investment services to wealthy private and business customers in the UK and around the world. Our services include portfolio management, tax planning, and stockbroking.

4 _____

We offer a range of tailored products and services for small businesses, as well as providing a network of business advisors based in our branches. Our commercial subsidiaries offer specialist help in the areas of vehicle and property leasing and asset finance.

5 _____

This division supports the needs of large international companies, providing access to a full range of services in global financial markets, providing debt financing, risk management, and investment services. The STR group remains an important banking partner to major corporations and financial and governmental institutions around the world.

6 _____

This supports the activities of all the STR operations, developing and maintaining the infrastructure and IT technology to support our branches. It also manages our property portfolio and is responsible for our purchasing.

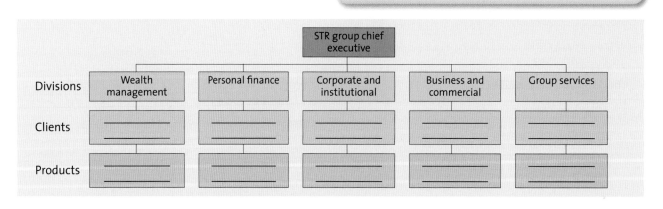

What message do you think these banks were trying to communicate by using these slogans?

The listening bank (Midland Bank, now HSBC)

One idea among millions (Santander)

Citi never sleeps (Citigroup)

By your side (Sberbank)

The bank for a changing world (BNP Paribas)

The bank that bridges East and West (RZB)

Thinking today about tomorrow (Deutsche Bank)

Vocabulary

Banks and their products

1 Look back at *Reading* and find the words or phrases in the text to describe

  1 the main office of a bank (paragraph 1)

  2 the different sections of activity in the bank (paragraph 1)

  3 the different types of products they offer to clients (paragraph 2)

  4 the names under which the bank trades (paragraph 2)

  5 money lent to buy property (paragraph 2)

  6 loans given to clients without a guarantee, e.g. on a credit card (paragraph 2)

  7 the services they offer:
    a) to manage investments (paragraph 3)
    b) to buy and sell shares (paragraph 3)

  8 products aimed at a specific customer group (paragraph 4)

  9 the office for customers it has in every city (paragraph 4)

  10 a financial service that allows companies to obtain machinery, property, or vehicles without the cost of buying these items (paragraph 4).

2 Your manager has asked you to write a profile of STR as part of an *equity research report* (a report which analyses a company for potential investors). Complete the profile by choosing from the words in **1**.

> STR is a major provider of banking and insurance products, with a complete _____[1] of financial services. With its _____[2] in the UK, it also has a substantial business in the USA and is further represented across large parts of continental Europe. The bank has five main _____[3]. It has _____[4] in all major cities in UK and has many _____[5] products for special customer groups. Its services include _____[6], to allow customers to buy and sell shares, and _____[7], to help manage clients' investments. The bank's commercial division also offers specialist services to companies, like _____[8] of equipment or vehicles. Its _____[9] names include STR Insurance, Reach Bank, USA, and Customer First.

Writing

A bank profile

The STR profile at the end of *Vocabulary* is written as a piece of equity research. But if it appeared on a website as a marketing communication to customers, it might be worded differently.

1 Look at the marketing text below. What differences do you notice in the language and style of the text compared with the previous equity research? Think about these points:

  ● How are the bank and the customer referred to?

  ● Are the words and expressions formal or informal?

  ● How does it use personal pronouns?

> **At STR, we can offer you all the financial services you need for every stage of your life.**
>
> And it's so easy! By phone, online, or in any of our branches, check out our market leading offers, like our award-winning current accounts.
>
> If you're a student paying for your university, a family buying your first house, or even a pensioner managing your savings, we have tailored our products to suit your needs. Call in to one of our branches and find out more from our specialist advisors.
>
> From our base in the UK, we operate through all of continental Europe, or even in the USA. Wherever you are, we're there to support you. Come in and ask or visit us online!
>
> *Look out for our familiar names like* **STR Insurance**, **Reach Bank**, **USA**, and **Customer First**.

2 Using the model profiles of STR above, work in pairs.

Student A, write a profile of the bank you have researched in the *Webquest* as a piece of *equity research*. In your profile, you should focus on the financial features that would interest an investor.

Student B, write a profile of the bank you have researched in the *Webquest* as a *marketing communication* to customers of the bank. In your profile, you should focus on selling the bank's services to its customers and users.

Work together and compare your results.

Know your credit terms

credit limit: the amount of money a bank is prepared to lend to a customer

credit history: a history of the client's previous and current borrowings and repayments

cross-selling: selling extra services to customers in addition to what they already use

credit check: a bank will investigate a client's previous borrowings and current debts before agreeing to provide any new loans

loan schedule: a timetable showing the amount of interest to be paid each month and the conditions for repayment of the loan

It's my job

1 Before you read, discuss the questions in pairs.

1 What do you think the job of a loan officer in a bank involves?

2 What skills would you need to do the job?

2 Read the interview and find the answers to the questions in **1**.

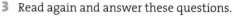

Ursula Grzelski

Job Loan officer
Works for Bank of Poland, Warsaw

How is your department organized?
We have three different teams responsible for different kinds of loan. One team is for consumer loans, which includes personal loans, educational loans, and loans to buy a car; a second team deals with commercial loans for small businesses; and the third team is responsible for mortgage lending to clients who want to buy a flat. I work for the commercial team for small businesses.

That must be a lot of responsibility.
Well, not really, because part of my job is just routine. I help the client to complete the loan application forms, and then see if the application meets the credit limits set by the bank. I have to check if the client will be able to repay the loan. For example, we have to know how much profit the company really makes, what other expenses or debts it has. So, we have to check their credit history. Do they usually pay their suppliers on time? Are they good at collecting payments from customers? That kind of thing. Then I have to work out a loan schedule for repayment. If the analysis is good, then I send the complete application with my calculations to my supervisor for checking.

What is the most difficult part of the job?
Oh, when I started work after university, the worst part was contacting clients to try to sell them additional services, in other words, cross-selling.

3 Read again and answer these questions.

1 What is the difference between 'consumer loans' and 'commercial loans'?

2 Why are banks so interested in the 'credit history' of a client? What does it tell them?

3 Which of the three teams in Ursula's department would be most interesting to work for? Why?

Professional skills

Selling on the telephone

Selling on the telephone sometimes requires different skills from face-to-face selling.

1 Here are some of Ursula's tips about selling on the phone. Which three are the most important?

1 Prepare the call carefully before you make it. Make a list of the points you want to cover during the conversation.

2 Keep a good database – record all your information on the client and have it ready when you start the call.

3 Always begin by checking that it's a convenient time. If it isn't, make an appointment to call back later.

4 'Small talk' can be useful: for example, a change in the client's business could be a selling opportunity.

5 Don't ask too many questions that they can answer with just 'yes' or 'no'.

6 Imagine the person you're talking to is in the room; concentrate on what they are saying and don't do other things at the same time.

7 Build a relationship. Keep in regular touch with the client even if nothing special is happening.

8 At the end of a call, repeat what you have agreed and fix a time for another call.

2 Can you think of any other tips for selling on the phone? Are there things you shouldn't do?

● **Language spot**

Verb patterns

When you learn a new verb in English, it is important to look at how the verb works. If a verb is followed by another verb, different patterns are possible. Some common patterns are:

verb + *to* infinitive   *The third team is responsible for mortgage lending to clients who **want** to buy a flat.*

verb + *-ing*   *When I started work after university, I **hated** selling!*

verb + object + *to* infinitive   *I **help** the client to complete the loan application forms.*

Some verbs, like *want*, *help*, and *ask*, can belong to more than one category:
*I **want** to arrange a mortgage.*
*I **want** you to arrange a mortgage for me.*
*She **helped** to arrange my mortgage.*
*She **helped** me to arrange my mortgage.*

>> Go to **Language reference** p.123

1 Complete the following article about starting a company by putting the verbs into the correct form.

Do you want ___to be___ [1] (be) an entrepreneur?

Have you ever considered _____[2] (*start*) your own business? Can you imagine _____[3] (*make*) a lot of money or _____[4] (*be*) an entrepreneur? Or maybe it is not worth taking the risk?

If you decide _____[5] (*start*) your own business, this will probably involve _____[6] (*borrow*) money from friends or family, or even from a bank. If you choose to borrow from a bank, you should arrange _____[7] (*see*) a bank manager to discuss the terms of a loan. But, you can expect _____[8] (*have*) a lot of work. Before you arrange _____[9] (*have*) a meeting with the bank, you will have to spend a lot of time researching your idea and preparing all your figures.

The bank will certainly want _____[10] (*see*) a business plan. This will involve _____[11] (*prepare*) a

2 Imagine you are chatting online to a friend about different jobs in finance. Write some sentences of your own, using the three verb structures, for example

*If you want to be an accountant, this **involves studying** for two years.*

*If you want to be a(n) analyst, this **involves** ... -ing*

*Retail banking is a good/bad job if you **like / hate / enjoy** ...-ing*

*Equity trading is a good/bad job if you **want / decide / hope / choose** to ...*

*Investment banking is a good/bad job if you want **to help / enable** people/companies to ...*

*As a loan officer you will need **to convince / help / force** people to ...*

*As a branch manager you often have to **agree / arrange / refuse** to ...*

3 Write six sentences about some bad experiences you have had with a bank.

EXAMPLE
The bank refused to give me an overdraft.

1 The bank failed ...   4 The bank didn't mention ...
2 The bank denied ...   5 The bank forced me ...
3 The bank delayed ...

lot of information. You will need to define the objectives of the company and prepare a cash flow forecast which shows how much money you expect _____[12] (*make*) in the first three years, plus how many customers you hope _____[13] (*win*). It's also a good idea to make a study of the competition and the prices you expect _____[14] (*charge*). You will also have to decide what kind of security you want _____[15] (*offer*) the bank.

If the bank agrees _____[16] (*give*) you a loan, your problems don't stop there because the bank will often require you _____[17] (*update*) them on your progress. The business plan allows them _____[18] (*see*) if you are meeting your forecasts and, if you fail, they may want _____[19] (*have*) the money back. Of course, if you agree _____[20] (*borrow*) the money, you will have to repay the loan plus interest. That can be the hardest part ...

Speaking

Commercial lending

1 Work in small groups or as a class. Discuss what kind of information a bank wants to know before it gives a loan to a business customer. If you are not sure, think about these points:

- What risks does the bank take when it grants a loan?
- How can it reduce these risks?
- What does a loan officer mean when he / she asks for 'security' on a loan?

2 Choose the five factors that are most important in assessing a loan application.

- the objective of the loan
- the size of the company
- the assets (buildings and machinery) owned by the business
- the experience of the managers
- the level of profit this year and next year
- the security they can offer
- the ability to pay interest from profit
- the turnover or total sales of the business
- the amount of other debts
- how long they have been a customer of the bank

3 Now work in pairs. Explain your list and the reasons for your choices to a partner. Work together and decide on the best five factors between you.

4 You work as a loan officer in the branch of a bank and you are going to interview a client about a loan for their business. Your boss has told you to make sure you check these details.

1 the objective of the loan
2 the amount required
3 the turnover of the business (total sales this year)
4 the profit this year
5 the expected profit next year
6 the security offered

Complete the questions below using the question openers. Then match each question with the point being checked 1–6. (The first one is done for you.)

How much	How much do you
~~What is the~~	What is your
What is your	What kind of

a _What is the_ purpose of the loan?   ☑ 1

b _____ security can you offer?   ☐

c _____ profit this year?   ☐

d _____ want to borrow?   ☐

e _____ profit do you expect to make next year?   ☐

f _____ turnover this year?   ☐

5 Work in pairs. Student A, you are the loan officer. Student B, you are the client. Go to p.118.

Student A

You are a loan officer. Look at the table of possible loan offers.

Amount of loan	Interest rate	Repayments	Loan period
£80,000	8%	£11,600 per year	10 years
£80,000	10%	£12,600 per year	10 years
£50,000	8%	£7,250 per year	10 years
£50,000	10%	£8,000 per year	10 years

Interview your partner, the business client, using the questions in **4**. As a loan officer you need to get the best terms you can with the minimum risk. Are you confident that the client can repay the interest on the loan this year and next? If the risks are high, you need more security or a higher interest rate. Or you may need to offer a smaller loan.

From the information your partner gives you, decide if you will grant the loan, how much you are prepared to offer, and what kind of security you need.

Now change roles. You are now the client. Look at the details of your loan application below. Answer your partner's questions and try to get the best loan you can for your business. You want £600,000, but you would like to pay off the loan quickly over five years and want to secure the loan from the existing properties you own (value £200,000).

LOAN APPLICATION

Name of company: Atlantic Villas

Type of business: villa rentals for the holiday market

Purpose of loan: (1) to convert three old properties currently valued at £200,000 to holiday villas with an estimated cost of conversion of £400,000
(2) to build a fitness centre, estimated cost £200,000

Amount required: £600,000

Turnover/total sales: £440,000

Profit this year: £170,000

Estimated profit next year with the new villas: £300,000

Security you can offer: Existing old properties (value £200,000). You also have a farmhouse worth £700,000 but don't want to offer this if possible.

Checklist

Assess your progress in this unit. Tick (✓) the statements which are true.

- I can describe the different types of bank and their customer groups
- I can check, clarify, and reformulate in a discussion
- I can explain what the different divisions in a retail bank do
- I can write a profile of a bank's activity
- I can use different verb patterns
- I can negotiate the basic terms of a loan with a customer

Key words

Nouns
branch
brand
business plan
commercial bank
credit
division
investment bank
leasing
loan officer
loan schedule
network
organigram /
organization structure

portfolio
product line
retail bank
secured loan
security
stockbroking
tailored products
terms (of a loan)
unsecured loan

Verb
involve

Look back through this unit. Find five more words or expressions that you think are useful.

8 Stock mark

Countdown

1 What is the difference between a private company and a public company? Which of them is listed on a stock market?

2 What information does a stock index, like the *FTSE 100* or *S&P 500* contain?

3 Where can you find the stock market indices below? Match the indices with the cities where they are based, one of the cities matches with two indices.

1	Dow Jones	6	Hang Seng
2	FTSE 100	7	NASDAQ
3	Nikkei	8	Bovespa
4	CAC 40	9	MICEX
5	DAX	10	Straits Times Index

4 Look at the news items below. Which sectors of the market would they affect the most? Would they have a positive or negative effect on these sectors?

Central bank cuts interest rates

Oil prices hit a 2-year high

Consumer debt levels continue to rise

London wins Olympic bid

5 Who do you think are the biggest investors in the stock markets?

6 What is the main index in your country? What are the biggest companies in it?

... ity broker ... stock ... find out
supercomm.ch

Look at the list of questions students submitted online below. First, work in pairs and see how many of the questions you can answer together before you read the text.

1 What is the difference between a *share* and a *stock*?
2 What rights do you get if you buy a company's shares?
3 What is a dividend?
4 Who decides how much dividend to pay?
5 Why do some companies not pay dividends?
6 What are the two main ways shareholders make money from shares?
7 How does a company become a listed company?
8 What is an IPO?
9 What does it mean when an investment bank 'underwrites' a company's shares?
10 What is the difference between a primary listing and the secondary market?
11 What is the role of the market regulators?
12 What is a rights issue?
13 When a company makes a rights issue, the share price usually goes down. Why is that?

2 You are going to work together by sharing information to check your answers to the questions in 1.

Student A

Read your extract from the text of the broker's speech and check your answers to the questions in **1**. Make notes.

Every day people buy and sell about £16bn of shares on the stock market in London. But what exactly are they buying?

Basically, when you buy a share you become an owner of part of that company. The English markets use the word 'share', the American markets also use the word 'stocks'. As a shareholder or stockholder, your investment gives you rights to vote at the annual company meeting (the AGM) and to receive a percentage of the profits that a company will hopefully make.

The profit is distributed to you as a dividend, usually paid twice a year. This is because the Board of Directors who run the company decide each year how much of the profit to give back to the shareholders as a return on their investment and how much to retain for the company to use to invest in new projects. Some very big companies do not pay dividends because they feel that the profit made by the company is better retained in the company to grow that business. That way, the shareholder benefits long term because if the company succeeds, the shares will increase in value. So when they sell the shares they will get a higher price.

That is why an investor in shares expects to make two kinds of return: a dividend and a capital increase when they sell. The value of the shares, of course, changes every day as people trade the stock, and so the market capitalization or total value of the company is never constant.

Student B

Read your extract from the text of the broker's speech and check your answers to the questions in **1**. Make notes.

What do they do on the stock market every day? Basically, the biggest markets in the world, like Wall Street, try to value companies every day according to the economic prospects of the company and the progress of the economy. A company that wants to offer its shares to the public must first come to the market through an IPO, an Initial Public Offering. When it has this 'listing' the price of the shares can be 'quoted' every day in trading.

This initial offer to investors is organized by an investment bank which supports the company and organizes the first day of trading. They work, of course, with the market regulators, like the Financial Services Authority (FSA) in the UK or the Securities and Exchanges Commission (SEC) in the US, to make sure that the company follows all the regulations and the company is not trying to defraud investors. The investment bank will 'underwrite' the shares by promising to buy the shares if no other investors are interested. Market participants call this first offer a primary listing. Once a stock has a quoted price, investors can buy and sell the stock every day, so the stock exists in what they call 'the secondary market'.

Sometimes companies need to raise more capital to grow their business and then they can issue new shares in what is called a rights issue. By selling new shares, the company, of course, is getting new money, but at the same time it also means that each individual share in the company is now worth less because it represents a smaller percentage of the whole company.

3 Now work together and check each other's answers. Discuss (as a class) any of the questions you still aren't sure about.

Ownership of UK shares

Foreign investors hold ²/₅ of UK shares

Rest of the world
Insurance companies
Pension funds
Individuals
Unit trusts
Investment trusts
Other financial institutions
Charities
Private non-financial companies
Public sector
Banks

0% 10% 20% 30% 40% 50%

Listening

Why do stock markets move?

What do you think are the main factors behind the daily movements of a stock market?

1 Which **three** of these factors have the biggest effect on the performance of a company's share price?

- Company announcements
- The views of analysts
- Movements in interest rates
- Inflation data
- Business / consumer confidence surveys
- Sector outlook
- Company financial results
- Performance of competitors

2 🎧 Listen to an interview with a fund manager who is explaining why stock markets move. Complete the two slides that she uses to explain the stock market.

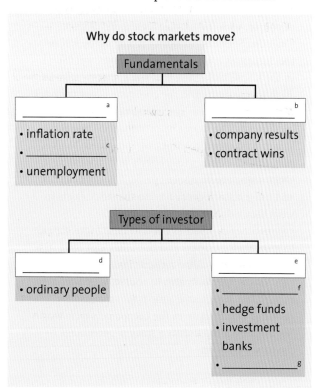

Why do stock markets move?

Fundamentals

a _____
- inflation rate
- c _____
- unemployment

b _____
- company results
- contract wins

Types of investor

d _____
- ordinary people

e _____
- f _____
- hedge funds
- investment banks
- g _____

3 🎧 Listen again and write T (true) or F (false).

1 The New York market was up today, but the London market was down.
2 A fall in interest rates will boost the stock market.
3 Analysts upgrade a stock because they want to attract buyers.
4 The share price tells you about the probable future profits.
5 Retail investors have the biggest influence on profits.
6 Hedge funds make about 30% profit per year.

Pronunciation

Vowel sounds

Here are three vowel sounds in English which are easy to confuse:

/ɒ/ as in *stop, not, top* – these are short vowels.

/ɔː/ as in *four, talk, store* – these are long vowels.

/əʊ/ as in *know, growth, OK* – these are double vowels (= diphthongs).

1 These words were all used in *Listening*. Put them in the right column.

long	macro	most	show
ordinary	rose	shops	short
stock	volume	whole	important
cause	economy	fall	obvious

/ɒ/	/ɔː/	/əʊ/

2 🎧 Now listen and check your answers.

3 🎧 Practise saying these sentences aloud. Then listen and check your answers.

1 Stock values have fallen following problems caused by slow growth.
2 Lower levels of domestic borrowing are important for the economy.
3 Obviously, when prices in the shops rose, this caused a drop in the volume of sales.

In 2008, the US investor **Warren Buffet**, the so-called 'Sage of Omaha', was ranked by *Forbes* magazine as the richest person in the world with an estimated fortune of $62 billion. His philosophy to investing is as follows: *'The basic ideas of investing are to look at stocks as business, use the market's fluctuations to your advantage, and seek a margin of safety.'* Simple if you know how!

Professional skills

Investment strategies

Online brokers' websites are full of discussion boards for investors to discuss their investment strategies. Have you ever visited one?

1 Look at these tips from an online forum in which people explain their investment strategies. Work in pairs. Which **three** of these strategies do you think could be the most successful? Why would they work better than the others?

a If you want to invest in the markets, you should spread your risks by investing in several companies in different sectors. That way you reduce your exposure to any one company.

b I believe that it is best to invest in large international companies with strong brands. Small companies are just too risky.

c Take Warren Buffet's advice (the famous US investor): 'Be fearful when others are greedy and greedy when others are fearful'.

d The only way to make money on the markets is to invest your money for at least five years. Buying and selling quickly – or day trading – is just a way to lose your money.

e The best way to invest in the stock market is to invest in a general fund, in which a manager decides which shares to buy or sell.

f Watch the discussion boards for good stories about companies. Then 'buy on the rumour, sell on the news'.

2 Work in pairs. Discuss these questions.

1 Do you think it is worth investing in shares? Or is it just 'gambling', like the lottery?

2 Which companies or sectors would you invest in today? Why?

● Language spot

Describing consequences

When we talk about the consequences of events we can use first conditional sentences with *If …* . We can ask and answer questions in this way:

What will happen if the government nationalizes the biggest banks?
If the government nationalizes the biggest banks, shareholders will lose their money.

We can change the probability by using these modal verbs:

should – high probability
If the government nationalizes the biggest banks, customers should feel more confident.

may / might – lower probability
If the government nationalizes the biggest banks, top managers may lose their jobs.

Write three different answers for these questions using the modal verbs above and the phrases below each question.

EXAMPLE
What will happen if the Chinese economy slows down?
    investors
If the Chinese economy slows down, investors will / may sell their shares.

1 What will happen if the Chinese economy slows down?
   a company profits
   b the price of steel and metals
   c unemployment

2 What will happen if a flu virus spreads around the world?
   a shares in airline companies
   b sales of pharmaceutical drugs
   c business travel and trade

3 What will happen if the US government does not support its car industry?
   a workers
   b car suppliers
   c foreign car producers

>> Go to **Language reference** p.124

Speaking

News briefings

If you work as a trader on the stock market, every day will start with a news briefing in which the analysts interpret the day's news for the share traders.

1 Look at the morning news announcement from *Reuters*, the news agency, below and the analyst's notes on the probable effects that follow. Mark each of the effects P (positive) or N (negative).

> Supermarkets and shop owners protest as government bans all petrol-driven cars from city centres.

Analyst's notes
- the demand for electric vehicles _____
- profits of big supermarkets in city centres _____
- the share price of car battery manufacturers _____
- sales of petrol car manufacturers _____

2 Look at how one analyst presents their comments in a morning briefing. Complete the model using the information from the news announcement and analyst's notes above.

MORNING BRIEFING

Reuters today announced _____
_____ 1

This will have a significant impact on share prices this morning.
POSITIVE EFFECTS
On the one hand, this will probably **lead to** an *increase* / *decrease* in
_____ 2

Equally, this will probably **result in** an *increase* / *decrease* in
_____ 3

NEGATIVE EFFECTS
On the other hand, this will certainly **lead to** an *increase* / *decrease* in
_____ 4

At the same time, this will **result in** an *increase* / *decrease* in
_____ 5

CONCLUSION / RECOMMENDATION
As a result, we believe we should buy _____ 6,
and we should sell _____ 7

3 🎧 Check your answers by listening to the recording.

4 Work in pairs. Student A, go to p.111. Student B, go to p.118.

It's my job

1 Work in pairs. Discuss the questions.
1 Have you ever used Internet blogs to find out about a job you would like to do in finance?
2 What can you learn from blogs that you can't learn from a job advert?

Jim Chung

Job Junior equity analyst at an investment bank
Location New York

I just wrote this blog to give other students an idea of my life on the stock markets here as a typical equity analyst in New York. Here's my routine:
6:00 Check the computer for early morning news announcements. I have to prepare a report on a small technology company for the morning briefing with the sales team at 7. Have to chase company data on sales. Deliver the report successfully and have time to grab a coffee before returning to my desk.
9:30 As the market opens, I watch to see what happens to the share price of the company I just reported on. I got it right! The stock is up and the phone begins to ring as sales people want info on the company.
1:00 Lunch with the head of another fast-growing software company at Juno's Bistro. Order a great meal but I have no time to eat it, since I am asking questions all the time and trying to reach a conclusion about the company's prospects to tell my boss.
2:00 Draft a report to my boss on the meeting. Check the market again for any news announcements. Prepare some figures on a possible takeover.
4:30 Market closes but then there is a news announcement from one of the companies I am responsible for. That means a long night since I know my boss will want to discuss it before he leaves so I won't get back home before 10. No time for the gym!

2 Which things does Jim find most exciting and which are most frustrating? Make notes and compare with a partner. Do you both agree with Jim's view?

Nick Leeson lost over **$1.3 billion** through unauthorized trading on Asian futures markets while working as a manager in the Singapore office of Barings Bank. Because of Leeson's actions, Barings cash reserves were used up and, after more than 230 years in business, the bank was finally sold for just **£1**.

He was sent to prison in Singapore in December 1995, and was released four years later, suffering from cancer. His book, *Rogue Trader*, was turned into a film starring Ewan McGregor.

Nick Leeson is probably the world's most famous rogue trader. But why and how did he do it?

Vocabulary

Reading the financial press

If you want to research a company to invest in, you can look online or in a newspaper at the *share price tables*. But what kind of information do you want to know?

1 Work with a partner and make a list of **four** key things you need to know about a company before you consider investing in it.

EXAMPLE

1 *the share price*

2 _____

3 _____

4 _____

2 Share price tables use a lot of financial expressions. Look at the table below and match the labels in the table with the definitions 1–9. Put the correct numbers 1–9 in the spaces in the table. One of the items in the table doesn't have a matching definition. Which one?

1 the number of shares traded yesterday
2 the percentage return you can expect to receive each year for investment in each share
3 the price you must pay for one share today
4 the total value of the company yesterday
5 the code you need to look up the shares online
6 if the share price increased or fell yesterday
7 the area of industry in which the company works
8 the relation between the earnings made by the company on each share and the current price of the shares
9 the highest price paid by investors for a share this year

3 Now, using the information in the table, answer these questions.

1 If you wanted to buy 200 shares in BP today, how much would it cost you? (Note in the UK share prices are quoted in pence so 100p = £1.)
2 If you bought the shares at the lowest price for the year, how much did you pay?
3 If you sold the same shares today, how much money have you made?
4 If you bought 200 shares today, how much money would you expect to earn in dividends?
5 How many shares in BP were traded yesterday?

Webquest

You are going to research the share price performance of the IT company *Microsoft*.

1 Find the 'financial markets' section on an Internet website such as *Yahoo*, *Google*, or *MSN*.

Enter the stock code for *Microsoft*: (**msft**)

2 Find

- the current share price. Is it up or down today?
- the 52-week high and low of the price.
- the one year target price analysts expect it to reach.

3 Use the **charts** section and look at the graphs. Find what has happened to the stock in the last 12 months? Has it gone up or down?

4 Find the 'company news' section and find the latest reports from the company.

Make a note of any important news announcements or product launches that may affect the share price.

(____) Sector: oil & gas

(____) Symbol	(____) Current price	(____) Change on day	(____) 52-week high	(____) 52-week low	(____) Dividend yield	(____) p/e Price/ Earnings ratio	(____) Market cap. £UK	(____) Volume 000s
BP	450p	+23	657	347	9%	5.2	81bn.	72,848

Writing

An analyst's report

Stock market analysts, who often work for investment banks or brokers, write regular reports on companies to update clients on recent performance. They then publish recommendations to *buy*, *sell*, or *hold* the stock. These reports strongly influence stock market prices.

1 Read the analyst's report on Boggle below. Look at the four headings and write each heading in the correct place in the report.

Sector outlook   Share price performance
Recommendations   CEO's statement

2 Look at the expressions *in italic* used in the report below. Match the expressions a–k with the fuctions 1–6 below. Some of the functions match with more than one expression.

1 companies giving news and information about themselves

2 predicting the future

3 describing recent share price performance

4 making comparisons

5 describing consequences

6 making recommendations

3 Your boss has asked you to update the information on your company's website. Check the recent press releases from the software sector below.

Microphose shock!
Microphose reports big fall in profits and rise in investment costs. Share price down from $24 to $21 this morning. Fall now is 40% over 12 months compared with 22% fall for the NASDAQ.

Outlook poor for Microphose
Analysts turn negative on the computer sector as sales forecasts show only 5% growth over the next 3 years.

Chairman's warning
Chairman warns of difficult market conditions as mobile applications begin to take market share from traditional personal computer market. Promises to invest in new products to boost profits.

Analysts advise 'sell'
Analysts move recommendations on Microphose from buy to sell setting a target price of $23 per share. Analyst Dave Sweetman at Goldman Sachs explained that the high cost of investing in new products will result in lower profits over the next few years.

4 Now complete the analyst's report for Microphose using the language expressions from the Boggle report and the information in the press releases above.

Analyst report

Company name: BOGGLE
Sector: Internet technology
Current share price: 390 **target price**: 480
52-week high: 570 **52-week low**: 330
Recommendation: (buy) / sell / hold

1 _____
Over the last six months, Boggle's share price has increased by 20%[a]. This is due to a sharp rise in advertising revenue and a big increase in new customers.
The performance compares with a fall[b] for the S&P 500 index of 18%.

2 _____
The outlook looks positive[c] for the whole Internet sector. *Most analysts remain bullish*[d], with Internet advertising taking market share from traditional press and TV commercials. *The online sector is projected to grow*[e] by 60% over the next three years.

3 _____
At a recent press conference, *the company announced*[f] that Boggle was facing difficult economic conditions in the global market. However, *CEO Eric Bulwark commented that*[g] the launch of new projects, like the upgrade of Boggle phones, *will certainly lead to*[h] a rise in sales. At the same time, Boggle has promised to cut costs and reduce investment in equipment and property. This *will probably result in*[i] an increase in profits.

4 _____
We believe that Boggle's shares will outperform the S&P 500 index over the next twelve months. We have moved Boggle from hold to buy and *we recommend buying*[j] up to a $480 target share price. *We would advise clients to buy*[k] now on weakness.

Company name: *Microphose*

Sector: _____ [1]

Current share price: _____ [2]

Target price: _____ [3]

52-week high: $32   **52-week low**: $20

Recommendation: buy / sell / hold[4]

Share price performance

Over the last twelve months, Microphose's share price
_____ [5].

This is due to _____ [6].
The performance _____ [7]
for the NASDAQ index of _____ [8]
over the same period.

Sector outlook

The outlook for the computer software sector looks
_____ [9] over
the next twelve months. Most analysts remain _____
_____ [10].

The total computer sector _____ [11]
grow by _____ [12] over
the next three years.

Chairman's statement / recent news

At a recent press conference, the company Chairman
_____ [13].

However, the Chairman promised _____
_____ [14]. This will probably
_____ [15] an
increase in profits in the long term.

Recommendations

We believe that Microphose's shares will underperform
the NASDAQ index over the next twelve months. We have
moved Microphose from _____ [16]
to _____ [17] and we have set
a target price of $_____ [18].
We would _____ [19] now on
current prices.

Key words

Nouns
analyst
briefing
bullish
dividend
exposure
hedge fund
institutional investor
IPO (initial public offering)
market capitalization
retail investor
return
rights issue
share / stock
stock market index. / (pl. indices)
tip

Verbs
issue shares
list
outperform
project
quote
spread
underwrite

Adjectives
bullish

Look back through this unit. Find five more words or expressions that you think are useful.

9 Company internal finance

Countdown

All companies need money every day to run their business. But where does the money come from? Look at the diagram of the typical cash-flow cycle of a company below.

1 Find the three sources from which a company gets its money.

2 Work in pairs. Decide which of the items below bring a flow of cash into the company and which mean cash flows out. Mark each item 'In' or 'Out'.

 a bank loans
 b salaries and rent
 c a bank overdraft
 d selling products to customers
 e owners' capital
 f taxes and dividend payments
 g interest payments on loans
 h buying stocks and raw materials

3 Use the information from 2 to complete 1–8 in the diagram below.

4 What happens to this cycle if a company sells a product today (1st July) on 90 days' credit?

 1 On what date does the company get paid?
 2 What kinds of problem can this create for a company?
 3 How can a company control its cash flow?

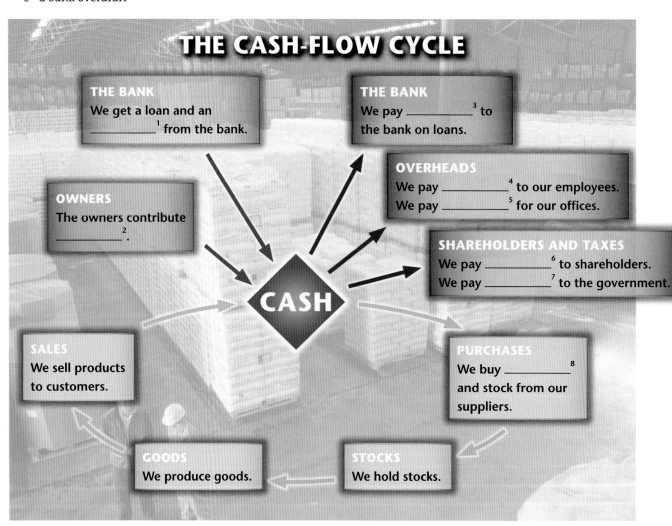

THE CASH-FLOW CYCLE

THE BANK
We get a loan and an _____ [1] from the bank.

THE BANK
We pay _____ [3] to the bank on loans.

OWNERS
The owners contribute _____ [2].

OVERHEADS
We pay _____ [4] to our employees.
We pay _____ [5] for our offices.

SHAREHOLDERS AND TAXES
We pay _____ [6] to shareholders.
We pay _____ [7] to the government.

CASH

SALES
We sell products to customers.

PURCHASES
We buy _____ [8] and stock from our suppliers.

GOODS
We produce goods.

STOCKS
We hold stocks.

In this unit
- cash-flow cycle
- writing a first reminder for payment
- 1st and 2nd conditionals
- insisting on payment
- financing decisions
- profit and loss account / income statement

Listening

Cash flow

You are going to listen to a meeting in which the directors of a company are discussing a cash-flow problem in the company. There are four directors at the meeting:

Carrie O'Connor – Managing director

Nick Wilson – Sales director

Rémy Danet – Purchasing director

Sandra Chan – Finance director

1 Listen and complete the key financial information about the company's problem.

Last month:
- costs rose by _____ [1]
- sales increased by _____ [2]
- the credit period increased from _____ [3] to _____ [4]
- the company increased production by _____ [5]
- purchasing costs for raw materials increased by _____ [6]

2 Listen again and mark these statements T (true) or F (false).

1 The managing director believed that sales were good.
2 The sales team were following company policy on credit terms.
3 The sales targets were not easy to achieve.
4 The sales team reduced the credit period for customers because of competition.
5 The company has recently introduced new products.
6 The cost of materials increased because of demand from competitors.

Writing

A reminder for non-payment

You are a credit control manager in APT, the company in *Listening*. You have identified two unpaid accounts: one is five days late and the other 70 days. You decide to deal with the first one by emailing **a first reminder** to the customer.

Usually, your colleague deals with all the international correspondence but she is away for this week and has left you a few notes. Complete your email reminder below using the following expressions a–i.

a We appreciate that this delay may be due to a mistake
b We look forward to hearing from you soon
c We would appreciate it if you could
d Invoice no. FG/647/10
e Please find attached
f Best regards,
g could you look into the problem and inform us of the reason for the delay.
h I am writing with reference to
i We note from our accounts

File   Edit   View   Tools   Message   Help

Reply   Reply All   Forward   Print   Delete   Previous   Next   Addresses

email reminder

Our ref: _____ [1]

Dear Mr Sanchez,

_____ [2] invoice number FG/647/10 for $50,000. _____ [3] that the invoice has still not been paid. Given your previous record of prompt payment, we were surprised at this delay. _____ [4] at the bank or in your payment system. In any case, please _____ [5].

_____ [6] give this matter immediate attention and send us the payment by bank transfer.

_____ [7] a copy of the original invoice for your reference.

_____ [8]

_____ [9]

J. Martin

Credit Control Manager

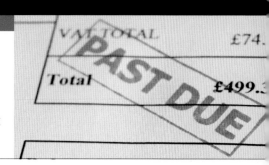

The cost of late payments

A 2009 survey has shown that small and medium-sized companies in the UK are owed an amazing **£25.9 billion** in overdue payments. This was after overdue payments increased by almost 40% over the last year, up sharply from £18.6 billion. This works out at a national average of £38,000 per business. The most common cause of late payment is cash-flow problems. Almost a quarter of businesses (24%) say this is the excuse they're given when they are chasing late payments.

● **Language spot**

First and Second Conditionals

1 Look at these two comments about the company's cash-flow problems in *Listening*.

A *'If the customers pay on time, we will have no problem with cash flow.'*

B *'If the customers paid on time, we would have no problem with cash flow.'*

1 In which situation does the speaker think payment is **possible**: A or B?

2 In which situation does the speaker think payment is **unlikely**: A or B?

3 Which finance director has the biggest problem: A or B?

2 Now complete the rules about conditional sentences.

1 We use __*If*__ + _____ + _____ for a situation in the future that we think is possible. This is called the First Conditional.

2 We use __*If*__ + _____ + _____ for a situation in the future that we think is unlikely to happen. This is called the Second Conditional.

3 Look at these sentences from *Listening*. Discuss the differences in probability between the sentences.

1 If we don't get some cash quickly, we won't be able to pay our suppliers.

2 If we didn't have to get the stock quickly, we wouldn't have to pay more.

3 If they paid us on 30 days' credit, we wouldn't have a problem.

4 If we can reduce the price we are paying for materials, we'll be able to make some savings.

4 First Conditional

The finance director is looking at different options to improve the cash flow in the company. Look at the options and match them with the consequences.

Options	Consequences
1 reduce our stock of materials	a lose orders from customers
2 increase our overdraft	b stop delivery
3 offer incentives for quick payment	c pay more interest to the bank
4 cut our advertising budget	d customers pay more quickly
5 delay paying our suppliers	e have problems with production

Now use the information to write five sentences using the First Conditional.

EXAMPLE

If we reduce our stock of materials, we will have problems with production.

5 Second Conditional

The finance director is now talking to her team and imagining some of the things that could go wrong in the next twelve months. Match the risks she imagines with the consequences.

Risks	Consequences
1 need to raise capital	a switch to green energy
2 lose a major customer	b import materials from China
3 oil prices rise by 50%	c change our bank
4 the bank stops the overdraft	d sales collapse next year
5 cut salaries and bonuses	e ask our shareholders for help
6 local suppliers increase their prices	f workers go on strike

Now use the information to write six sentences using the second conditional.

EXAMPLE

If we needed to raise capital, we would ask our shareholders for help.

>> Go to **Language reference** p.124

to hedge *(v)* to protect your money against movements in the value of currencies, interest rates, etc.

working capital *(n)* the money, stocks of goods, etc. that a company uses for its daily business activities.

factoring *(n)* a financial arrangement in which a company sells a debt that is owed to it at a reduced price to another company (=a factor) in order to receive cash immediately. The factor is then responsible for collecting the debt in full.

Speaking

Insisting on payment: the final reminder

1 When invoices are not paid on time, sometimes the company owed money will telephone, as well as write. In the dialogue below, Renate from PBS is calling Marius from Polstock Products about an unpaid invoice. Match the expressions (1–6) with their possible answers (a–f).

Renate	Marius
1 Hello, this is Renate from PBS. I'm phoning about an unpaid invoice, reference: FG/584/310. ↓ Marius' reply _e_	a Well, I'm afraid we cannot do anything until the network is working again.
2 We emailed you twice last week, but haven't received any reply. ↓ Marius' reply ___	b OK, I'll contact you again soon. Thank you for your call.
3 I see. How can we resolve this issue of the outstanding invoice? ↓ Marius' reply ___	c Oh, I'm sure legal action won't be necessary.
4 I appreciate your problem, but I'm afraid I must insist on payment in the next three days. ↓ Marius' reply ___	d Sorry, we're having problems with our computer network at the moment so I haven't received any emails.
5 Very well but if we don't receive payment by July 27, I'm afraid we'll have to pass this on to our legal department. ↓ Marius' reply ___	e Oh, hello. I was planning to phone you about that invoice.
6 We hope so too. So, I'll look forward to receiving your payment. ↓ Marius' reply ___	f OK, let me talk to my boss and see what we can do.

2 Work in pairs. Role-play the dialogue from **1**. When you finish, swap roles.

It's my job

The treasury department of a company is often a small team, but it plays an important role in making sure the company always has enough cash to pay its bills. Birgit joined the treasury department of a German company after doing an internship there.

1 Read the text. What does a treasury department do? What did Birgit learn from her internship?

Birgit Vanderbeke

Job Treasury department assistant
Location Bavaria, Germany
Company Melstock: German dairy company

What did you learn most from the internship?
It was real work experience. My boss took me to all the meetings with the banks to discuss loans and credit terms and always asked my opinions of the negotiations after every meeting. He even forced me to do the calculations. I didn't know anything about negotiating loans but had to learn quickly. It was a surprise to find how different banks wanted different types of security as a guarantee for loans and how my boss would calculate the different advantages before making any decision.

What sort of responsibilities do you have today?
I'm the assistant to the director in the treasury department. Our main task is to manage the cash flow in the company. As we now have operations all over Eastern Europe, this is not so easy because we have over 150 different bank accounts in twelve countries. That means we have to move money around the company every day to meet the needs of different parts of the group. But as they all have different currencies we have to use a technique of hedging to protect the value of our money against movements in other currencies.

My main tasks now are to manage the working capital so that that we have the money to pay our suppliers, even if the customers don't pay us for 90 days. We use a system of factoring to get the cash we are owed immediately rather than wait for the customer to pay us.

2 What would be your ideal internship?

Reading

Financing the company

Companies need different types of financing for different activities. They need *short-term* financing for daily operations, like paying their bills to suppliers, but they also need *medium* and *long-term financing*, for example, to buy properties, machinery or to expand into new markets.

1 Look at these four different problems of company financing below. Decide which of the problems need short-term and which need long-term financing. Mark each company file **S** (short-term) or **L** (long-term).

Plasnia is a plastics company based in Brazil. It needs to invest heavily in new machinery. Its machines have to be replaced every three years because of new technology and this uses up a lot of its profits every year.

Claw Valley is a health food company. Its biggest customer (40% of sales) is a major supermarket, but the supermarket often takes 120 days before it pays its bills to the company.

Schlink, a German family company, owns its own engineering factory, but the building in a city centre is old and not adapted to modern production or truck delivery. The site is worth $20m, but badly needs modernization and the company doesn't have the funds to do the work.

■ **Mitlink** is a software start-up company in Cambridge, Mass. which sells devices for mobile phones. Sales are expanding fast, but it often has problems paying its rent and even salaries at the end of each month because it is short of finance.

2 Find out what kind of financing these companies could use. Look at the text and match the types of financing 1–7 with the explanations a–g given below on the website.

1 bank overdraft

2 trade credit finance

3 bank loans and term loans

4 property and machinery leasing

5 factoring of sales invoices

6 bonds / debentures

7 mortgages

a A system of borrowing in which you take out a loan by offering the guarantee of some asset, usually a building, as a security. This can be much cheaper than other forms of loan.

b If your company is owed cash by customers who take a long time to pay you, why not sell the debts to a bank in exchange for immediate payment? The bank will charge you a commission fee but it gives you immediate cash.

c A system by which a company borrows money from a bank for an agreed medium or long-term period and pays interest each year on the debt plus final repayment of the capital.

d An arrangement with a bank that allows you to spend more money than you have in your account for a short time to pay bills or expenses. Talk to your bank and arrange a 'facility' but remember this can be an expensive way of financing your business and is not a long-term solution.

e An arrangement between a company and a bank or specialist finance company in which the bank buys machinery, cars, trucks, etc. for the company and charges the company a regular fee to use this equipment. This saves you from making big long-term capital investments.

f A larger company can borrow money from the financial markets by issuing debt or 'paper' to the financial markets. It borrows the money from long-term investors and agrees to repay with interest over a given period. This can give real long-term stability to your company.

g Have you thought of negotiating with your suppliers to get short-term financing by buying on credit and paying 30/60 days after they deliver the goods? This is a common arrangement if you place regular orders with a supplier and they trust you.

Where's the best place to start up?

Every year, the World Bank produces its *Doing Business* report on which countries are the best for starting small businesses. In 2009, they surveyed 181 countries. They look at how easy it is to legally set up a business, hire workers, get credit, pay taxes, enforce contracts, and declare bankruptcy.

The top three countries in 2009 were Singapore, New Zealand, and the United States. The country that introduced the most business-friendly reforms was Azerbaijan, which moved up 64 places in the overall ranking to 33rd place.

3 Work in pairs and decide together which form of financing would be best for each of the companies mentioned in **1**. Write your decision into the file and give any reasons you have for it.

	Best solution	Reasons
Plasnia		
Claw Valley		
Schlink		
Mitlink		

Webquest

Governments around the world all offer a lot of advice to small start-up companies. In the UK, the government's website *www.businesslink.gov.uk* gives young business entrepreneurs a lot of financial advice about setting up and managing a small business.

Look at the business case study below and see what solutions you can find to help a young English woman, Sandy, to get finance to start her business.

Sandy is a young businesswoman who wants to set up a company to sell eco-friendly men's cosmetics that are natural and good for the environment. She has made a business plan, found good suppliers, and now needs to set up an attractive website to begin selling. She has approached several banks for a loan of £30,000 to start up, but so far without success.

1 Go on the Internet and search for 'finance for small business + uk government support' or go to the government website: *www.businesslink.gov.uk* and find out what other sources of finance she could try.

2 Find out who these people are and how they might help small businesses.

business angels (try:*www.bba.org.uk*)
venture capitalists

3 Now work in groups of four. Report back your results to the class and discuss together the advantages and disadvantages of your solutions. Then decide together what you would recommend Sandy to do.

Professional skills
Negotiating

1 What kind of things have you negotiated about in the last week – for example at home, with companies, or in shops? Make a list and explain to a partner what you did. Did you get what you wanted?

2 Now read the advice on negotiating below. Do you agree with it?

What do you think of when people talk about negotiating? Buying a car and arguing over the price? Negotiating over the rent of your flat? Deciding with your friends which film to see tonight?

In fact, most people think first of price negotiations. This leads them to think there must be a winner and a loser in every negotiation. 'I will start by asking a really high price and then negotiate down. I know what my bottom line is: I won't sell for less than that.'

But is it the same in a business negotiation? Business research suggests that when companies negotiate with a supplier over a contract, both sides have to live with the results for years. If one side feels that it has got a bad deal, does that make for a successful commercial long term partnership? Probably not.

That is why management experts now believe that the best solution is to think of all professional negotiations as part of building a partnership. So, in a professional negotiation you should:

■ set clear objectives about what you want to achieve
■ focus on the issues and not on personalities
■ try to understand the needs and fears of the other side
■ not get emotional, be negative or blame people. It doesn't help.
■ always prepare options in advance – you will never achieve everything you want.

"That's good enough for me. I don't need the specifics!"

WE MADE A FORTUNE

Vocabulary

Income statement / profit and loss account

Every year, by law, a public company has to present its audited financial results to its shareholders and publish them in the annual report. But to understand how much profit (or loss) a company has made we need to turn to the income statement or profit and loss account. The income statement is made up of three parts:

1 the trading performance
2 the operating performance
3 the distribution of profit.

1 Look at the income statement for NBS (a UK company) and write the titles 1–3 above in the correct sections a–c in the statement.

2 Look at the first part of the income statement (**a**) and find the accounting words they use to show you

1 the money spent on raw materials and components for production
2 the total sales last year
3 the total sales minus the material costs.

3 Now in the second part (**b**) find the words for

1 the tax paid on profit
2 the fixed costs of running the business
3 the profit made after deducting all the costs of running the business
4 the final profit it made after paying tax
5 the cost of paying interest on all the bank loans.

4 Now find the words in the third section (**c**) that show

1 the money it kept for future investment
2 the amount it paid shareholders based on each share they owned
3 the amount of profit made for each share in the company.

5 Finally, see if you can work out the profit the company made: do the calculations.

1 What was the gross profit?
2 What was the operating profit?
3 What is the profit after tax?
4 Which of these figures do you think is most important in deciding how successful the company is?

NBS Group
Income statement for the year

	£ 000	
a		
revenue / turnover	6,067	*this shows the total sales they made for the year*
cost of sales	(1,601)*	*the cost of buying the materials they added to the stocks to produce the goods*
= GROSS PROFIT	_____ 1	
b		
overheads / expenses	(2,743)	*the 'fixed costs' that they had to pay to run the business (wages, rent, etc.) independent of how much they produced*
= OPERATING PROFIT	_____ 2	
net interest paid	(27)	*the money paid to the bank as interest on its loans*
corporation tax	(283)	*the money paid to the government as a tax on their profit*
= PROFIT AFTER TAX	_____ 3	
c		
dividends	324	*the money paid to shareholders from their profit as a return on their investment*
retained profit	1,089	*the profit kept in the company to fund investment*
earnings per share	4.6 pence	*the profit made for the year divided by the number of shares*

*Figures in brackets are negative

6 Now complete the following text from a finance handbook. Circle the correct answer A or B.

	A		B	
1	A	overheads	B	revenue
2	A	fixed costs	B	cost of sales
3	A	operating profit	B	gross profit
4	A	overheads	B	cost of sales
5	A	operating profit	B	retained profit
6	A	overheads	B	interest
7	A	corporation tax	B	administration tax
8	A	retained tax	B	profit after tax
9	A	retained profit	B	dividends
10	A	earnings	B	dividends

How do you know if a company is making a profit?

There are many different ways in which to look at the profits a company makes because accountants need to measure the efficiency of different activities in the business. So, if, for example, we want to find out how well a company is trading we need to look at the figures for total sales, the _____[1], and then subtract from that the amount the company paid suppliers to purchase these goods, the _____[2]. This gives us a figure for the _____[3].

However, a company also has many other permanent 'fixed' costs that are not affected by the sales volume. It has to pay for rent, salaries, and administration and these _____[4] have to be deducted to give us the _____[5]. It is this figure that most analysts focus on each quarter.

But to understand the risks of investing in the company the investor also needs to look at the outgoings from the company to pay the _____[6] on the bank loans and the level of _____[7] (the company tax paid to the government). Once these have been deducted we are left with a figure for _____[8].

Finally, we need to look at what happens to the money the company earns. This money can be kept by the company as _____[9] to invest for the future. But the directors also have to consider what level of return to offer to the shareholders when they decide the level of _____[10] to pay out.

Checklist

Assess your progress in this unit. Tick (✓) the statements which are true.

- ☐ I can understand the terms for cash flow of a company
- ☐ I can write a first reminder to a customer
- ☐ I can use conditionals
- ☐ I can call a customer to insist on final payment
- ☐ I can advise on financing decisions
- ☐ I can understand the accounting terms in an income statement

Key words

Nouns
cash flow
cost of sales
earnings
excuse
factoring
fixed costs
income statement /
profit and loss account
inflow
operating profit
outflow
overheads
reminder
revenue
stocks (of materials)
target
turnover
working capital

Verbs
appreciate
delay
insist (on)
negotiate

Adjective
outstanding

Look back through this unit. Find five more words or expressions that you think are useful.

10 Company reporting

Countdown

1 Here are some ways in which companies report to us about their activities. What do you think is the purpose of each of the communications?

trade fairs and exhibitions

annual general meetings

analyst meetings

the annual report

open days and factory visits

2 Work in pairs. Choose one of the companies below and make a list of things you would like to know if you were

● a shareholder in the company
● an employee
● a green campaigner
● a customer.

1 An oil company, e.g. *Shell*
2 A car manufacturer, e.g. *Chrysler*
3 A tobacco company, e.g. *British American Tobacco*

3 Discuss your ideas together as a class. Which of the communications above would tell you this information?

Reading

The annual report

The annual report of a company is a long document that contains a lot of complex information, such as the financial accounts of a company. When you read these documents you need to learn two reading skills:

1 How to **skim** articles quickly to find the main themes of each paragraph. A good technique is to read only the first sentence of each paragraph first.
2 How to **scan** a text to find facts, such as names, dates, figures, and titles, for example, the amount of profit the company made or the name of the chairman.

Look at the text opposite, which is about how to read annual reports.

1 First skim the text opposite and find out which paragraph contains the information below. Write the paragraph number next to each item.

● how to get an overview of the company's activities ☐
● the financial statements of the company ☐
● the way a company is managed ☐
● the opinion of the auditors ☐
● the notes explaining the accounts ☐
● what the law says a company report has to contain ☐

2 Now scan the text opposite to identify the titles of the main sections in the annual report (a–g below). With a partner, see who can find and <u>underline</u> all the section titles first.

a chairman's statement
b outlook
c corporate governance
d statement of directors' responsibilities
e independent auditor's report
f financial statements
g notes to the accounts

3 Which sections of the report are of most interest to

1 a shareholder?
2 a regulator?
3 an analyst?

Why?

What should I look for in the annual report?

1 By law, all public companies have to publish an annual report every year, and to send a copy to all shareholders. The contents are mostly defined by law.

2 To see how the company is performing, one good place to start is the chairman's statement, sometimes called 'a letter to shareholders'. It gives a quick view of the company's performance over the last year – often by reviewing the different sectors of the business. At the end of this section there is also an outlook statement: analysts check this to see how confident the board feels about the future.

3 In the middle sections of a UK report there is now a section called corporate governance, which explains the way the company is managed by its board of directors and how it follows the codes for good governance. These codes do not have the force of company laws but they are recommendations on how a company should be managed.

4 Then there are the statement of directors' responsibilities and the independent auditors' report. The former tells you of the legal responsibilities of the board in preparing the accounts. The latter is of interest to regulators because it gives the opinion of external auditors on the accuracy of the published financial figures.

5 At the end of the report, you will always find the financial statements: these contain essential information for investors. If you want to know about the value of the company (its assets and liabilities), you should turn to the balance sheet. However, to see how the company is performing (the profit or loss it is making), you should turn to the income statement and look at the operating profit.

6 The financial statements are supported by detailed notes to the accounts. These are of interest to professionals like equity analysts or accountants, who want to see them, as they show how all the figures were calculated.

Speaking

What should companies include in an annual report?

In many countries today governments are keen to improve the information companies report to the public such as the effects of their activities on the environment, the bonuses they give top management, and the way the companies are managed.

1 You have been asked to attend a discussion forum on company reporting to the public. Decide which of the items below you believe companies should be forced by law to publish in their company reports. Tick (✓) the items you think they should publish.

> Points
>
> ☐ their policy on health and safety of workers, e.g. accidents, child labour
>
> ☐ the effect of their activities on the environment, e.g. recycling materials, air travel
>
> ☐ their use of energy and resources
>
> ☐ how much their management is paid
>
> ☐ money they spend on TV commercials and other forms of marketing
>
> ☐ money they give to political parties
>
> ☐ statistics on the gender, race, and age of their staff and their recruitment policy
>
> ☐ risks of investing in their business
>
> ☐ how they help local communities (e.g. funding of local charities, schemes for employees to do voluntary work)

2 Work in groups of four and hold a meeting to discuss your conclusions.

1 Appoint a chairperson and someone to make a note of your decisions and the reasons for them.

2 Discuss each point that group members have ticked and try to agree on a final list of the three most important things companies should report on.

3 When you have finished, discuss as a class the conclusions you have reached.

Chairman, CEO, MD: Who's who?

- **Chairman**: The person chosen to lead the Board of Directors and chair board meetings.
- **The CEO (Chief Executive Officer)**: The person in charge of the running of the company. In the UK this person often has the title of **Managing Director (MD)**.

In a public company that is quoted on the stock exchange the roles of Chairman and Managing Director are normally separated. A chairman who is involved in the normal running of the company is called an **executive chairman**. A chairman who is appointed from outside the company is a **non-excecutive chairman**. Similarly, members of the Board can be **executive** or **non-executive directors**.

It's my job

When a company reports to the public about its activities, it is the role of the company secretary to make sure that the company follows all the laws and regulations that exist for a public company.

1 Isabel is a company secretary. Read the interview and underline all the information that describes Isabel's job responsibilities.

Isabel Mendoza

Job Company secretary, Novespa Mining
Location Santa Cruz, Patagonia

What is a typical day like?
Really there is no typical day. Basically, I have to organize all the meetings of the board and **send people the list of topics they plan to discuss**[a]. As the company secretary, it's my job to **keep the official records of all the discussions and decisions they make**[b]. Then I have to **keep a lot of other records like the list of all directors and shareholders**[c] and make sure we keep them all informed about changes in the company.

By law, a company has to **send its annual reports and accounts to the financial authorities**[d] and it is my job to make sure that we do this on time.

What do you like best in your job?
The real advantage of my job is the chance to work daily with the top management of the company. I also have to talk to many of the main shareholders to keep them up to date on the company's activities. And I like **preparing information to send to the press**[e].

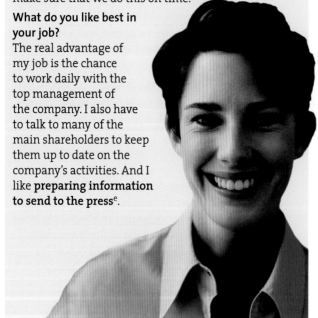

2 Work in pairs. Look at the expressions taken from a job advertisement for a company secretary. Match the technical words 1–5 with the expressions a–e in **bold** in the text.
1 to take the minutes of the meeting
2 to circulate the agenda.
3 to prepare a press release
4 to keep the shareholder register up to date
5 to file the annual accounts

3 Isabel's job is very much about communicating with managers and shareholders. Would you like this job?

Vocabulary

Forecasting adjectives

When we talk about our expectations for the future we often use different kinds of language to **make forecasts** (= predict what will happen).

1 Look at the text below about a company's forecasts. Underline all the **adjectives** that are used to forecast performance. Are they positive or negative?

> Looking ahead, the outlook for the Asian market next year looks bright. We have made an encouraging start to the year, sales are expected to grow by 30% and forecasts are promising. Prospects for our new product range are also quite encouraging, especially in the Chinese market.
>
> However, the outlook for the US market is poor. Sales are expected to grow by only 2% and profits are forecast to fall. In Europe too, the current outlook is gloomy. Economies are projected to decline by another 2% next year and forecasts of consumer spending remain bleak. The German market, in particular, looks grim. We expect sales to fall in all major European markets.

2 Now complete the table below using the words you have underlined. (Three have been done for you.)

The outlook is	bright	Very positive
	encouraging	Positive
	poor	Negative
		Very negative

In 2007, *Marks and Spencer* launched its PLAN A, which promises to report on the company's environmental impact. They describe it as '*Plan A because there is no Plan B*'. Plan A includes aims for M&S to become carbon neutral, send no waste to landfill, extend sustainable sourcing, be a fair trading partner, and help customers and employees to lead healthier lifestyles. Critics say, '*It's just marketing.*' What do you think?

Listening

The chairman's statement at the AGM

The annual general meeting of a company (AGM) often starts with a speech from the chairman or CEO of the company about the company's performance last year and its prospects for the future.

1 🎧 You are a shareholder attending an AGM. You have made a list of the things you want to find out (see below). Listen to the chairman's speech and complete the information on the right-hand side of your list.

Find out about …

	Up (↑) or Down (↓)?
Sales revenue	_____
Costs	_____

	Positive [+] or Negative [-]?
Markets:	
Asia	_____
China	_____
Europe	_____

New products	Partnership with _____ ?
Awards	How many mentioned? _____
Acquisitions	Where? _____
Share issues	Raised $ _____ m ?

2 🎧 Now read the notes made by an analyst at the AGM meeting. Listen again and correct any mistakes she made.

FINANCIAL RESULTS
- *Sales revenue up from $500m to $700m*
- *Costs increased by 2%*
- *Achieved by closing research and development department*

MARKETS
- *Sales in Asia to grow by 13% this year*
- *Sales in China up 8%*
- *Europe outlook poor. Sales to decline by 6%. Increased spending on marketing*

NEW PRODUCTS
- *Launched several new projects*
- *Partnership with Microsoft to sell personal computers*
- *Market to expand at 30% over next 5 years*

AWARDS
- *from Forbes magazine for best new security software*

ACQUISITIONS
- *Bought 'Best Ticket' to sell tickets for music concerts and sports events*

FUNDING
- *Raised $2m by issuing new shares at a price of 43 pence to finance acquisitions*

PROSPECTS
- *Outlook bright, except in Europe, supported by high levels of consumer spending*

• Language spot

Forecasting

Look at these two sentences from the text in *Vocabulary*:

We expect sales to fall in all major markets.
Sales are expected to grow by 30%.

The first sentence is **active**. The predicting verb can be followed by a verb in the infinitive (with *to*) or by a future verb with *will*.

*We expect sales **to** fall in all major markets.*
*We expect sales **will** fall in all major markets.*

The second sentence is **passive**. The predicting verb can only be followed by a verb in the infinitive (with *to*)

*Sales **are expected** to grow by 30%.*
Sales are expected will grow by 30%.

We can use the verb *forecast* in the same way:

*We **forecast** sales **to fall / will fall** in all major markets.*
*Sales **are forecast** to grow by 30%.*

1 Change the company forecasts below from the active to the passive.

EXAMPLE

We expect the sector to recover next year.
The sector is expected to recover next year.

a   We forecast sales of our new range to be strong.
b   Analysts expect the market will decline by 2%.
c   We expect profits to rise by 20%.
d   We forecast costs will fall over the next quarter.
e   The sales team expect demand will improve.

When we talk about the **probability** of something happening in the future, we can use other expressions.

2 Look at these comments about the chances of things happening in the future. Match the expressions 1–4 with the probability a–d.

a   certain to happen
b   strong probability
c   low probability
d   zero probability

1   Profits **are unlikely to** recover this quarter.
2   Prices of raw materials **are bound to** rise.
3   There **is no chance of** winning any new contracts before January.
4   Growth **should** pick up next year.

3 Complete the sentences below using the expressions of probability in **2**.

1   Our new product range has received great reviews in the press; it _____.

2   Consumer demand is beginning to improve. Next year, sales _____.

3   There is a real shortage of steel in the market; prices _____

4   Our biggest customer has gone bankrupt; there _____

5   Trading in the USA is poor. Profits _____ _____

6   The banks have refused to lend us any more money; there _____ _____

4 🎧 Now listen again to these extracts from the speech in *Listening* and complete the sentences.

In Europe, by contrast, _____[1]
in the short term. We are _____
_____[2]
any increase in sales of our software for the next twelve
months and sales _____[3]
decline by 6%. As a result we have cut our sales team and
our marketing budget for the next year.

This market _____[4]
at a rate of 30% per year over the next five years.

Looking ahead, we believe the outlook for our company
_____[5].
Although _____[6]
some weakness in Europe next year, we believe
worldwide growth _____[7]
as a result of the high levels of government spending,
especially in China.

>> Go to **Language reference** p.125

Profits warnings

If a company listed on a stock market recognizes its profits will be less than it had previously forecast to the markets, it must issue a profits warning. This usually causes a big fall in its share price.

The number of profit warnings issued gives a good picture of a country's economy. In 2008, there were 449 profit warnings in the UK: an increase of 17% on the previous year.

Writing

A press release

When a company is involved in a news story, it will often issue a press release to journalists, either to attract their attention or to control what information reaches the public.

1 Read the tips below from a public relations agency about how to create a good press release.

1 What do they mean by a 'catchy headline'?
2 Why do they advise you to use third-person forms like 'it' and 'they'?
3 Why is a quotation important?

How to write a good press release

- Put a date and time for release of the story.
- Indicate the types of journalist who will be interested in the story and the sector of business.
- Write a 'catchy headline' that will attract attention and use short paragraphs to divide up the text.
- Include a good quotation from the company that journalists can use in quotation marks ('…').
- Use a formal style with the third person 'they', 'she', 'he', and 'it' – not first person pronouns 'I' or 'we'. Keep the language objective and avoid typical sales expressions, like 'amazing' or 'terrific'.
- Keep to the facts and not your impressions. Any conclusions you make need information to support them. Provide sources for information.
- If you use the Internet, include hyperlinks to help the journalist access the information quickly. Links to social websites (e.g. *Twitter*) or to news agencies (e.g. *Reuters*) are also a good idea.
- Include an address and Internet contact.

A good press release should have the following structure:

references
- date for release
- for the attention of

story
- headline
- story
- quotation
- business sector

- contact address
- links / bookmarks

2 Work in pairs. Read the press release below and using the tips in **1** decide what is wrong.

- Is the choice of language appropriate? <u>Underline</u> examples of words you think are too informal and suggest alternatives.
- Does it use third person pronouns?
- Are all the points relevant? Cross out information that is not relevant.
- Does it give good references or contact links?

Arno technologies announces amazing new headquarters in Maldevise

Journalists will be very interested in the news that we have now finished building our headquarters in Maldevise.

The building looks really great and is full of state of the art technology like solar panels and wind turbines for electricity. We are really excited.

The Prime Minister of Maldevise will open the building next week in a cool ceremony. We invite all the press and expect good reports on our wonderful architecture.

We will begin to use the HQ when the builders go. Our boss at Arno says it is a great advance for the company. We will move all the new research plus the sales and marketing department into the building. He says 'we estimate the building will save us $2m because it has new green technology.'

'We will recruit more young people and train them for good jobs, contributing to the local economy.'

Journalists and the public who are interested can find details if they want to ring the company or look at the website.

We welcome everyone to the ceremony.

3 Now use the information from the story to rewrite the press release. Feel free to change details or add information like dates, links, or references you consider appropriate.

Vocabulary

A balance sheet

A balance sheet shows us the value of a company at the end of the company's financial year.

On one side of the balance sheet, we find everything the company owns – its **assets**. These are both the things it has invested in, like property and machinery, and the cash they hold. Some of these assets are long-term investments and are difficult to sell quickly; these are described as **fixed assets**. There are other things, like stocks of materials that the company expects to use and to sell quickly, plus cash and debtors; these are described as **current assets**.

On the other side of the balance sheet are the **liabilities**: all the money the company still owes and must pay to other people such as the banks, creditors, and other forms of debt. These are also divided into **short-term liabilities** that the company must pay soon, and **long-term liabilities**, like bank loans and shares issued.

If we put the two sides together, we can see the net value of the company at the date of the balance sheet. As the company is owned by the shareholders, this represents the value of the shareholders' funds.

In the UK, a balance sheet is presented in vertical form.

1 Look at the balance sheet for Reklam opposite and find the accounting expressions for

1. the investments made in machinery and property
2. the long-term debts of the company
3. the value of raw materials and components owned by the company
4. the money owed to the company by customers
5. the money the company owes on its overdraft and to its suppliers
6. the total assets minus the total liabilities.

2 One of Reklam's competitors is thinking of buying the company. Using the information in the email about Reklam, complete the balance sheet below.

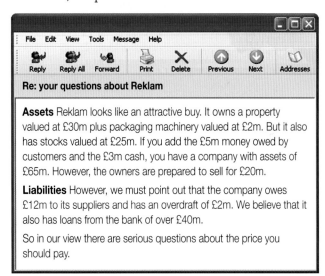

Re: your questions about Reklam

Assets Reklam looks like an attractive buy. It owns a property valued at £30m plus packaging machinery valued at £2m. But it also has stocks valued at £25m. If you add the £5m money owed by customers and the £3m cash, you have a company with assets of £65m. However, the owners are prepared to sell for £20m.

Liabilities However, we must point out that the company owes £12m to its suppliers and has an overdraft of £2m. We believe that it also has loans from the bank of over £40m.

So in our view there are serious questions about the price you should pay.

REKLAM

Balance sheet: as at 31 March

FIXED ASSETS _____ a (£m.)

CURRENT ASSETS
   stock _____ b
   debtors _____ c
   cash _____ d

LIABILITIES
   current liabilities _____ e
   long-term liabilities _____ f

= TOTAL NET ASSETS 11m

CAPITAL AND RESERVES
   share capital 8m
   reserves 3m

TOTAL SHAREHOLDERS' FUNDS 11m

3 What do you think are the biggest problems Reklam has with its balance sheet?

Webquest

Go to the home page of a big international bank (e.g. *Barclays Bank*) and find their annual report.

1 Scanning Use the information from your reading about the different sections of an annual report (see *Reading* on p.84) to find the right sections of the report and try to find answers to these questions.

1 How much profit did the bank make last year?
2 How much was the dividend?
3 How many people are there on the board of directors?
4 Who is the chairman?
5 Who are the company's auditors?

2 Skimming Find an example of a recent press release from the bank. Make notes on the key information and report back to the class.

Checklist

Assess your progress in this unit. Tick (✓) the statements which are true.

- I can identify the main sections in an annual report
- I know the job responsibilities of a company secretary
- I can explain what happens at an AGM
- I can make forecasts about the future
- I can write a press release
- I can understand the key terms in a balance sheet

Key words

Forecasting	Reporting
bleak	circulate an agenda
bound to	file accounts
bright	minutes of a meeting
gloomy	press release
grim	profits warning
outlook	
prospects	
unlikely to	

Accounting
assets
balance sheet
code
creditor
debtor
liability
owe
own
regulator

Look back through this unit. Find five more words or expressions that you think are useful.

11 Accountancy and auditing

Countdown

One of the best ways to start a career in finance is to work for one of the **big four** accountancy firms.

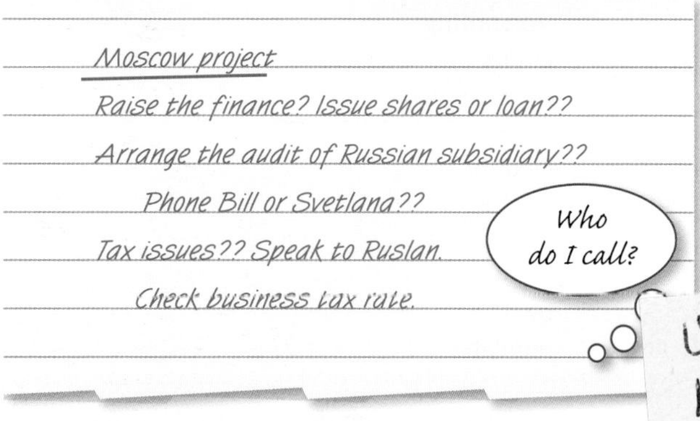

Moscow project

Raise the finance? Issue shares or loan??

Arrange the audit of Russian subsidiary??

Phone Bill or Svetlana??

Tax issues?? Speak to Ruslan.

Check business tax rate.

Who do I call?

1 How many of the big four firms can you name? Here are the first letters:

1 K _ _ _

2 D _ _ _ _ _ _ _

3 E _ _ _ _ & Y _ _ _ _

4 P _ _ _ _ _ _ _ _ _ _ _ _ _ _ Coopers

2 Look at the web page below. Complete the headings 1–3 by matching the names of the divisions below to the activities of the firm:

Tax   Advisory   Audit

3 Which division would you join if you wanted to work as

1 a consultant on company strategy?
2 an investigator of company's accounts?
3 a legal specialist?

4 Which division is responsible for

1 checking the accuracy of a company's accounts?
2 reorganizing a company's finances?
3 helping companies with mergers or acquisitions?
4 interpreting new changes in tax laws?
5 testing for accounting fraud and errors?
6 advising on accounting standards?
7 advising on budgets and cost control?
8 reducing a company's tax costs?

5 Work in pairs and compare the ... ions.

... k they do?
... to your
... n it.

Home	Careers			us

1 _____

We can support your decision making:

- on loans, debt, capital restructuring, planning your finance needs for the next 5 years
- when buying or selling other companies
- when deciding which sectors and markets to work in
- to improve the way you manage your budgets and cost accounting.

2 _____

Our team of aud...

- to achieve hig... bookkeeping
- to detect fraud
- to test the inte... staff's work
- to make sure yo... accounting stan...

... , we can
... s in tax

... g your

... n to

... of differences between countries' tax laws.

[Handwritten note:]
Unit 11   Accountancy + auditing.
KPMG, DELOITTE, ERNST+ YOUNG.
PRICE WATERHOUSE COOPERS
1- Advisory 2 Audit 3 Tax
(3)   1   2   3
(4) 1 Aud 2 Adv 3 Adv 4 Tax 5 Aud
6 Adv 7 Adv 8 Tax
1 purchase 2 delivery 3 proof 4 autho
5 inspect 6 defective 7 wd 8 AO 9 settle
10 issue.

Vocabulary

Documents and billing records

All companies need to keep accurate records of their financial transactions: when they buy something, pay someone, or sell items. Every transaction must be recorded in both paper and electronic format, so that they can prepare the accounts and auditors can inspect them. This means that if you work in the **accounts department** of a company, you will see many kinds of billing documents, like a sales invoice or a delivery note.

Study the flow chart, which shows the main steps for a company to complete a simple order. Complete the following definitions with these financial expressions from the diagram.

amount owed	authorized	inspect
delivery	proof	purchase
issue	wrong delivery	
settle	defective	

1   To buy goods for a company is to _____ them.
2   The confirmation that goods have arrived is given by a _____ note.
3   A delivery note will give the purchaser _____ of delivery.
4   Someone who has the authority to sign a document to place an order is an _____ purchaser.
5   To check the goods is to _____ them.
6   Goods that are damaged are _____.
7   Goods that arrive but were not ordered are a _____ _____.
8   The money that has not been paid yet is the _____.
9   To pay what is owed in an account is to _____ the account.
10 To print or publish an official confirmation record is to _____ a document.

ISSUED BY PURCHASER

purchase order – an internal document that lists items to buy and is signed by an authorized purchaser.

Order placed

ISSUED BY SUPPLIER

delivery note details the items delivered and is signed by the purchaser as proof of delivery

Goods delivered

goods received note (GRN) – issued after the goods are inspected for damage or wrong delivery

sales invoice issued to the purchaser requesting payment and describing all items purchased
additional documentation:
- **credit note** issued if the purchaser returns any items as defective goods or wrong order
- **statement of account** gives the client a summary of all their purchases for the month and the amount owed
- **remittance advice** used if you are requesting payment by cheque

electronic payment by bank transfer to settle the statement of account

Payment made

cash receipt – issued to confirm receipt of payment

pg 94 Unit 11. Time clauses.
(a) 1 1 will, 2 have tested 3 will
4 will 5 neg 6 pp 7 are
8 arrives 9 pp.

about one of

• Language spot

Time clauses: describing stages of a process with *when*

Look at the two sentences below. Which one is correct: a or b?

a When we receive the goods, we will sign your delivery note.
b When we will receive the goods, we will sign your delivery note.

When a sentence has two parts that refer to the future, we normally use:

When + Present Simple – future with *will*

The two parts of the sentence can be reversed:
We ***will sign*** *your delivery note* ***when we receive*** *the goods.*

When a sentence refers to a process that has to be completed in the future before something else can happen, we use:

When + Present Perfect – future with *will*:

When we ***have checked*** *the goods,* ***we will*** *issue a goods received note.*

1 Put the verbs in brackets into the correct tense.

1 When we visit the suppliers next month, we ________ (check) their quality.
2 When we ________ (test) their quality, we will place our order.
3 We ________ (ask for) a price list when we begin discussions.
4 When we have studied the price list, we ________ ________ (decide) the size of our order.
5 When we ________ (negotiate) the contract, we will need translators.
6 When they ________ (finish) production, they will package the goods for us.
7 They will begin the shipment when the products ________ (be) ready.
8 We will check the details when the invoice ________ ________ (arrive).
9 When we ________ (check) the details, we will arrange the payment.

Accounting and auditing

1 Before you read, work with a partner to test what you know about the differences between accounting and auditing. Circle the correct option for each sentence.

1 *Accountants / Auditors* prepare the financial accounts of a company.
2 *Accountants / Auditors* investigate and test the accuracy of the accounts.
3 *Accountants / Auditors* are appointed by the shareholders.
4 *Accountants / Auditors* prepare the statutory accounts at the end of every financial year.
5 The *accounts / auditor's report* record(s) the financial results of a company.

2 Now work together to find out more about the differences. Student A, read the text opposite. Student B, go to page 116.

Student A: Accounting

Read the following text about the purpose of accounting and write notes to answer the questions below. You will need to use these notes to explain to your partner what accountants do.

1 What information can you find in the books or ledgers of a company?
2 What is the purpose of the management accounts?
3 What is the reason for having the statutory financial accounts?
4 What are accounting standards? Give three examples.
5 What is the role of the IFSA?

Arthur Young was born in Glasgow, Scotland but moved in 1890 to the US to pursue a career in accounting. In 1906, he formed an accounting firm, *Arthur Young & Company*, with his brother Stanley.

Alwin C Ernst was born in Cleveland, USA. After leaving school he worked as a bookkeeper. In 1903, he and his brother Theodore started *Ernst & Ernst*, a small public accounting firm. Alwin Ernst and Arthur Young never met in life, but died within days of each other in 1948. In 1989, the firms they created combined to form *Ernst & Young*.

Accounting

In the past, a company's financial records were kept in real books or ledgers – hence the term bookkeeping – so a company kept a separate **sales ledger** for sales made, a **purchasing ledger** for things bought, a **cash ledger**, and others. Today, of course, these records are mostly kept on computers in electronic form.

Even today, the company accountants may use these books to prepare the **management accounts**. These are prepared monthly, or even weekly in very big companies. They are not published outside the company, but provide information for controlling the business by giving an up-to-date statement of the company's current financial trading. They help to answer questions such as: 'Are sales going to plan?' and 'What is happening to our costs?'

But a modern company is also regulated by laws (e.g. the Companies Acts in the UK), and these laws require a company to publish official financial statements for regulators and shareholders to inspect. This means that the accountants have to prepare a second annual summary set of accounts, the **Statutory Financial Accounts** which include a balance sheet, income statement, and cash-flow statement, according to recognised accounting standards.

These statutory accounts summarize the financial statements for the last year. But the accountants must make sure that the company reports its official results according to the accounting standards created by the accounting profession. For example, the company must follow a principle of '**consistency**' (it cannot keep changing its accounting systems every year); it must be '**prudent**' (careful) in its estimate of the value of things it owns; and the directors must believe that the company has enough money to continue trading next year as a '**going concern**'.

These basic principles have been incorporated into national accounting standards in different ways in different countries. But globalization has created a growing pressure for all companies worldwide to use the same reporting standards developed by the international accounting organization, the IFSA.

3 Now work in pairs to explain the system you read about to your partner. Student A, using your answers to the questions on p.94, explain to your partner what kind of accounts companies keep. Student B, using your answers to the questions on p.116, explain to your partner what an audit is.

4 Go to p.114.

Listening

The steps of an audit

1 🎧 Listen to a presentation in which the leader of an audit team explains to a client the steps of the audit he will carry out in the company. Write down the sequence of steps by putting the numbers (1–6) in the first column of the table.

Steps in the audit		What the client needs to do
a do substantive tests	☐	show us _____ and _____ and talk to _____
b define the scope of the audit	☐	arrange interviews
c sign off the audit report	☐	report the results to _____ _____ in your company's _____ _____
d examine the accounting system	☐	give access to company's books, e.g. _____ and _____
e write a management letter	☐	to make a plan of _____ _____
f examine the internal controls	☐	provide two things: (a) _____ and (b) _____, e.g. sales invoices and purchasing documents

2 🎧 Listen again and make a note in the second column of what preparation the company should do for each step.

Speaking
Presenting a sequence of steps in an audit

You are the head of a team of auditors. You are going to plan a first presentation to a client on the steps in an audit.

1 🎧 Listen to the first part of the listening again and complete the sentences with the expressions used at the start of the presentation.

> In this opening meeting, _____¹ the steps in the audit of your company so that your staff will know what to expect.
>
> _____² there will be three of us in the team – I think you have all met them by now – and _____ _____³ about three weeks.

2 🎧 Now listen to the way the presentation ends and complete the sentences.

> When _____¹, we will sign off the audit report ... So, that's what happens from start to finish. In total, we expect _____² about two months.
>
> Is _____³ for everyone? Are there any questions? No? Good. Well, _____ _____⁴ of the audit stages.

3 Now you are going to prepare your own presentation. Look at the **presentation plan** on this page.

1 Using the expressions for an introduction and for a conclusion from *Listening* above, complete the first part a–c and last part d–g in your presentation plan.

2 Now complete the main part of the presentation 1–6 using the sentences below:

- define the scope of the audit
- do the substantive tests
- examine the internal controls
- look at your accounting system
- sign off the audit report
- write a management letter

Presentation plan

Introduction:

a In this opening meeting _____¹ the steps in the audit.

Background:

b _____², there will be three of us in the team…

c _____³ about three weeks.

Main part of presentation:

1 First of all, we will _____⁴.

2 Then, we will _____⁵.

3 After that, we will _____⁶.

4 In the next step, we will _____ _____⁷.

5 When we have finished our tests, we will _____ _____⁸.

6 When we have completed these tasks, we will _____⁹.

Summary and questions

d So, that's what happens from start to finish. In total, we expect _____¹⁰ about two months.

e Is _____¹¹ for everyone?

f _____¹² questions?

Conclusion

g Well, that _____¹³.

4 Work in pairs. Student A, using your plan make your presentation to your partner. Student B, as you listen to your partner's presentation, make notes to assess them using the questions below.

> 1 Which parts of the presentation were not clear to you?
> 2 Did they signal each step clearly?
> 3 Have they left out any steps?
> 4 Did they speak loudly / clearly enough?

Give your comments to your partner. When you finish, swap roles.

It's my job

1 Have you ever been to a recruitment fair? What is the purpose of them? What can you learn there?

2 Sofia Angeles is an auditor who works for Broughton and Stewarts, Senegal. Read her story. Do you think she made the right decision?

3 Discuss the questions.
1 What do you think of Sofia's decision? Would you choose to do the same?
2 Auditing can involve a lot of international travel. What are the advantages and disadvantages of this?
3 Sofia's career was partly decided by accident. How often do you think this happens?

Webquest

Visit the website of one of the big four accountancy firms or a large accountancy firm based in your own country, and find out information on job applications.

1 Find answers to these questions.
1 How do you apply for a job in the firm?
2 What kind of skills are they looking for?
3 What qualifications do you need to become an accountant in your country? How long does it take?
4 Does the firm you've looked at offer you any help with preparing for the exams?
5 What do some of the people who work at the firm think of their jobs? Choose one person and make notes to report back on why they like the job.

2 Report back to the class on the firm you have visited.

Sofia Angeles

Job Auditor
Company Broughton and Stewarts
Location Senegal

Sofia, you studied in France. Why did you return to Senegal?
Oh, that was a wonderful accident. After my studies in France I began working as an auditor for Broughton and Stewarts in Paris. Then, as usual, I went back to Senegal for my summer holidays. One day, my sister asked me to go with her to a local recruitment fair because she was looking for a job.

At the fair, I noticed a stand for Broughton and Stewarts. I went over for a chat. The guy running the stand explained how working in Senegal I could be part of a small team and have a creative role in planning the audit and tests. That's the really interesting part of auditing. He even offered me a job in the Senegal office.

I had never thought of returning to Senegal so I rejected the idea at the time, the salary was 40% below my salary in France! But coming back to Paris I felt very lonely and I wanted a more interesting challenge. So I began to think again.

What made you change your mind?
Well, after a long miserable month I decided it was more important to be happy and do an interesting job than to earn a big salary. By going back to Senegal I had to take a big pay cut but in the end I realized I could still live very well in Senegal and the job is far more interesting.

And why did you choose to go into auditing?
I always think it's a bit like being a detective. Sometimes people working in a company want to present financial information in a way that makes the company look good. But as the auditor, I'm responsible to the shareholders. I have to make sure that the accounts show 'a true and fair view'.

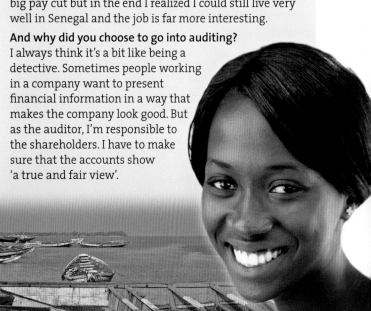

Accountants, like other companies, often have values statements on their websites. Here are some examples from the *KPMG* website.

- We lead by example.
- We work together.
- We respect the individual.
- We seek the facts and provide insight.
- We are open and honest in our communication.
- We are committed to our communities.
- Above all, we act with integrity.

Writing

The auditor's letter to management

When the auditors have completed their audit, they will usually write a formal **letter to management**, explaining the problems they have found in the accounts and any weaknesses in the control systems.

1 Read the letter opposite and match the descriptions 1–7 with the underlined expressions in the letter.

1 asking for a plan from the management to solve the problems
2 introducing a list of the main problems discovered
3 identifying specific problems and weaknesses (3 expressions)
4 explaining the limits to the auditor's work
5 a reminder of necessary accounting practice
6 making recommendations (2 expressions)
7 the purpose of the letter

2 Using the notes below and the expressions identified above, write a letter to the management of 'Yeovil Plastics, explaining the results of your preliminary audit.

Notes on Yeovil Plastics Audit (14 June)

- audit completed: June 10
- limits to audit: time and available resources
- outline of key points
- main findings:

– Two machines recorded in the balance sheet accounts had been sold but there was no record of money received in the cash ledger.

– Sales staff took clients to restaurants and were refunded by a secretary from the petty cash in the office. This was against company rules which state that all expenses must signed for by a sales manager.

recommendation: Make one senior sales director responsible for all client entertainment expenses.

Request a plan from the management about how they propose to solve the problems.

RBT Partners
AUDITING DIVISION
Cheviot House, 167 Bishops Gate
London EC4W 6JH

Dear Sirs,

Following the completion of our audit on November 22, we are writing to inform you[a] of the first results of our checks on your company.

   We must point out that for reasons of time and resources we may not have identified[b] every failure in your systems.

   We would like to draw your attention to[c] the following weaknesses identified in your systems.

Invoices

1   During our checks on your Sales Ledger we discovered[d] six examples in which sales had been recorded in the ledger without corresponding paper invoices or documents. We must remind you that[e] all sales records must be matched by real physical documents.

Credits

2   We also found three cases[f] where credit was given to customers who were already more than 60 days late in their payments. This showed a serious failure by staff to comply with the rules as stated in your company handbook. We would advise you to[g] make one manager responsible for checking that all rules are followed by staff.

Salaries

3   Our investigations showed that[h] there were a number of examples in which extra wages were paid to employees without any proof in the 'time sheet' that these hours had really been worked by the employee during the period. We recommend that[i] in future a department manager should check and sign all salary claims before payment is made.

Could you please inform us of the steps you intend to take[j] to solve these problems before our next meeting on December 16?

Yours faithfully,

Jan Houten

Jan Houten
Audit Team Manager

Professional skills

Accountancy and professional ethics

Read the text below and then discuss these questions.

1   Do you think that accountants need ethical standards in the same way as doctors and lawyers?
2   What is the difference between tax planning and tax avoidance?
3   Should we allow some countries to offer low tax rates to attract international companies?

A lot of professions today require high ethical standards of their staff to avoid corruption and to protect the public. Accountancy firms, in particular, promote their integrity and honesty.

But accountancy firms have to compete in the real world. If they refuse to do what clients want, they may lose them as clients. But if they are flexible in interpreting standards, they risk breaking the law. So how does an accountancy firm reconcile these conflicts?

For accountant Tim Cox, the answer is clear: 'Accountancy firms must first respect the law, then develop and apply high professional standards of conduct. If, for example, an international company decides to move part of its business to another country to take advantage of lower tax rates, we would ask: Are they really going to do business there? Will they employ people and use local services? If the answer is yes, we would view that as legitimate tax planning.'

'But if a company decided to move its business address offshore only to avoid taxes, we would be suspicious. If they employ no one there and do no business, we would call that tax avoidance. They may not be directly breaking any laws, but we would not want to assist a client whose intention is only to avoid tax. It is a question of professional standards.'

12 Insurance and risk

Countdown

1 Look at the photos of typical risks people face.

   1 What kinds of risk do you associate with each photo?

   2 Match the photos a–g with the types of personal insurance you can take 1–7.

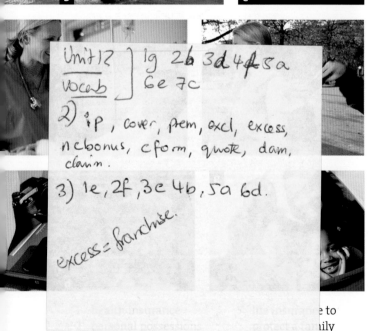

2 Discuss with a partner. Which of these features should a car insurance policy include and which could be excluded? Mark them I (include) or E (exclude).

   1 protection against theft ___

   2 your medical costs if you have an accident ___

   3 paying compensation if you cause damage to another vehicle ___

   4 full cost of all repairs to your car ___

   5 a refund of the original price of your car if it is destroyed ___

   6 a free replacement car if your car breaks down ___

3 What features would you expect a travel insurance policy for a holiday to include? Work in pairs and make a list then discuss your results together.

Vocabulary

Personal insurance

1 Match the key insurance terms with their definitions.

1 a claim	5 no-claims bonus
2 an excess	6 an exclusion
3 a premium	7 the cover
4 insurance policy	

a a discount the client can get if they make no claim for a period of time

b the fixed sum of money the client must pay towards the costs of a loss before the insurance company pays compensation (e.g. 'the first £200')

c the things you are protected against by the insurance policy

d the charge you pay annually or monthly to the insurance company

e something that is not covered by the insurance

f the written contract that defines the terms of your insurance

g informing the insurance company about a loss and requesting compensation (= 'making _____')

3 motor insurance

4 travel insurance

insurance

6 property insurance

7 credit card insurance

In this unit
- types of personal insurance
- terms of an insurance contract
- how companies manage risk
- insurance for a natural disaster
- writing a report on an insurance claim
- Lloyd's of London insurance market

2 Complete the advice from a broker's advice site with the insurance expressions in the list.

claim	claims form	cover
damage	excess	exclusions
quote	no-claims bonus	premiums
insurance policy		

If you drive a car, go on holiday or rent a flat, you need to take out an _____¹ in order to get protective _____² against losses or accidents.

You can usually reduce the _____³ you pay each year if you select only the cover you need. But it's important to read the policy carefully because many companies impose _____⁴ which do not pay for some risks. Others require you to pay an _____⁵, a fixed amount of any claim you make, before they pay you compensation.

If you make no claims, however, you can often build a _____⁶ that gives you a discount on the premiums, the costs you pay each year.

If you have to make a claim, it's important to notify the insurance company as quickly as possible and fill in a _____⁷.

Often they will require you to obtain a _____⁸ from different service providers for the cost of repairing the damage and the insurance company may send out a <u>loss adjustor</u> to assess the value of the _____⁹ or losses you have suffered.

When the work is completed, the insurance company will settle the _____¹⁰ by either sending you a cheque or paying the provider directly.

3 Match the verbs with the nouns to create word partnerships for these insurance expressions.

1 build up	a a claim
2 fill in	b a quote
3 impose	c exclusions
4 obtain	d an insurance policy
5 settle	e a no-claims bonus
6 take out	f a claims form

Professional skills
Tips on getting the best insurance policy

1 Look at this tip sheet from an insurance broker on finding the best insurance policy. Which of the tips are new for you? Which do you think are most effective?

What kind of cover do you really need? Many people find they pay more than they need for their insurance because they don't take the time to **compare prices** from different companies. But you can find a whole range of quotes very quickly by going online.

Look at all the exclusions. Often people think they have obtained a cheaper quote but find when they want to make a claim that they are not insured for that risk.

See if you can reduce the cost by **increasing the excess**, the amount you agree to pay before the insurance company gives you compensation for your loss.

Think about putting all your insurance needs with one company. Often you will get a better quote if you insure your possessions, flat, and car with the same company.

Build up a no-claims bonus. That will often give you a big discount. Remember if you make a lot of small claims on your policy, you may lose your no-claims bonus.

Understand how the insurance companies work. The higher the risk, the more you pay. If you are young and want motor insurance for a fast car, you will probably pay top prices. But you can cut the cost if you keep the car in a secure location like a garage, or you can install anti-theft devices on the car. Or switch to a smaller car!

2 Discuss the questions.
1 Do the tips above apply to where you live?
2 Which areas of personal insurance are important for a family to have in your country (e.g. health, life, etc.)?

Hedging your bets: Companies often try to lower the risk of losing money due to changes in commodity prices, exchange rates, interest rates, etc. This is called **hedging** and it's big business. Nowadays, complex forms of **derivative** such as **futures**, **swaps** and **options**, which can be used to limit risk, are traded on exchanges all over the world.

Reading

How do companies manage risk?

1 All companies face many types of risk in running their business. Look at the four examples below. What kind of risks should companies consider when planning these activities? What could go wrong?

- a bank lending money to customers to buy property
- a car company launching a new model of car
- a construction company building a high-rise office tower
- a food company producing cooked food for sale in supermarkets

2 To eliminate or manage risks, companies carry out regular risk audits of their business. A risk audit usually divides risks into four categories. What do you think these categories refer to?

financial risks   natural disaster risks
operational risks   strategic risks

Now read the text opposite on managing risk and match the four categories to the correct paragraphs. Write the title above each paragraph.

3 In which category of risk would you place each of these problems ? Mark each item **O** (operational), **S** (strategic), **F** (financial), or **N** (natural disaster).

1   launching new products _____
2   computer virus attacks _____
3   human errors _____
4   managing customer credits _____
5   takeovers and mergers _____
6   understanding consumer trends _____
7   compliance with health and safety regulations _____
8   key staff resignations _____
9   flooding or fire _____

4 Work in pairs. Student A, go to p.114. Student B go to p.118.

Managing Risk

1 _____
A first priority for every risk manager conducting a risk audit is to identify the risks that could affect the daily working of the business. For example, any failure in the system, loss of data, or virus attack can quickly damage the business. Also staff can make mistakes, commit fraud, or resign unexpectedly. A company must make sure that it follows government health and safety regulations, both for employees and also the products it sells to consumers.

2 _____
But managers in all companies have to make daily decisions about their product range and markets. What new products do we want to launch? What kind of clients should we target? Do we want to buy any other companies? In each case, they must compare the opportunities with the risks of failure. In a fast-moving consumer market, like mobile phones, failing to understand consumer and design trends can eliminate a company permanently from the market.

3 _____
The biggest cause of bankruptcy in small businesses is the failure of companies to manage their cash flow and credit operations. If a customer does not pay on time, if a bank stops the overdraft facility, if it is impossible to borrow any money, can the company survive?
For any company working on the financial markets sudden changes in prices of shares or commodities create special daily risks. A broker must know at every moment what is the 'value at risk' – that is to say, how much money the company could potentially lose if things go wrong.

4 _____
But if a catastrophe happens, a hurricane or flooding, even the best-managed companies are at risk. Companies must plan ahead to survive. Staff must know what to do and be ready to move to safe locations. Computer systems must be backed up to remote servers. Companies can then ask their insurers to help restore their operations when the crisis is over.

In the early days of cinema, actors like **Harold Lloyd** often used to do their own stunts. In one incident, Lloyd lost several fingers on his right hand and in later films had to wear an artificial hand! Nowadays, film companies rarely let actors do stunts as insurance companies refuse to insure them.

● Language spot

should have done and Third Conditional

1 Work in pairs. Look at the newspaper headlines below about companies whose risk strategies failed. Discuss the questions.

1 What do you think the company did wrong?

   EXAMPLE
   They sold water with chemicals in it.

2 What should the companies have done?

   EXAMPLE
   They should have tested the water properly before they sold it.

> **Drinks manufacturer announces huge product recall after chemicals found in product**

> **BANK COLLAPSES AS ROGUE TRADER LOSES $ BILLIONS**

> **Record losses at US car company as customers reject big engine cars**

> **TWO WORKERS DIE AFTER CHEMICAL COMPANY STOPS SAFETY CHECKS**

> **CEO resigns as advertising campaign fails to attract new customers**

When we talk about mistakes people made in the past, or things they didn't do correctly, we can use *should have* + **past participle**.

*They **should have backed up** their computer system.*

(= 'They didn't back up their computer system. It was a mistake not to do it.')

*They **shouldn't have launched** the software without more tests.*

(= 'They launched the software without more tests. It was a mistake to do it.')

2 Look at these mistakes which companies made in the past and write one or two sentences about each mistake using *should have* or *shouldn't have*. The first one is done for you.

1 The company rented a warehouse near the river and didn't check the risk of flooding.
   They shouldn't have rented the warehouse.

[handwritten notes overlaying text:]

Language spot   Unit 12

2 They should've checked the customer's credit position

3 They should've ~~checked~~ tested for safety for children and labelled it

4 They should've tried alternative suppliers

5 The company should've issued safety glasses to prevent injuries

1 They didn't test the software so they didn't find the faults.
2 They didn't practise the fire drill so workers didn't know the fire procedure.
3 They didn't respect the safety guidelines so they received a big fine.
4 They didn't maintain the machines so the machines broke down.
5 They didn't visit the factory so they didn't see the working conditions.

>> Go to **Language reference** p.125

Listening

Insurance claims from a natural disaster

On 4 September 2010, a major earthquake hit the city of Christchurch in New Zealand. There were no deaths but the earthquake and its aftershocks caused extensive damage to buildings and roads. *New Century* is an international chain of hotels that has two hotels in the city. Donna works in the finance department of New Century and is responsible for arranging insurance for the hotel chain. She flew out to New Zealand immediately after the incident and is now updating the CEO of the company on the damage.

1 What sort of insurance would you expect companies to have to cover such disasters?

2 Match the types of loss and damage 1–5 with the insurance cover a-e in the table below. Now listen to the conversation between Donna and the CEO and check your answers.

LOSS OR DAMAGE SUFFERED	INSURANCE COVER
1 Property damage to hotel	a Employer's liability insurance
2 Loss of business due to hotel closure	b Private medical insurance
3 Personal injuries to guests	c All risks policy
4 Injuries to staff at work	d Business interruption insurance
5 Hospital expenses	e Public liability insurance

3 🎧 Now listen again and write T (true) or F (false).
1 The earthquake happened in the afternoon.
2 None of the hotel guests or staff were injured.
3 Guests are still staying in the city centre hotel.
4 The loss adjustor thinks that the repairs will cost about NZ$500,000.
5 Repairing the hotel will take up to three months.
6 All the guests at the city centre hotel have been moved to the airport hotel.
7 The hotel followed the health and safety regulations.
8 All the hotel staff have private medical insurance.

4 Discuss these questions.
1 What sort of short-term and long-term help do you think people need after a disaster such as an earthquake? Who should provide it?
2 What role in reconstruction after major disasters can be played by
   ● insurance companies?
   ● the government?
   ● relief agencies, e.g. the International Red Cross and Red Crescent?
   ● other countries?

3 Would you visit an area (as a tourist or for your work) if it had recently suffered a natural disaster?

Writing

Reporting on insurance claims

You work for New Century, the hotel chain in *Listening*. You have just visited the site of the earthquake in New Zealand and must now use your notes to write a report for the company directors. The purpose of the report is to update them on possible insurance claims resulting from the earthquake.

Read the notes below and decide what information to include under the different sections of the report outline below. When you have finished, write a short report using the headings and language in the outline to help you. Your report should summarize the losses suffered by the company and explain the type of insurance policy that covers each loss.

Notes on visit to New Zealand – September 2010

HOTEL GUESTS AND STAFF
- No injuries reported among 155 guests
- Guests staying at city centre hotel transferred to our airport hotel and other local hotels.
- Future compensation claims from guests for personal injury unlikely, but if this happens, we're covered by our public liability insurance.
- Any future claims from staff for injuries at work covered by employer's liability insurance (but not expected).
- Employees would receive treatment through public healthcare system and senior staff have private health insurance provided through company.

BACKGROUND
Earthquake hit Christchurch on 4 September 2010. First struck at 4.30 a.m., but aftershock risk throughout following week. No deaths or serious injuries, but serious damage to buildings in city centre. Power and water supplies restored but at risk from aftershock.

PROPERTY DAMAGE
- Airport hotel unaffected; damage limited to our city centre hotel.
- Structural engineer's report says building is structurally safe.
- Repairs to chimneys, cracked walls, and window replacement needed. N.B. all property damage to hotel covered by 'all risks' policy.
- Repair work to take up to 3 months. Estimated cost NZ$700K (= US$500K).

IMPLICATIONS FOR FUTURE BUSINESS
- Hotel in city centre can't be used during repairs.
- Company will have to cancel and refund advanced bookings (40% of rooms) or offer rooms in airport hotel. Estimated cost: NZ$300K.
- Need to consider compensation from business interruption insurance for loss of future business.
- Serious damage to city and region for holidays/ tourism?

CONCLUSION
Overall it's fortunate that no staff or guests injured and one of our hotels functioning normally. All major claims (actual and possible) covered by our insurance.

RECOMMENDATIONS
- Check other hotels round the world. Are they designed to withstand earthquakes?
- Plan publicity campaign (+ special price offers) once hotel reopens and city has recovered.

Title: *Internal report on …*
For the attention of …
Objectives: *The purpose of the report is to …*
Background: *On 4 September 2010, …*
Damages and insurance claims:
1) **Public liability insurance**: *We are glad to report that none of the 155 guests were injured in the earthquake. Therefore we do not expect claims for _____ . However, if there are claims from guests in the future, they will be are covered by our public liability insurance.*
2) **Property (all risks) insurance**: *The hotel …*
3) **Employer's liability insurance**: *We are glad to report that …*
4) **Business interruption insurance**: *We expect the hotel …*
Conclusion / recommendation: *Fortunately, the overall effects of the earthquake were limited … We recommend that … In addition …*

In 2009, **Lloyd's**, the world's leading specialist insurance market, insured the tongue of Gennaro Pelliccia, *Costa Coffee*'s Italian Master of Coffee, for £10 million.

Gennaro Pelliccia personally tastes every single batch of raw coffee beans at the company's roastery in London, before they are roasted and shipped to its stores.

This is not the first time Lloyd's has insured a tongue. Wine tasters for supermarkets and wine merchants have also taken out policies. And in 2008, a Dutch wine maker, Ilja Gort, last year insured his nose for €5m.

Webquest

Lloyd's of London is a specialist insurance market. It insures against risks that no ordinary insurance company will cover. Lloyd's started out in Edward Lloyd's Coffee House over 300 years ago. It insures everything from oil rigs and hurricanes to the body parts of famous people; from airlines and space travel to major sporting events.

1 Find out how the Lloyd's market works. Visit the website and match the jobs 1–3 with what they do a–c.

  1 brokers
  2 managing agents, underwriters
  3 a syndicate, members, 'names'

  a They provide the capital to guarantee the insurance.
  b They represent clients and bring business to the market.
  c They evaluate the risks and decide the premium to pay.

2 Find examples of the kinds of insurance Lloyd's offers for
  ● sport and sports events
  ● climate change
  ● space travel.

3 What is 'reinsurance' and how does it work?

It's my job

1 Joanna works for an insurance brokers in London. Read her blog and find out what activities she does in her job.

2 Now answer and discuss these questions:
  1 Which team is Joanna working in?
  2 What do you think 'emerging risks' are?
  3 What other examples of emerging risks can you think of?
  4 Why do you think insurers study history?
  5 How can insurance help to contribute to safety?

Joanna Rodgers

Trainee risk manager

Insurance brokers

When I go to a party and tell people that I work in insurance they are often unimpressed. But when I tell them I am working on the effects of climate change on sea levels they suddenly get excited. In fact, there are some three billion people in the world whose lives could be dramatically affected by a rise in sea levels. That's why insurance can be so exciting.

When I joined the company my first placement was in the risks department and in our team we are studying emerging risks like extreme weather conditions. It's our job to advise the underwriters – the people who assess risks and evaluate their financial impact – on the probability of events that may happen in the future. With this information they can decide if the company wants to take on the risk and what level of premiums to charge for providing insurance cover.

This means talking to experts in insurance and universities, and researching historical records, in order to build a picture of the damage caused by previous events, so the underwriters can quantify the financial impact.

Currently, in the risk department, we are also working on a project to study the potential insurance risks for the next World Cup football championship. We have to look at all the things that could go wrong: terrorist attacks, the collapse of a stadium, or the effects of extreme weather conditions like flooding or storms. Some of our clients in the construction sector have to understand these risks not just to insure the company against losses but also to design the buildings so as to protect the public. In this way, as insurers, we are also helping to make the world safer for people to enjoy great events.

Checklist

Assess your progress in this unit. Tick (✓) the statements which are true.

- I can describe the types of personal insurance
- I know the main terms used in a personal insurance contract
- I can identify the categories of risk management
- I can describe past mistakes
- I know about the insurance for natural disasters
- I can write a report on an insurance claim
- I know what the Lloyd's insurance market does

Speaking

Insuring risks at Lloyd's

Lloyd's insurance market is famous for insuring unusual risks, e.g. the voices of famous pop singers, the legs of great footballers, or being hit by meteorites.

1 Work in pairs as a broker (Student A) and as an underwriter (Student B).

Both students, think of three unusual things you would like to bring to the Lloyd's market to find insurance cover.

Student A, present your items to your partner, the underwriter.

Student B, decide if you want to accept the risk and what kinds of conditions you would want to apply if you offered insurance.

When you have finished, swap roles.

2 Work with a partner and make a list of some of the disasters that could happen at a major event like the Olympic Games. Collect together your ideas as a class and discuss what kind of insurance you would need to cover these risks. What would you include and exclude in the insurance?

Key words

Nouns
cover
damage
earthquake
excess
exclusion
flood
fraud
insurance policy
loss adjustor
no-claims bonus
operational risk
premium

reinsurance
risk audit
strategic risk
virus attack
write-off

Verbs
back up
make a claim
rebuild
renovate
settle a claim

Look back through this unit. Find five more words or expressions that you think are useful.

Speaking activities

Unit 1 p.8

What can you expect from a career in banking?

Student A

Read the text about Angus and find the answers to the reporter's questions on p.8.

Angus Fraser (2004–07) Customer advisor

After university, I joined the Glasgow branch of Fleetwood Bank as a trainee customer advisor. It is a client-facing job, meeting customers who come in to the branch and advising them on how to manage their money. That means I need a good knowledge of savings accounts, loans, and mortgages, but we have weekly meetings to learn about these products.

In this work, you must have good relationship skills because the customer gives you private information and must trust the advice you give. It is also important to be systematic and accurate because you have to enter the information in electronic forms.

On a typical day, I can see about 50 customers in private interviews and it makes a long day. I usually start at 9.00 a.m. (by checking my appointments diary) and finish at 6.00 p.m. So I work about eight hours, but it takes another 45 minutes to get home.

The salary (£20,000 p.a.) is not great, but it is very satisfying to work with people and know that you have helped them to plan their financial decisions well.

Unit 2 p.15

Financial check-up

Student A

You are a customer at the bank. You are a 50-year-old government employee. You are very cautious about money. Answer the bank employee's questions, using the notes below. Each number 1–5 refers to the sections on the interview form on p.14.

1 **SPENDING** You don't use cash machines, but prefer to get cash in the branch. You have a debit card, but prefer using cash or cheques in stores. You don't have a credit card: they cost too much to use.

2 **PAYING BILLS** You pay all your bills by cheque. You don't use standing orders and direct debits because you can't control what you're spending. You use bank transfers to send money to your son in Australia, but it costs a lot in charges.

3 **SAVING** You keep most of your money in your current account. You have a savings account, but think the interest rates are very low.

4 **BORROWING** You don't have an overdraft and have never taken out a bank loan. You have paid off your mortgage.

Unit 4 p.31
Presenting data

Student A

1 Using the graph below and your signal expressions, give a mini presentation to your partner on the movements of oil prices, 1988–2006.

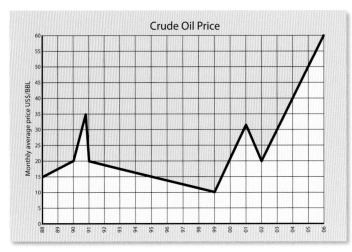

2 Now listen to your partner's presentation and draw the graph they describe for the Dow Jones index of US stocks, 1998–2008.

Dow Jones index (1998–2008)

Unit 4 p.32
Explaining trends and their causes

Student A

You are going to interview your partner to find out about how life has changed in the UK since 1957.

Work with Student B and complete the table. Take turns to ask for and give the missing figures. Then read back the statistics you have written to your partner and check if they are right.

1 Interview your partner and complete the table.

	1957	Today	Causes
Food			
Housing			
Fuel and power			
Clothing			
Tobacco	6%	1%	Health campaigns
Alcohol	3%	3%	Lower taxes
Leisure	2%	6%	Increase in family income
Transport	8%	16%	Increase in car ownership

EXAMPLES
How much did families spend on food in 1957?
What has happened to spending on food since 1957?
What is the reason for the change?

2 Now answer Student B's questions from the information in your table. (Answer with complete sentences and use some of the expressions from *Language spot* p.32 in your answers.)

Unit 6 p.46

Competing in the global economy

Student A

2 Read the report on the Chinese economy and make notes on the strengths and weaknesses of each sector. In order to do this, you will need to

1 find the examples given for each sector
2 find the strengths mentioned
3 find the weaknesses mentioned
4 add the information in note form.

There is an example of how to do this in the first paragraph of the table. When you have looked at this, read the rest of the report and complete the table in the same way. Then complete 3 on the next page.

THE CHINESE ECONOMY

In the primary sector of the Chinese economy, agriculture has benefited from the move to private or village farms, creating new specializations, especially in the coastal regions near Hong Kong. Farming is very intensive, more productive per acre than the US, and produces significant exports of rice, wheat, and meat. However, productivity is achieved by human labour and small farms lack machinery and capital for investment and often suffer from the effects of pollution and problems of water.

In the secondary sector, the opening of the country to foreign investment and technology has played a big part in modernizing Chinese industries. China is now a leader in electronics, textiles, and consumer products. Manufacturers still enjoy the benefit of a huge low cost workforce and relatively cheap land. However, a lot of the country's capital is invested in old state sector industries, often with great waste and inefficiency. The whole sector suffers from poor infrastructure, bureaucracy, and shortages of electric power and raw materials.

The service sector in China includes marketing, software, and customer services but it is still underdeveloped and businesses lack finance and technical knowledge. However, with the rise in living standards and a huge boom in Internet use, demand for services has increased dramatically. Private companies have used their own capital to develop, giving these companies great flexibility and independence from government control.

CHINA	Examples	Strengths	Weaknesses
Primary sector	• Agriculture	New specializations following move to private / village farms Farming more intensive and more productive than US	Human labour used Lack of machinery and investment capital Pollution and water problems

Secondary sector	• _____ a
	• _____ b
	• _____ c
		Benefits from: • _____ d
		    • _____ e
			Too much capital invested in _____ f
			
			Problems: • _____ g
			    • _____ h
			
			Shortages of: • _____ i
			    • _____ j

Service sector	• _____ k
	• _____ l
	• _____ m
		Demand for services _____ n
		because of : • _____ o
		    • _____ p
		Private companies use: _____ q
		giving them • _____ r
		    • _____ s
			Businesses lack: • _____ t
			    • _____ u

3 Now complete the table below on the British economy, by asking your partner questions.

Examples

What are the key industries in the primary sector in the UK?
What are the weaknesses in the primary sector?

UK	Examples	Strengths	Weaknesses
Primary sector	• _____ a	Mechanized Produces _____ c% of food needs	employs _____ e%of workforce? Profitability of farming: _____ f
	• _____ b	High reserves _____ d	Future prospects: _____ g
Secondary sector	• _____ h • _____ i • _____ j	advantages of specialist engineering: • _____ k • _____ l	Weak industries include: • _____ m • _____ n Secondary Sector performance in the last 20 years: _____ o
Service sector	• _____ p • _____ q • _____ r	Benefits from: • _____ s • _____ t	Dependent on: _____ u Infrastructure problems, e.g. _____ v

Unit 8 p.72

News briefings

Student A

You are going to practise presenting the results of an analyst's report to your partner.

Look at the morning news announcement opposite from *Reuters* and the analyst's notes on the effects.

1 Decide which of the effects are positive and which are negative. Then decide what recommendations you would make.

2 Use the model on p.72. to prepare your presentation.

3 When you have finished, make your presentation to your partner.

Hurricanes hit US destroying factories and power plants

US government announces big reconstruction project for houses and highways as well as financial help for food producers.

• share price of house builders and construction companies
• growth of the US economy this year
• profits of farmers and food producers
• share price of insurance companies

Unit 3 p.22
Making requests

Student A

1 You are Student B's assistant. Listen to your manager's requests, agree to help, and offer other help with one of the suggestions below.

1 convert the money today or next week?
2 include new workers we expect to hire this year?
3 look at UK grants or EU grants as well?

2 Now change roles. You are now the manager and Student B is your assistant. Ask your assistant to do the tasks on the list. Use expressions from *Language spot* p.21 to help you and make sure your requests sound polite (see *Pronunciation* p.22).

1 Work out the cost of buying new machinery.
2 Talk to the investment bank about raising money.
3 Check if the payment has arrived in the Nestlé account.

Unit 4 p.34
A report

Report on the Kazakh economy

Title _____
written for ABS fund management team.

Executive summary: The Kazakhstan economy offers great opportunities for investment, especially in the oil and natural resources sectors. Growth is currently 7% per year and domestic consumption is rising sharply.

1 Objectives:
The purpose of the report is to analyse _____
_____

2 Findings
Section 1: Background
  Since 2003, GDP _____
  _____

  The inflation rate _____
  _____

  The exchange rate _____
  _____

Section 2: Current situation
  Oil: _____
  _____

  Risks: _____
  _____

  Reforms: _____
  _____

  The banking sector: _____
  _____

3 Recommendations
Given the strong growth forecasts I would recommend that our fund _____
_____

Unit 4 p.28

Interpreting data

Student A

Take turns to ask for and give the missing figures. Then read back the statistics you have written to your partner and check if they are right.

Economic indicators	Turkey	Poland
a Population		38.4m
b Gross domestic product	US$ 861.6bn	
c Growth rate		1.1%
d Interest rates	25%	
e Unemployment rate		11.0%
f Inflation	5.9%	
g Exchange rate:		US$ 1 = PLN* 3.1 * Polish zlotych
h Balance of trade	US$ -12.54bn	

Unit 5 p.37

Recession and recovery

Student A

Match these effects of a recession (1–5) with the explanations (a–e). Make notes using this structure. *In a recession ... fall(s)/rise(s), because ...*

In a recession ...

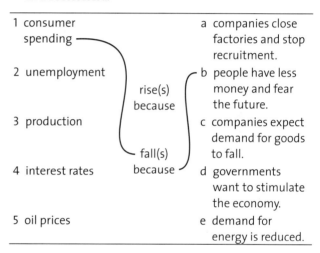

1 consumer spending

2 unemployment

3 production

4 interest rates

5 oil prices

rise(s) because

fall(s) because

a companies close factories and stop recruitment.

b people have less money and fear the future.

c companies expect demand for goods to fall.

d governments want to stimulate the economy.

e demand for energy is reduced.

Now go back to **4** on p.37.

Unit 11 p.95
Accounting and auditing

Work together and decide if these statements are true or false. Mark them T (true) or F (false). You will need to look at both the texts on pages 95 and 116 at the same time.

1 At the end of an audit, the auditors will always sign off the accounts.
2 A purchasing ledger tells you about things a company sells to customers.
3 Auditors will ask about the rules a company has for recording transactions.
4 Accounting standards are the same all over the world.
5 Auditors are appointed by the managers to check accounts.
6 By law, a public company has to publish its statutory accounts every year.
7 Companies use books or ledgers to prepare the accounts.
8 Auditors want to know if a company's accounts offer a 'true and fair view'.
9 The management accounts are prepared once a year.

As a class, compare your answers and discuss together the differences you have found.

Unit 12 p.102
How do companies manage risk?
Student A

You are going to open a restaurant in your home town. Make a list of the risks you anticipate in each of the four risk categories – **operational**, **strategic**, **financial**, and **natural disaster**. Explain to your partner how you would manage the risks.

Unit 2 p.15

Financial check-up

Student B

You work for Southern Star Bank. Look at the interview form and ask questions to find out which of the services the customer uses. Tick the services in the box. Then use the advice notes to offer suggestions about other options.

Southern Star Bank plc

Category	Southern Star product / service used	Customer name _____	Advice for customers
1 Spending	Cash withdrawal at branch counter	☐	If you use a cash machine: no queues
	Cash machines	☐	You can also get statements and pay cheques in a cash machine
	Debit card	☐	The quickest way to pay in stores. Safer than carrying cash
	Credit card	☐	Our credit cards are free now and have 0% interest for 6 months
	Cheque book	☐	Much slower than debit card and many shops now don't accept them
2 Paying bills	Standing order	☐	Use standing orders and you don't need to write a cheque every month and use the post. Plus, they pay the bill even when you are on holiday
	Direct debit	☐	Many companies give a discount if you pay by direct debit
	Bank transfer	☐	Take advantage of our 2% discount foreign currency rate if you have an account with us
3 Saving	Deposit account	☐	Move your money from a current account and earn high interest rates
	Online savings account	☐	Pay 1% more than deposit account
4 Borrowing	Overdraft	☐	Free to organize, then if you go overdrawn by mistake there are no charges.
	Mortgage	☐	We have the cheapest fixed rates on the market. Use your house to borrow money more cheaply
	Other loans	☐	Use a loan to improve your house, take a dream holiday or buy a car

Unit 11 p.94

Accounting and auditing

Student B: Auditing

Read the text opposite about the purpose of auditing and write notes to answer the questions below. You will need to use these notes to explain to your partner what auditors do.

1 Why do the owners of a company appoint external auditors?
2 How often does a public company have to do an external audit?
3 Who do the external auditors work for?
4 What kinds of documents do the auditors inspect?
5 What is the purpose of the substantive tests?
6 How do the auditors report the first results of their tests?
7 What do the auditors do if they are not happy with the results of their audit?

Auditing

How do the owners of a company know if the management are really telling them what is happening in the company's finances and not hiding information or even committing fraud?

The answer is that every year the owners appoint an 'external auditor' to check the company's accounts and to write a report on the accuracy of the financial statements: the auditor's report. This is now a legal requirement for public companies.

The auditors must give an independent opinion of the accounts and make tests to see if the accounts are properly prepared according to accounting standards, and if they give '**a true and fair view**' of the company's finances.

The auditors will look at all the company's documents, like invoices and receipts, the books and bank statements and check if these have been recorded properly. Have the staff really followed both the accountancy standards and the company's rules? Are there systems in place to prevent mistakes or fraud?

It is also important to know if the assets a company claims to own really exist. So the auditors will run '**substantive tests**' and will visit the factories and warehouses to physically see items recorded. Because of the quantity of information, the auditors will usually test this by taking samples of information, rather than looking at every document.

At the end of their tests the auditors write a letter that they send first to the management – the **letter to management** – describing what they have found and what needs to be corrected before they are happy to '**sign off**' the accounts. They can then complete the audit report in which they declare that '**in their opinion**' the accounts are accurate and give a '**true and fair view**' of the company's position.

If, occasionally, they are unable to demonstrate this, they will issue a '**qualified opinion**' in which they will point out the things that they could not prove. This, of course, will give a serious warning to the company's owners and investors.

Unit 4 p.31

Presenting data

Student B

1 Listen to your partner's presentation and draw the graph they describe for the movement of oil prices, 1988–2006.

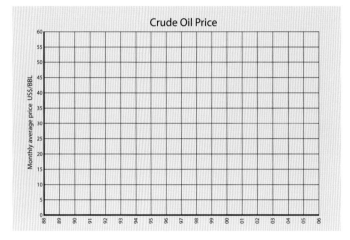

2 Using the graph below and your signal expressions, give a mini presentation to your partner on the movements of The Dow Jones index of US stocks, 1998–2008.

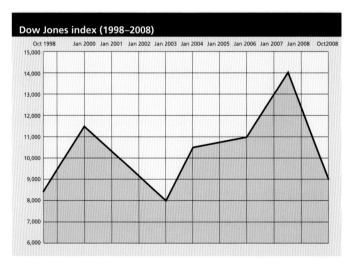

Unit 4 p.32

Explaining trends and their causes

Student B

You are going to interview your partner to find out about how life has changed in the UK since 1957.

Work with Student A and complete the table. Take turns to ask for and give the missing figures. Then read back the statistics you have written to your partner and check if they are right.

1 Use the information from your table to answer your partner's questions. (Answer with complete sentences and use some of the expressions from *Language spot* p.32 in your answers.)

	1957	Today	Causes
Food	33%	15%	Development of intensive farming
Housing	9%	19%	Rising costs of materials and land
Fuel and power	6%	3%	Demand from new developing economies
Clothing	10%	5%	Cheap foreign imports
Tobacco			
Alcohol			
Leisure			
Transport			

2 Now interview your partner and complete the table.

EXAMPLES

How much did families spend on tobacco in 1957?
What has happened to spending on tobacco since 1957?
What is the reason for the change?

Unit 7 p.66

Commercial lending

Student B

You are the client. Look at the details of your loan application below. Answer your partner's questions and try to get the best loan you can for your business. You want £80,000 for rent and new stock but don't want to offer much security if possible.

loan application
Name of company: Stella Fashions
Type of business: fashion retailing
Purpose of loan: to rent a second shop for one year and pay for stock
Amount required: £80,000 (£50,000 for rent, and £30,000 for new clothes stock)
Turnover/total sales: £300,000
Profit this year: £11,000
Profit next year with the new store: £18,000
Security you can offer: two business vans (worth £50,000)

Now change roles. You are now the loan officer. Look at the table of your possible loan offers.

Amount of loan	Interest rate	Repayments	Loan period
£600,000	8%	£145,000 per year	5 years
		£87,360 per year	10 years
£600,000	10%	£152,000 per year	5 years
		£95,160 per year	10 years
£400,000	8%	£97,300 per year	5 years
		£58,300 per year	10 years
£400,000	10%	£102,000 per year	5 years
		£63,400 per year	10 years

Now interview your partner, the business client, using the questions in 4 on p.66. As a loan officer, you need to get the best terms you can with the minimum risk. Are you confident that the client can repay the interest on the loan? If the risks are high, you need more security or a higher interest rate. Or maybe you need to offer a smaller loan.

From the information your partner gives you, decide if you want to grant the loan or not, how much you are prepared to offer, and what kind of security you want from the client.

Unit 8 p.72

News briefings

Student B

You are going to practise presenting the results of an analyst's report to your partner. Look at the morning news announcement from Reuters and the analyst's notes on the effects that follow.

OPEC (organization of oil-exporting countries) increases oil prices by 20%

- demand for green energy
- manufacturing and transport costs
- share price of oil companies
- growth in the economy

1 Decide which of the effects are positive and which are negative. Then decide what recommendations you would make.
2 Use the model on p.72 to prepare your presentation.
3 When you have finished, make your presentation to your partner.

Unit 12 p.102

How do companies manage risk?

Student B

You are a manager in an entertainments company responsible for organizing a musical event in a concert hall. Make a list of the risks you anticipate in each of the four risk categories – **operational**, **strategic**, **financial**, and **natural disaster**. Explain to your partner how you would manage the risks.

Language reference

1 Question types, Present Simple v Present Continuous

Question types

yes / no questions

These are closed questions. They don't begin with a question word, and generally require a 'yes' or 'no' answer. With *yes / no* questions, we change the order of the subject and verb from a positive to a question form (auxiliary verb + subject).

***Did** you **study** business or finance at college?*
***Is** your job interesting?*

Information questions

When we need to have more information, we ask open questions, often beginning with a question word such as *where, what, when, how, why*. The word order is generally the same as for *yes / no* questions.

***What aspect** of the course **interested** you most?*
***By how much did** the market **fall**?*
***Where do** they **work**?*

However, the word order does change depending on whether the question word is the subject or the object.

> ***Who pays your salary?*** ~ 'My company.'

subject + verb + object

> ***Who do you pay*** for your flat? ~ 'My landlord.'

object + auxiliary + subject + verb

NOT *Who does pay you for your flat?*
This generally applies to the question words *who* and *what / which*.

Present Simple v Present Continuous

Present Simple

We use the Present Simple to talk about:

- skills and abilities
  *She **is** an excellent communicator.*
  *He **hasn't got** / **doesn't have** strong analytical skills.*

- daily routines
  *We **go** to the canteen for lunch.*
  *I **don't leave** work before 7.00 p.m.*

- facts and things that are generally true
  *Sales of these products **tend** to peak in June.*
  *Retail banks **offer** a lot of financial services.*

We can also use the Present Simple with an adverb of frequency (*always, sometimes,* etc.) to talk about things that happen regularly. Frequency adverbs go before the main verb, but after *be*.

*I **often** work at the weekends.*
*She is **never** late for meetings.*
*What do you **normally** do for lunch?*

Present Continuous

We use the Present Continuous to talk about:

- something that is happening at the time of speaking, or around that time
  *It's now 10 a.m. in New York and the bond market **is falling** fast.*

- temporary situations and arrangements
  *We**'re working** together on this project.*

We don't generally use the Present Continuous with verbs of perception (*know, see,* etc.) or verbs such as *need, want, hate, like, prefer.*

It's urgent so I want to talk to you now.
NOT *I'm wanting to talk …*

Note that some verbs change their meaning when used in either tense, e.g. *think* and *have*.

Present Simple: *think* = have an opinion
Present Continuous: *think* = consider

*We **think** that is an excellent idea.*
*We're **thinking** of expanding our operation.*
When *have = have got*, we only use it in the Present Simple.
NOT *He's having good analytical skills.*
But
*We**'re having** a meeting to discuss this tomorrow.*
*We **have** too many meetings in our company.*

We often use the Present Continuous with time expressions, such as *now, at the moment, this morning, these days, currently,* etc.

*The market **is rising at the moment**.*

2 Suggestions and advice

There are several ways of making suggestions and giving advice. They are followed either by the infinitive, the infinitive with *to*, or the *-ing* form.

+ infinitive

- *I think you should ...*
  I think you should arrange *to see a financial advisor.*
- *Why don't you ...?*
  Why don't you pay *your bills online?*
- *Perhaps / Possibly you could ...*
  Perhaps you could discuss *your problem with the bank.*
  Possibly you could arrange *an overdraft facility.*

+ infinitive with *to*

- *The best thing to do is ...*
  The best thing to do is to pay *your gas bills automatically.*

+ *-ing* form

- *How about ...?*
  How about paying *by direct debit?*
- *Have you thought about / considered ...?*
  Have you thought about applying for *a credit card?*
  Have you considered applying for *a credit card?*

Note that some expressions are questions and others are in the positive form, so the correct punctuation must be used.

Why don't you pay your bills online?
NOT ~~Why don't you pay your bills online.~~

3 Requests and offers, Modals of obligation and permission

Requests

There are many ways of making requests. The way in which we make requests and ask people to do things for us depends on the situation and who we are speaking to.

Formal

- *I'd like you to* + infinitive
  I'd like you to *contact Steven Walker at head office for me.*

This is more of an instruction than a request. In a work situation, you normally only use this with staff who work for you.

- *Would you* + infinitive
  Would you *call me back this afternoon?*
- *Could you* + infinitive
  Could you *let me have your email address, please?*

These can be instructions or requests. They are more polite than *I'd like you to ...*, and can be used with colleagues as well as with staff who work for you.

- *Would you mind* + *-ing* form
  Would you mind *filling in this form, please?*

This is very polite and can be used with clients or visitors to a company.

Informal

- *Can you* + infinitive
  Can you *give me Matilda's phone number?*
- *Don't forget to* + infinitive
  Don't forget to *call me when the meeting is finished.*

We normally use these when talking to a friend or colleague.

Offers

When we respond to a request, we sometimes agree and then offer to do something else. These offers are all followed by the infinitive.

Formal

- *Of course. **Would you like me to** ...?*
  *Could you try to finish the presentation for the conference today? ~ **Of course. Would you like me to** change the introduction?*

- *Certainly. **Should I** ...?*
  *I'd like you to send this letter off urgently. ~ **Certainly. Should I** send it recorded delivery?*

Informal

- *Sure. **Shall I** ...?*
  *Could you cancel this afternoon's meeting? ~ Sure. **Shall I** reschedule it?*

- *No problem. **Do you want me to** ...?*
  *Can you get some insurance quotes from the company on this list? ~ **No problem. Do you want me to** contact all of them?*

Modals of obligation and permission

We can use modal verbs to express obligation and permission. Modal verbs do not have an auxiliary verb, and have no *s* in the third person singular. The following modals are used to talk about obligation and permission: *must / mustn't, can / can't, may / may not, need / needn't.*

We also use *have to,* which does use auxiliary *do* in negatives and questions.

*You **don't have to** give a presentation.*

The verb *need* has a non-modal form which has the same meaning as *needn't.*
*You **don't need to** contact all the people on the list.*

Use

- When something is necessary:
  must
  *You **must** send those figures today.*

  have to
  *You **have to** finish the report by the end of the week.*

  need to
  *You **need to** call her back urgently.*

- When something isn't necessary:
  don't have to
  *You **don't have to** work this weekend.*

  don't need to / needn't
  *You **don't need to / needn't** send these letters by courier.*

- When something is permitted:
  can
  *You **can** use the computer in my office.*

  may
  *You **may** go as soon as you've finished.*

- When something is not permitted:
  mustn't
  *You **mustn't** leave your laptop in the office overnight.*

  can't
  *You **can't** leave those boxes in the corridor.*

  may not
  *You **may not** download games onto your office computer.*

We can use other expressions to talk about permission: *be allowed* (*to*), *be permitted* (*to*). Unlike modal verbs, we can also use these expressions in the passive:

*You **aren't allowed / permitted** to use this printer.* = You must not use this printer.
*Smoking **is** no longer **allowed / permitted** anywhere in the building.* = You can't smoke in the building.

4 Describing change and cause

Change

We use the Past Simple and Present Perfect to talk about change in the past.

Past Simple

We use the Past Simple to talk about a past situation that is finished, with no connection to the present.

*After three years of decline, incomes **rose** by 3.4%.*

We use time expressions such as: *in, last, from ... to ..., at the start of ..., for,* and *then.*

In 1999, the company expanded its operations.
Last year, we increased our market share by 10 per cent.
From 1998 to 2003, the bank opened offices in twelve new countries.
At the start of this century, the CD industry started to decline.
I worked for them for five years before I decided to change jobs.
At first, sales decreased slightly then fell dramatically.

Present Perfect

We use the Present Perfect to talk about a situation in the past which continues into the present.

*We **have increased** production to meet demand.*

We use time expressions such as *since ...* and *so far this ....*

Since 2001, we have been the market leader in our field.
So far this year, inflation has been stable.

Some expressions, such as *for, during,* and *over,* can be used with either tense, depending on the context.

*We **sold** this product in China **for five years**, but we don't sell it there now.*
*We **have sold** this product in China **for five years**: it's our most successful export.*

*In 2008, sales fell sharply but **in / over /during the next two years** they recovered well.*

In / over / during the last three months, sales have performed well.

The time expression *recently* can be used with either tense with a similar meaning.

*Sales **fell** / **have fallen** recently, despite a strong marketing campaign.*

Cause

To ask why a situation has changed, we use the following expressions:

What's behind ...?   *How do you explain ...?*
What's the reason for ...?

To describe the reasons for a change in a situation, we use the following:

This is due to ...   *This is because of ...*
This is the result of ...

***What's behind** the increase in petrol costs? ~ **This is the result of** increased demand from developing countries.*

***How do you explain** the rise in unemployment? ~ **This is due to** the recession.*

5 Predictions: probability

When we talk about future outcomes, we use modal verbs such as *will, should, could, may, might.*

- *will / won't*
  *Inflation **will** rise because shops have increased their prices.*
  *Interest rates **won't** rise until the economy recovers.*

- *should / shouldn't*
  *Unemployment **should** fall as the economy improves.*
  *There **shouldn't** be an oil price increase, as demand has fallen.*

- *could*
  *This scheme **could** cause a decline in car sales.*

Note that we don't use *couldn't* to talk about predictions. We use *may not* or *might not.*

- *may / may not*
  *It **may** be some time before we see a cut in interest rates.*
  *The markets **may not** recover in time to avoid a crisis.*

- *might / might not*
  *There **might** be more redundancies in the company.*
  *Many firms **might not** recover from the recession.*

We often use probability adverbs such as *certainly, probably,* and *possibly* to modify the force of the prediction. These adverbs are most commonly used with *will / won't.* Note that the position of the adverb is different in the positive and negative.

*The project **will probably** be finished by the end of the year.*
*The economy will improve this year, but it **certainly won't** recover completely.*

6 Contrasting information

We use several expressions to contrast information.

- **but**
  But is used within a sentence, after a comma.
  They did everything they could to keep all their staff, **but** *eventually had to make people redundant.*

- **although**
  Although can be used within a sentence, after a comma.
  The scheme will be successful, **although** *it will take time.*

  Other expressions similar to although are *though* and *even though*.
  The scheme will be successful, **though** *it will take time.*

  We use *even though* when we talk about a surprising or unexpected circumstance. It is closer to 'despite the fact that'.
  They rejected our offer for the company, **even though** *it was very high.*

  Although, though, and even though can also be used at the beginning of a sentence to introduce two contrasting ideas or situations.
  Although / Though / Even though *the banks refused to offer us a loan, we still secured the funding.*

- **despite**
  Despite is followed by a noun, and can be used in the middle of a sentence or at the beginning.
  Despite *the economic climate, she decided to start her own business.*

  We can also use *in spite of* with the same meaning and in the same position as *despite*.

  We use *in spite of* + noun phrase.
  In spite of *all expectations, the company performed well.*

  We use *in spite of the fact that* and *despite the fact that* before a clause.
  Consumer spending increased, **in spite of the fact that / despite the fact that** *prices were very high.*

- **however**
  However is used to begin a new sentence that contrasts with the previous one.
  The company sold a lot of products. **However,** *it didn't make any profit.*

7 Verb patterns

Verbs can be followed by different structures.

- Verb + *to* infinitive
  These include the following: *agree, aim, appear, arrange, ask, choose, continue, decide, expect, fail, help, hope, intend, manage, need, offer, prefer, prepare, propose, refuse, seem, start, try, want.*

  Consumer spending **seems to be** *increasing.*
  The bank **refused to lend** *us the money.*

  Note that we can use the negative infinitive *not to*.

  They decided **not to invest** *in a new office system.*

- Verb + *-ing* form
  These include the following: *admit, appreciate, avoid, be worth, can't stand, consider, continue, delay, deny, dislike, enjoy, finish, hate, imagine, involve, keep, like, mention, prefer, risk, start, suggest, try.*

  Have you **considered applying** *for a job in banking?*
  It's **worth checking** *the recruitment websites every day.*

- Verb + object + *to* infinitive
  These include the following: *allow, ask, convince, enable, force, help, like, persuade, require, want.*

  The M&A department of an investment bank **helps companies to buy** *other companies.*

Note that some verbs, e.g. *continue, help, like, prefer, start, try* and *want*, can belong to more than one pattern.

This action **helped to safeguard** *most of the jobs.*

The recruitment website **helped me to** *find a job.*

Have you **tried to discuss** *this with your financial advisor?*
Have you **tried discussing** *this with your financial advisor?*

8 Describing consequences

We can use first conditional sentences to describe the consequences of situations or actions. We can say how probable we think the consequences are by using the modal verbs *should*, *may*, or *might* instead of *will*. *Should* expresses high probability (we think that something is likely to happen), while *may* and *might* express lower probability (we think it's possible that something will happen, but we aren't sure).

*A fall in interest rates **should** boost the stock market.*
*If current trading conditions continue as they are, we **might** need to rethink our strategy.*

We can also use the negative forms *may not* or *might not*.

*If we lose our biggest customer, the company **may not** survive.*

Another way to talk about consequences is to use *lead to* or *result in* + noun.

*Investing in new equipment and machinery will **lead to** greater efficiency.*

*We are not convinced that higher spending on advertising will **result in** an increase in sales.*

We can add adverbs such as *possibly*, *probably*, *certainly*, and *definitely* to modify the degree of probability.
*The company failed to win the contract. This will **probably** lead to redundancies.*
*The country is going into recession. This will **certainly / definitely** result in higher unemployment.*

9 First and Second Conditionals

First Conditional

We use the First Conditional to talk about a possible situation and the probable result.

if-clause	main clause
*If we **reduce** our stock of materials, we **will have** problems with production.*	

= *If* + Present Simple + *will* + infinitive

We use a comma after the *if*-clause when it begins the sentence. When the *if*-clause follows the main clause, there is no comma.

We will have problems with production if we reduce our stock of materials.

Either or both of the clauses can be in the negative.

*If we **don't get** some cash quickly, we **won't be able to** pay our suppliers.*

We can use *be going to* rather than *will* in the main clause.

*If we don't reduce the credit period, we **are going to** have real problems.*

Second Conditional

We use the Second Conditional to talk about a possible situation and an unlikely result.

if-clause	main clause
*If we **needed** to raise capital, we **would ask** our shareholders for help.*	

= *If* + Past Simple + *would* + infinitive

As is the case for the First Conditional, the clauses can be reversed. Note that there is no comma when the main clause begins the sentence.

We would ask our shareholders for help if we needed to raise capital.

Either or both of the clauses can be in the negative.

*If we **didn't have to** get stock quickly, we **wouldn't have to** pay more.*

unless

We use *unless* as an alternative way of expressing a condition. *Unless* replaces *if* in the *if*-clause, and is always followed by a positive verb. The main clause can either be positive or negative.

***Unless** we reduce the credit period, we are going to have real problems.*

As with other conditional sentences, we can reverse the order of the clauses.

We are going to have real problems unless we reduce the credit period.

We can use *unless* in First and Second Conditionals.

*We wouldn't consider cutting jobs **unless** it was absolutely essential.*

10 Forecasting

We can use different ways to make forecasts or predictions.

Verbs

We can use predicting verbs such as *expect* and *forecast* to introduce predictions. These verbs can be used in the active and passive.

In the active, there are two forms:

*We **expect** profits **to rise** this year.*

= *expect* + noun + *to* infinitive

*We **expect** profits **will rise** this year.*

= *expect* + noun + future with *will*

We use *forecast* in the same way.

*We **forecast** sales **to increase** next quarter.*
*We **forecast** sales **will increase** next quarter.*

In the passive, there is one form:

*Profits **are expected** / **forecast to fall** sharply.*

= noun + Present Simple of *be* + past participle + *to* infinitive

Expressions

- *be bound to* + infinitive (= certain to happen)
  *Consumer demand **is bound to** improve this year.*
- *should* (= strong probability)
  *Confidence **should** begin to return soon.*
- *be unlikely to* (= low probability)
  *We **are unlikely to** see an increase in profits over the next quarter.*
- *no chance of* + -*ing* (= zero probability)
  *The company has **no chance of** recovering.*

11 Time clauses: describing stages of a process with *when*

We can use *when* to describe the order in which events take place.

time clause	main clause
When you **make** a tour of the plant, you **will see** our new machines.	

= *When* + Present Simple + future with *will*

NOT *When you will make your tour ...*

The two clauses can be changed round, but *when* always introduces the first action in the process. Note that there is no comma when the main clause begins the sentence.

You will see our new machines when you make your tour of the factory.

When we want to describe a process that has to be completed before something else can happen, we use:

time clause	main clause
When we **have collected** the data, we **will make** a list of points.	

= *When* + Present Perfect + future with *will*
NOT *When we will have collected the information ...*

12 *should have done* and Third Conditional

We use *should / shouldn't have* + past participle to talk about things that went wrong in the past and alternative courses of action.

*We **should have invested** our money more carefully.*
*You **shouldn't have invested** so much in that company.*

We use the Third Conditional to talk about the possible outcome of an imagined situation in the past.

if-clause	main clause
If we **had invested** in banks last year, we **would have lost** a lot of money.	

= *If* + Past Perfect + *would have* + past participle

As is the case for the First and Second Conditionals, we can reverse the order of the clauses.

We would have lost a lot of money if we had invested in banks last year.

We can also use a negative form in either or both clauses.

*If we **hadn't tested** the software, we **wouldn't have found** the faults.* (But we did test them, so we found them.)

Listening scripts

Unit 1

Pronunciation

Exercise 1
1 Is your office in London?
2 Where do you work?
3 Can you earn a lot?
4 How much can you earn?
5 Do you work for Paribas?
6 Who do you work for?

Exercise 3
1 What did you study at university?
2 Do you work at weekends?
3 Is your job well paid?
4 Does your job involve a lot of travel?
5 Why did you decide to work in finance?
6 How many people work in your company?

Listening

TOSHI
I was born in Hokkaido, an island in the north of Japan.

I was never very good at school and I could not go to university. So my dad advised me to get a professional qualification.

My first job was at a retail bank. But I didn't like banking because I am really quite shy and I don't want to talk to customers all day. I prefer to work on a screen with figures. So I joined an accountancy firm. The training took three years and was very hard. I had to go to classes three evenings a week.

Now I spend a lot of my time working with small companies, managing all their financial accounts and preparing quarterly reports. It's very satisfying work, my clients are always very happy if you do things well. I really feel at home in the firm and, most importantly, people respect my work and my professional status. My family are very proud of me because I now have a good job with a good career. One day I may even become a partner in the firm.

DANIELLA
I was brought up near Naples and went to business school in Rome. But even at school I began to dream of going to

London. I really wanted to travel and be independent. So I decided to go to London and try and join an investment bank. I didn't know much English then but I came and studied for six months in the UK. Then I began to apply for jobs.

The interviews I had were terrible, three rounds plus another final weekend interview when I had to give a presentation for twenty minutes to senior bankers. It was really stressful but they gave me a job and offered me £45,000 a year starting salary. I could finally get a flat in London and begin my real life!

What's it like? Well, you work really hard – I often do a twelve-hour day. But they give you great training from day one in accountancy, tax, and company finance, and this is very important for me. And you learn fast – after only one month I gave my first presentation on financial strategy to a big company boss. And now it's easy to stand in front of managers and present ideas. I still have a lot to learn but, in the long run, I would like to take the experience and become the Chief Financial Officer of a big company. That's the dream.

ABDULLAH
After school, I went to university in Riyadh to study business studies. I had a lot of fun there with my friends but I didn't take my studies very seriously. Then in my last year we had a new teacher who taught finance. He made us think about the future of our country. Our economy is increasingly opening up to foreign companies. So when I finished university, I decided to join a bank because I wanted to help the country to grow.

I decided to join Citigroup because my teacher said we needed to learn about finance. At first, they sent me to a very small branch in the suburbs with nothing to do. But I was lucky because soon they began to develop the area for business. A lot of new companies began to arrive and we were suddenly very busy and we grew very fast. My boss appreciated my work and one day he asked me if I wanted to be a manager. He offered to send me to the UK to learn

English for a year and then to sponsor me to do an MBA. At first, I was nervous about leaving Saudi but when I came to England I loved it and I did my MBA in Guildford near London. So, now I am happy to return and, as the manager of a big branch, I can help young people like me to start companies in Riyadh.

Unit 2

Listening

Part 1
B=Bank employee, M=Man

B Thanks for coming to this interview, Mr Browne. Now I'd like to start with spending. I see you sometimes withdraw money at the counter in the branch as well as using the cash machines.

M Yes, I get money from the cashier when it's more than two hundred pounds.

B And do you have a Southern Star cheque book and a debit card?

M Yes, I do. I still have to write cheques sometimes.

B And what about a Southern Star credit card?

M I have a credit card, but not with this bank. I use a Marks and Spencer store card, because it gives me discounts on my shopping.

B OK. What about paying bills? Do you use standing orders and direct debits?

M Oh, I can never remember the difference!

B You use a standing order to pay the same amount every month, and direct debit means that you pay a bill automatically, whatever the amount.

M Oh yes, I use direct debit for gas and electricity bills, but I don't have any standing orders.

B I see you have a deposit account with Southern Star.

M Yes.

B But you haven't got an online account or an overdraft arrangement.

M No.

B And have you ever had a loan from the bank?

M No, apart from the mortgage on my new flat, which I set up here last year.

Part 2

B Well, Mr Browne, I'd like to make several suggestions. First, cash withdrawals. I see that several of your cash withdrawals at the counter are for between £200 and £300. In fact, you can withdraw up to £300 from our cash machines. Why don't you use the cash machines more? It will be much quicker and easier for you. Also, have you thought about using your debit card more and your cheque book less? The debit card is much more secure and payments are much faster.

M Yes, I'll definitely think about that.

B And how about applying for the bank's credit card as well? We offer very competitive rates.

M Well, I do like my Marks and Spencer card.

B Perhaps you could use our card as a second card if you want to keep your existing card.

M OK, I'll think about it.

B Do you use computers, Mr Browne?

M Yes, I do.

B Then I think the best thing to do is to open an online account. It's very easy to operate, and you can check your balance every day and make electronic payments. That means you won't need to use cheques to pay people and you can make sure your account is in credit.

M All right, I'll think about that as well. Is it safe to use?

B Absolutely. Millions of our customers use it without any problems. Also, have you considered setting up a small overdraft? Say £500? I can arrange it for free – there's no fee unless you use it. You probably won't use it, but it's useful to have an arrangement, so you don't have to pay charges to the bank.

M Yes, I think that's a very good idea.

Pronunciation

1	debts	7	savings
2	services	8	houses
3	shops	9	bills
4	problems	10	risks
5	offices	11	branches
6	banks	12	cards

Unit 3

Listening 1

D=Dave, H=Helen

D Hi, Helen. I'll be away tomorrow, so can we go through the appointments for next week?

H Certainly.

D Could you contact Russell at KPMG and arrange a meeting for Monday to discuss tax planning for the new store location?

H Sure, shall I make that for 9.00 a.m.?

D Yes, that's fine. On Tuesday I need to talk to John Kerry at Goldman Sachs about issuing shares to fund the takeover of Freshfoods. Would you set up a meeting for Tuesday afternoon? Say about 2.00 p.m.?

H Yes, of course. Would you like me to ask Bill along, too?

D Oh, yes, good idea. He can deal with the technical questions from investors. Oh and I'd like you to contact Phil and ask him to talk to AXA Commercial Insurance about the cost of the flood insurance. We need them to work out the costs. We'll need a meeting with AXA for next week too. We could do that on Wednesday at 3.00.

H OK, leave that with me.

D Then, on Thursday I really must talk to RBS commercial division to negotiate an increase in our overdraft facility. Can you set up something for the morning? I have a planning meeting at 8.00, so what about 10.00?

H Certainly. Should I book a meeting room, too?

D Yes, please. On Friday, I need to attend the fund management presentation at Merrill Lynch on pension planning. And I know it's a lot to ask, but would you mind phoning Pete for me and get him to put together some figures for us on the new company pension plan?

H No problem. Do you want me to ask for figures for last year as well?

D Oh, yes, good idea. We'd better have both. And I'll need to be at Merrill Lynch at 4.00 p.m., so please don't forget to organize a taxi for me.

H OK. Looks like a busy week again.

Pronunciation

Exercise 1

1 Could you contact Russell at KPMG?
2 Would you set up a meeting on Tuesday, please?
3 Would you mind phoning Pete for me?

Exercise 3

1 Can you call me a taxi for three o'clock?
2 Could you check these figures for me again?
3 Can we meet at four tomorrow afternoon?
4 Would you mind working late this evening?
5 Do you think you could explain the expenses system to me?
6 Can I speak to the head of department, please?

Listening 2

J=Journalist, D=Dave

J Can I start by asking you what kind of financial services you use?

D Well, we operate in Europe, America, and Korea so we have many different needs. To start with the cash management, we manage our day-to-day cash with the help of our commercial bank, RBS. Our treasury department is in daily contact with them. Every day we pay a lot of suppliers and we have to check that international payments are made on time.
The RBS pooled account is very useful because we can put all our money from around the world in one account. Then we can quickly see where we need money each day, or where to invest it.

J What about funding? How do you know where to find the money for the company?

D Well, if I have questions about funding, then I call our investment bank, Goldman Sachs. They know a lot about the financial markets and the best way to find money internationally.
We have to decide if it is better to borrow the money from a bank or

perhaps to issue bonds or shares. The investment bank also advises us of the best mix of funding to have between loans, bonds, and shares.

J How do you control all this money in the company?

D That's the responsibility of an in-house department, the financial controller's department. At the beginning of the year, we make a budget for each division. Then we collect them all into a single master budget for the whole company. Every week the financial controller's department checks if we are following the budget. If we aren't, then we have a chance to correct the situation.

J Do you use any other services? What about insurance or auditors?

D We need to insure all our buildings, equipment, even customers, against accidents. But we also have financial insurance against suppliers who don't deliver and what we call business continuity insurance: to protect us if we have to close operations for a time, for example, if we have a fire or flood. For commercial insurance, we use a European company, AXA Insurance. And then, finally, there are other services like auditing. Our auditors, PricewaterhouseCoopers, come in to check the company's accounts every year to see if they are correctly prepared and reported.

J And finally, what's the most interesting part of the job?

D Well, many people think Finance Directors spend their time looking at financial accounts but, in fact, the real excitement of the job is working on the long-term strategy, trying to plan and see how you can take advantage of changes you expect in your market in two, three, or even five years. That's fascinating.

Unit 4

Listening

Today, I would like to talk about the performance of the UK economy and explain why we think the UK now offers good opportunities for long-term investment.

Perhaps I should start with some background to explain the main trends we've seen in the economy since 2000. Then, I can move on to describe the recent inflation data in more detail. As you can see from the first graph, at the start of the year 2000, unemployment stood at only 6%. Over the next two years it decreased steadily to 5% in 2002. But following the stock market crash, unemployment rose again, back to 5.5% in 2003. Over the next three years, as the economy improved, unemployment fell to a new low of 4.5% in 2006. But with the start of the financial crisis, it rose dramatically to 6% in 2008 and then it hit a peak of 8% at the beginning of 2010. Since then it has begun to fall slightly.

Moving on to interest rates. As you may remember in the year 2000, interest rates were at a high of 5.5%. Over the next three years, with the collapse of the Internet boom, rates fell sharply to only 3.5 % in 2003. Then, as the economy began to recover, rates increased sharply from 3.5% to 5.5% in 2007. But, following the financial crash, the Bank of England cut rates dramatically to stimulate growth. They dropped sharply to 2% in 2008 and then they reached a new record low of 0.75% in early 2009. Fortunately, this helped the economy to recover from the crisis.

Finally, that brings me to the question of inflation. At the beginning of the year, inflation increased sharply from 1.8% in January to 2.4% in March. It then remained unchanged at this level for one month. After that, inflation began to fall to reach 2% in May. The fall continued for the next two months to a low of 1.6% in July. But with higher food prices in the summer, inflation went up sharply. In August, it rose to 2.4% and then in October to 3%. After that, the situation began to improve and inflation

decreased steadily to reach 2.2% at the end of the year.

So overall, the recent data demonstrates that, with interest rates at record lows and unemployment falling, the UK economy now represents an attractive place for long-term investment.

Unit 5

Listening

I=Interviewer, H=Historian

I What happened to the world economy in the 1920s? Was it a good period to live in?

H In the 1920s, the world economy began to recover from the First World War. Companies invested heavily, especially in new industries like the auto industry and radio, and there was a big expansion in world trade. Businesses were very optimistic that growth would continue so they borrowed money from the banks and built huge production capacity in their factories.

I It sounds like a great period! 'The Roaring Twenties' of the films?

H Yes, it was for a time … But the boom was really out of control. Share prices increased dramatically, but the end came with the great Wall Street Crash of 1929, when the stock market fell dramatically by 60% in twelve months and many businesses and people went bankrupt.

I How did the crash affect ordinary people?

H As a result of the crash, many people lost everything; their homes and all their savings. There was no money to buy anything in the economy. The banks were very weak and stopped lending to customers and so world trade also declined sharply.

I It sounds terrible. How did people manage?

H Well, yes, it was a terrible time. Prices, especially of food products and raw materials, fell sharply and farming and manufacturing became unprofitable. People, especially farmers and small businessmen, who had borrowed a lot of money, could not pay the banks and lost their businesses. This caused a further decline in production and consumption and many smaller banks in the USA went bankrupt too. By 1932, industrial production in Germany and the USA was only 53% of the 1929 period.

I   Terrible! And what about unemployment? What happened to that?

H   Global unemployment reached 30% of the workforce in 1932 and poverty and starvation were real. It was a terrible period in which to live, as the American writer John Steinbeck describes in his famous novels, like *The Grapes of Wrath*.

Pronunciation

1   The finance minister is meeting the IMF representative later today.
(IMF = International Monetary Fund)
2   The CEO is giving a talk for all employees at two o'clock.
(CEO = Chief Executive Officer)
3   The EU has announced new measures to control financial services.
(EU = European Union)
4   My country's debt is equivalent to 56% of its GNP.
(GNP = Gross National Product)
5   OPEC members are meeting to discuss an increase in production.
(OPEC = Organization of Petroleum Exporting Countries)
6   The RPI figures show that there has been a fall in inflation this month.
(RPI = Retail Price Index)
7   The VIP visitors are being met at the airport.
(VIP = Very Important Person)
8   The bank is holding an EGM to discuss the new share issue.
(EGM = Extraordinary General Meeting)

It's my job

I=Interviewer, E=Eric

I   Eric, could you tell us what motivates people like you to join an international organization like the IMF?

E   Yes, it is important for people to understand that. The thing I like most about my work is actually contributing to the economic

development of a poorer country like Laos, and helping to improve the quality of life of people here.

I   What are you responsible for?

E   My main responsibility is to develop the relationship between the IMF and the Lao PDR government. It's my job to explain very clearly the IMF point of view and the thinking behind our recommendations on the economy. But I also have to listen very carefully to what the Lao government is telling me and then advise IMF Headquarters on what is possible and what is not.

I   It's certainly an exotic place to work. How do you spend your time?

E   I arrive at work around eight a.m. and check all the emails from IMF Headquarters in Washington, DC, that arrive during the night. I try to do all my 'hard thinking' in the morning. To get answers for Washington I may have to arrange a meeting with the Director of Research of the Central Bank to find out about government economic policy – borrowing, spending, that kind of thing.

I   So is it all meetings?

E   Well, that is a large part of the job. I may arrange to have lunch with the local representative of the World Bank who I have been working with on a project to help finance a new dam.
At least two or three times a week, there is a social function to attend. That sounds just fun. But, in fact, they are still work. Social events are the best way of building contacts and looking for new information or ideas. By the time I get to bed and think back on my day, I realize that although by training I am a macro-economist, I spend only twenty per cent of my day as an economist. The rest seems to disappear in administration and diplomatic work.

Unit 6

Pronunciation

1   transportation

2   purchasing
3   industry
4   industrial
5   industrialization
6   competition
7   competitive
8   advertising
9   agriculture
10   agricultural

Listening

A   Thank you all for coming in. Has everybody got a copy of the agenda? I suggest we start with item one on the agenda: the decision about where to locate the new plant: China or the UK? John, could you give us your views from the finance department?

B   Sure, I'll try to be brief. Having looked at this from a financial perspective, I think the best option is certainly to locate in China. There are a number of reasons for this. First of all, there is the question of labour costs. A production worker in China will cost us only $2 per hour while in the UK it could cost up to $30. A significant saving. Secondly, if we choose the site in Shenzhen, we can buy the land for only $2m whereas in the UK this could cost up to $10m. Then there is the question of our suppliers. By moving to China we will be closer to our supplier base in the Pacific Rim. Delivery time will be cut to 45 minutes compared with 2 hours in the UK. This represents big cost savings of up to $100,000 per year in our stock levels. So overall, I'm strongly in favour of China.

A   Thanks, John. What's your view, Claire?

C   I'm afraid I don't agree with John on this issue. I'm not in favour of China. Although he is right about wage costs in China, I'd like to remind you of a number of other key points. Firstly, there is the question of recruitment. If we locate the new plant in China, we will have serious problems with finding the skilled workers we need for the production line. In the UK, by contrast, we can train new workers with our existing staff. Then there is the question of quality. I'm convinced that quality levels in China will be significantly lower than in the UK. Studies we have commissioned suggest that a typical Chinese plant will have defect levels of 30 per thousand compared with only 2 per thousand in the UK. That means higher costs. But crucially, there is the question of new product development. Currently, our research department is located in the UK and they work in daily contact with the production team on new products. If we move to China, there will be no communication between the two departments. This will seriously damage our ability to develop new products and to compete successfully in the market. That's why I'm very much in favour of locating the new plant in the UK.

A OK. Thanks for your contributions. It seems to me we have a serious disagreement. If I can summarize, what you seem to be saying is this. On the one hand, locating in China will be cheaper and allow us to get closer to suppliers. On the other hand, there is a risk that we will have problems finding workers and quality levels will fall. Also, we will have problems with design of new products. Is that a fair summary?

Exercise 4

1 Having looked at this from a financial perspective, I think the best option is certainly to locate in China. There are a number of reasons for this. First of all,...

2 So overall, I'm strongly in favour of China.

3 I'm afraid I don't agree with John on this issue. I'm not in favour of China. Although he is right about wage costs in China, I'd like to remind you of a number of other key points.

4 ...what you seem to be saying is this. On the one hand, locating in China will be cheaper and allow us to get closer to suppliers. On the other hand, there is a risk that we will have problems finding workers...

5 Is that a fair summary?

Unit 7

Listening

K=Karl, M=Marion

K I know many people think our system in Germany is complicated but I see that in the UK you have retail banks and commercial banks. Some banks seem to be both. What's the difference between them? Can you explain?

M Yes, it is very confusing. But, basically, retail banks are the banks you see in the high street of every town. In fact, sometimes they are called high street banks. They offer the ordinary customer the full range of financial services like your credit card, debit card, or customer accounts, plus, of course, mortgages and insurance. Commercial banks, by contrast, are focused on small or medium-sized businesses and they offer many additional business services like leasing or factoring. Today, however, many of the retail banks, like RBS or Barclays, also offer commercial banking so they provide both services. Is that clear?

K OK. So if I understand you, the same bank can be both a commercial and a retail bank? Is that right?

M Yes, exactly.

K Well in that case where do the investment banks belong? I thought they provided the commercial services to companies.

M Well, in a sense, you are right. But investment banks really work on the financial markets, like the stock market. They offer specialist advice to big international companies on raising money in bonds or shares. But they also have large M&A departments, that is to say, mergers and acquisitions, that help companies to buy or sell other companies. It's important to understand that investment banks don't lend money to customers or provide any of the other banking accounts that a company needs to manage its daily business. They make a lot of their money from fees by providing services to big companies.

K Sorry, I didn't get that about fees. Could you go over it again?

M Sure, the point I was trying to make was that investment banks don't actually lend money to companies. They make their money by arranging the borrowing for a company on the financial markets. For that they are paid an income or fees.

K OK, so what about the building societies? What's their role? They sound like our savings banks in Germany.

M Well, in the old days, building societies were basically savings and mortgage banks which focused on the ordinary customer. But building societies, unlike banks, are mutuals, which means that the customers own the bank. Every customer who has an account becomes a member and owner of the society.

K Interesting. So, you are saying that the customers are really the owners of the building society. Is that right?

M Yes.

K OK. But I see from your slide that there are other financial service companies like supermarkets. What do they do? How can a supermarket be a bank?

M Well, that's a good question. But it's an obvious development. Supermarkets have a lot of cash plus a large customer base who use their local retail shops every week. So, in the last ten years, they have introduced financial services for individual customers.

K What about other types of bank? I heard that the UK had Internet banks which don't have any branches but offer banking services to individuals only on the net.

M Yes, you're right Karl. Internet banks have become bigger and bigger because it's so much cheaper for banks to manage services online. In fact, some of them have no branches to visit and only exist on the Internet. These virtual banks may well be the future of banking.

K OK, so if I have got it right, there are about six different types of banks in the UK.

M Yes, exactly.

Speaking

Exercise 1

1 ...like RBS or Barclays, also offer commercial banking so they provide both services. Is that clear?

2 OK. So if I understand you, the same bank can be both a commercial and a retail bank? Is that right?

3 But they also have large M&A departments, that is to say, mergers and acquisitions,...

4 Sorry, I didn't get that about fees. Could you go over it again?

5 Sure, the point I was trying to make was that investment banks don't actually lend money to companies.

6 So, you are saying that the customers are really the owners of the building society. Is that right?

7 OK, so if I have got it right, there are about six different types of banks in the UK.

Unit 8

Listening

I=Interviewer, F=Fund manager

I Looking at the markets today, the Dow Jones index was up 200 points and the Footsie also rose by 70 points. Why do stock markets move like this every day?

F Well, it's a good question. On the whole, stock markets move on fundamentals and these can be of two kinds: macro data and micro data.
Firstly, there is the macro data, that is to say, the inflation rate, interest rates, unemployment figures, ... those kinds of things. If, for example, the market begins to expect a fall in interest rates, like today, this is good news for share prices because it will be cheaper to borrow money in the future. So it is more interesting for companies to invest and for consumers to spend.

I Yes, but surely investors are also looking at particular companies?

F Yes, that's right. That is what we call the micro data: the things that affect a particular company, like a company's results, or news of a big contract win.
If a company announces good financial results, the analysts will probably upgrade the stock, thinking it will make more profit in the future. This will attract buyers, so the demand for the stock goes up, and the share price will increase. The share price is simply telling you how much money people think the company will make in the future.

I So we should be reading company announcements carefully.

F Yes, of course, but we should also remember that a company's share price may be affected by the news of a competitor in the same sector. This can cause analysts to change their view of a whole sector. But institutional investors are really looking more at the longer-term trend: is it going up or down?

I OK. But who are all these investors?

F Well, generally speaking there are two kinds of investors. There are the retail investors, that means ordinary people, like you and me, who are buying and selling stock. And then there are the professionals, what we call institutional investors. Obviously, in today's markets the institutional investors are the most important and account for most of the day's volume.

I You mentioned these institutional investors? Who exactly are they?

F In general, there are four different kinds of institutional investors: first, there are the pension funds, then there are hedge funds, the third kind is investment banks, and finally there are insurance companies. All of them manage money for clients and make the investment decisions for them. In recent years, the new players here have been the hedge funds who now account for about 30% of daily trading in London.

Pronunciation

Exercise 2

long	volume	show
ordinary	economy	short
stock	most	important
cause	shops	obvious
macro	whole	
rose	fall	

Exercise 3

1 Stock values have fallen following problems caused by slow growth.

2 Lower levels of domestic borrowing are important for the economy.

3 Obviously, when prices in the shops rose, this caused a drop in the volume of sales.

Speaking

Reuters today announced a complete ban on petrol driven cars in city centres.

This will have a significant impact on share prices this morning.

On the one hand, this will lead to an increase in the demand for electric vehicles.

Equally, this will probably result in an increase in the share price of car battery manufacturers.

On the other hand, this will certainly lead to a decrease in the sales of petrol car manufacturers.

At the same time, this will result in a decrease in the profits of city centre supermarkets because shoppers will not be able to use their cars in the centre.

As a result, we believe we should buy the shares of electric vehicle and battery manufacturers, and we should sell shares in car producers and supermarket retailers.

Is that clear? Are there any questions?

Unit 9

Listening

C=Carrie, S=Sandra, N=Nick, R=Rémy

C I see from the figures you sent me yesterday that we have a real problem with our cash flow next month. Quite simply, if we don't get some cash quickly, we won't be able to pay our suppliers.
Last month our costs for buying raw materials increased from $50,000 to $70,000. That meant an increase of $20,000 in one month.
At the same time, the money we received from our sales increased by only $12,000. That surprised me, I thought sales were going well. Why aren't we receiving more money? Sandra, you're responsible for financial control. What's going wrong?

S You're perfectly right, Carrie. I'm afraid the problem is with the sales team. In the finance department, we're now having big problems with payment from customers because the sales team has offered customers longer credit periods. Sometimes they've increased from 30 days to 60 days. This means the cash is no longer coming in. Unless we reduce the credit period, we are going to have real cash flow problems. This, of course, is against all our company policy on credit terms.

C We need an explanation. Nick, what's going on in your sales department?

N Well, I think my sales team has done a great job. If you remember I said at the time that the new sales targets you gave us for this quarter were very ambitious. In order to meet these targets, they had to offer the same credit terms as our competitors. Sometimes that meant doubling the credit period to 60 days in order to win the contracts.
I don't think you can blame us. In my view, the real problem is not the credit period but the sharp increase in our purchasing costs.

C What's your reaction to this, Rémy?

R Well, I'm sorry but I don't think it is anything to do with us in the purchasing department. As you know, with the launch of our new product line we had to increase our production by 20%. Obviously, this meant buying components and raw materials quickly. Our costs have gone up because we had to buy the stock quickly. If we didn't have to get the stock quickly, we wouldn't have to pay more. There is nothing wrong with our stock control systems.

N I'm sorry, I can't accept that, Rémy. Why is it that we are now paying 40% more for our raw materials than last month?

R Quite simple. If you want quick delivery, you have to pay. There is no other solution.

N Well, it seems to me we have a real problem. What do you suggest we do, Carrie?

C Well, I think the finance department must begin to chase these debts. It's not acceptable that customers take more than 60 days to pay us. If they paid us on 30 days credit, we wouldn't have a problem.
At the same time, I think we must talk to our suppliers. If we can reduce the price we are paying for materials, we'll be able to make some savings. Rémy, can you talk to them and see if we can get any better terms of payment? Unless we get this sorted out, we may have serious financial problems.

Unit 10

Listening

I am pleased to report another very good year for the company despite the difficult economic conditions in world markets. Overall, sales revenue increased from $500m to $700m and at the same time we reduced our costs by 2%. This was done by closing two offices and locating our sales and marketing departments in our new headquarters in Malaysia.

I'd like to begin with a review of our markets. In our main Asian markets, we won a number of new contracts in Abu Dhabi and Kuala Lumpur. Sales in these regions are expected to increase by 30% this year and the outlook is very encouraging.

During the year we also expanded successfully into the Chinese market where we focused on the consumer market for personal computers. Sales of our software in China rose to $13m. This represented an 80% increase on the previous year. The Chinese economy is expected to grow by 8% this year and we are likely to see new opportunities in the personal computer sector.

In Europe, by contrast, the outlook remains poor in the short term. We are unlikely to see any increase in sales of our software for the next twelve months and sales are projected to decline by 6%. As a result we have cut our sales team and our marketing budget for the next year.

I'd now like to say something about our new products. During the year, the company launched several new products in the consumer market and we announced a new partnership with Microsoft to sell software for computer security. This market is expected to grow at a rate of 30% over the next five years as companies become more concerned about protecting their data.

We are pleased to announce that we won was the Goldshield award for the best new security software. At the same time, we were also given the Forbes magazine award for being one of the fastest growing companies in Asia.

Turning to acquisitions, in July we successfully bought Best Ticket, a company based in Hong Kong. This will allow us to sell our software for ticket reservation systems in the leisure market for music concerts and sports stadiums.

The company also raised money by issuing 2 million new shares at a price of 34 cents per share to raise $10m. This will give us the money to finance more acquisitions in the next year.

Looking ahead, we believe the outlook for our company remains bright. Although we are likely to see some weakness in Europe next year, we believe worldwide growth should increase sharply as a result of the high levels of government spending, especially in China.

Language Spot

Exercise 4

In Europe, by contrast, the outlook remains poor in the short term. We are unlikely to see any increase in sales of our software for the next twelve months and sales are projected to decline by 6%. As a result we have cut our sales team and our marketing budget for the next year.

This market is expected to grow at a rate of 30% over the next five years as…

Looking ahead, we believe the outlook for our company remains bright. Although we are likely to see some weakness in Europe next year, we believe worldwide growth should increase sharply as a result of the high levels of government spending, especially in China.

Unit 11

Listening

Thank you all for coming. In this opening meeting, I would like to explain the steps in the audit of your company so that your staff will know what to expect. As you know, when we do the audit, there will be three of us in the team – I think you have all met them by now – and we expect the audit to take about three weeks.

My team will start by defining the scope of the audit. All you will be required to do at this stage is to help us arrange interviews with your top management. When we have talked to your management about your business and its sector and looked at problems in previous audits of your company, we will make a plan and timetable for the audit. This will tell you what we will inspect and the methods we will use.

When we have defined this scope, we will begin to examine the accounting systems you use. This means we will check the figures you recorded in your financial accounts against the figures in your company's books and ledgers. So, at this stage, we will need to access your company's books, for example, the sales ledger, plus of course, the bank statements. Our main concern is to check that the accounts are accurate and to make sure that correct accounting standards have been used. This should take about a week.

In the next step, we will examine all the internal controls you have for recording information every day. For this purpose we will need to see the rule book you have for your staff which explains your systems. We can then check that the staff follow these rules in their daily work. Secondly, we will need to have a look at real documents, for example, the sales invoices you send to customers and the purchasing documents you use to record each purchase.

After that, we will need to visit your factory and offices to do substantive tests. This is when we make sure that all the assets that you show in your balance sheet really exist. So I'm afraid you will need to show us things like your machinery and of course the stocks you have. Hopefully, this will not cause too much trouble but we will also need to talk with some members of your staff during our visit.

When we have collected all this information we will discuss the results in our team and make a list of points we have found. The idea is to identify any errors and to help you to improve your systems in the future. We will put all this information into our first letter which we call: the letter to management.

When you have had time to study the letter, we will have meetings with your management to discuss your responses. So, you will need to make a plan of how you propose to change the systems to answer our questions.

When we have completed all these tasks, we will sign off the audit report and you will need to report the results to your shareholders in your company's annual report.

So, that's what happens from start to finish. In total, we expect the whole process to take about two months.

Is that clear for everyone? Are there any questions? No? Good. Well, that completes my presentation of the audit stages. Perhaps we could now move on and begin to discuss the timetable for all the steps.

Speaking

Exercise 1

Thank you all for coming. In this opening meeting, I would like to explain the steps in the audit of your company so that your staff will know what to expect. As you know, when we do the audit, there will be three of us in the team – I think you have all met them by now – and we expect the audit to take about three weeks.

Exercise 2

When we have completed all these tasks, we will sign off the audit report and you will need to report the results to your shareholders in your company's annual report.

So, that's what happens from start to finish. In total, we expect the whole process to take about two months.

Is that clear for everyone? Are there any questions? No? Good. Well, that completes my presentation of the audit stages. Perhaps we could now move on and begin to discuss the timetable for all the steps.

Unit 12

Listening

C = CEO, D = Donna

C So, how bad is it? I've only seen the pictures on the news. They looked terrible.

D Well, it's pretty bad, but it could have been much worse. The good news is that no one in the city was killed. The earthquake started at 4.30 a.m. on Saturday, so most people were asleep. If the earthquake had happened during the day, many more people would have been injured.

C And what's the situation with our hotels in Christchurch?

D Well, the first thing to say is that none of the guests or hotel staff were hurt.

C Thank goodness for that! That was my main concern. What about the hotels? Have you any idea of the damage to the buildings yet?

D Well, as you know, we have two hotels in Christchurch: one in the city centre and one at the airport. The airport hotel is outside the main earthquake zone and is operating normally. But I'm afraid the hotel in the city centre has suffered some damage and the guests have been moved out. The structural engineer has inspected the building. His report says the building is structurally safe, but we need to carry out some repairs before it can be reoccupied.

C I noticed that we have a limit on the property insurance for rebuilding and repair costs. Do you think it will cover all the costs?

D I don't expect a problem with the property insurance. It will all be covered by our all-risks policy which covers natural disasters like earthquakes, fire, or flooding.

C And do we have an estimate of the cost of repairs?

D I've been talking to the loss adjustor today and he's preparing a first estimate of the costs. At the moment he expects a claim of about seven hundred thousand New Zealand dollars for the property damage.

C What's that in US dollars?

D It's about five hundred thousand US dollars. But this might increase once he's done a more detailed inspection.

C How long will it take to repair?

D The engineers say it'll take up to three months to repair the hotel.

C And what happens to the guests in the meantime?

D Well, we have 155 guests at the moment. We've managed to transfer them all to the airport hotel or to other hotels in the city that are operating normally.

C That's good. What about our other bookings over the next three months? Won't we lose money while the city-centre hotel is closed?

D Yes, that might be a problem. But the good news is that our business interruption insurance covers us for the loss of business. We must now calculate how much income we expect to lose over the next three months and then we can make a claim.

C That's a good idea. I know you said that nobody was injured but what would happen if any of the guests decided to make a claim against us?

D Well, guests could only make a claim if they were able prove that the hotel was not safe, but we are covered against this risk by our public liability insurance.

C And the hotel staff?

D Again, the hotel staff could only make claims against us for injury at work if they were able to show that we hadn't followed all the health and safety regulations for employees. But we're very careful about safety and the hotel recently passed a safety inspection. Anyway, don't forget we have an employer's liability insurance for that kind of cost.

C OK. And what about medical costs?

D Yes, I've checked that. New Zealand has a public healthcare system so most of our hotel staff are covered by that. The hotel managers and senior staff are also covered by the private medical insurance that we introduced a few years ago. Our guests, on the other hand, will have to meet the cost of any medical care from their travel insurance.

Glossary

Vowels

iː	d**ea**l	ʊ	b**oo**k	aɪ	pr**i**vate
i	loyalt**y**	uː	**i**ssue	aʊ	dis**cou**nt
ɪ	l**i**st	u	stim**u**late	ɔɪ	empl**oy**
e	d**e**bt	ʌ	c**o**ver	ɪə	car**eer**
æ	t**a**x	ɜː	**ear**n	eə	sh**are**
ɑː	forec**a**st	ə	sect**or**	ʊə	sec**ure**
ɒ	c**o**st	eɪ	tr**ai**ning		
ɔː	sh**or**tage	əʊ	l**oa**n		

Consonants

p	**p**ay	f	pro**f**it	h	**h**ire
b	**b**ill	v	sa**v**e	m	**m**oney
t	**t**rade	θ	streng**th**	n	fu**n**d
d	**d**eal	ð	wi**th**draw	ŋ	meet**ing**
k	ban**k**	s	**s**tock	l	**l**end
g	**g**old	z	sale**s**	r	**r**evenue
tʃ	**ch**eque	ʃ	ca**sh**	j	**o**pinion
dʒ	**j**ob	ʒ	divi**si**on	w	**w**ork

accommodation /əˌkɒmə'deɪʃn/ *n* a place to live, work, or stay in

account (for) /ə'kaʊnt fə(r)/ *v* to represent an amount or proportion of something

accounting standards /ə'kaʊntɪŋ ˌstændədz/ *n* official rules that define the way in which amounts must be recorded in a company's financial records

accurate /'ækjərət/ *adj* correct in every detail; exact

acknowledge /ək'nɒlɪdʒ/ *v* **1** to admit that something is true **2** to inform somebody that you have received something that they sent to you such as a letter

advise /əd'vaɪz/ *v* to give somebody help and information on a subject that you know a lot about

agriculture /'ægrɪkʌltʃə(r)/ *n* the science or practice of farming

analyse /'ænəlaɪz/ *v* to examine something in detail, especially by separating it into its parts, in order to understand or explain it

analyst /'ænəlɪst/ *n* a person whose job involves examining information about particular companies, markets, etc. in order to judge their value

apologize (for) /ə'pɒlədʒaɪz fə(r)/ *v* to say that you are sorry for doing something wrong or causing a problem

apply (for) /ə'plaɪ fə(r)/ *v* to make a formal request, usually in writing, for something such as a job

appointment /ə'pɔɪntmənt/ *n* a formal arrangement to meet somebody at a particular time, especially for a business meeting

appreciate /ə'priːʃieɪt/ *v* **1** to be grateful for something that somebody has done; to welcome something **2** to understand that something is true

arrange /ə'reɪndʒ/ *v* to plan or organize something in advance

assets /'æsets/ *n* things of value that a person or company owns such as money, property, investments or a debt that is owed to it

back up /bæk 'ʌp/ *v* to make a copy of a computer file, program, etc. which can be used if the original one is lost or damaged

balance of trade /ˌbæləns əv 'treɪd/ *n* the difference in value between the imports and exports of a country

balance sheet /'bæləns ʃiːt/ *n* a written statement of a company's financial situation that lists its **assets** and its **liabilities**

be allowed to /bi ə'laʊd tə/ *v* to have permission to do something

billing /'bɪlɪŋ/ *n* the act of preparing and sending bills to customers

bleak /bliːk/ *adj* (of a situation) not encouraging or giving any reason to have hope

book /bʊk/ *v* **1** to reserve a room, seat, table, etc. for a particular date **2** to buy tickets for a flight, train journey, holiday, etc. in advance

bookkeeping /'bʊkiːpɪŋ/ *n* the activity of keeping an accurate record of the accounts of a business

boom /buːm/ *n* a period of rapid economic growth

borrow /ˈbɒrəʊ/ *v* to take money from a bank with the agreement that you will pay it back at a later time

bound to /ˈbaʊnd tə/ *adj* certain or likely to happen

branch /brɑːntʃ/ *n* a local office or store belonging to a large company such as a bank

brand /brænd/ *n* a name given to a product by the company that makes it, especially a trademark

break down /ˌbreɪk ˈdaʊn/ *v* to divide something into parts in order to analyse it or make it easier to do

briefing /ˈbriːfɪŋ/ *n* a meeting in which people are given instructions or information

bright /braɪt/ *adj* giving reason to believe that good things will happen; likely to be successful

budget /ˈbʌdʒɪt/ *n* the amount of money that is available to a person or an organization and a plan of how it will be spent over a period of time

bullish /ˈbʊlɪʃ/ *adj* connected with an increase in the price of shares or the expectation that this will happen

buoyant /ˈbɔɪənt/ *adj* (of a business, a market, demand, etc.) tending to increase or stay at a high level with a lot of financial success

business plan /ˈbɪznəs plæn/ *n* a formal statement of a company's aims and how it plans to achieve them, including a detailed description of the financial arrangements involved

candidate /ˈkændɪdət/ *n* a person who is applying for a job or position

capacity /kəˈpæsəti/ *n* the quantity of goods that a factory, machine, etc. can produce; the number of people that a company can provide a service to

career /kəˈrɪə(r)/ *n* the series of jobs that a person has in a particular area of work, usually involving more responsibility as time passes

cash flow /ˈkæʃ fləʊ/ *n* the movement of money into and out of a business, especially when considering the availability of cash to pay debts

cash machine / ATM /ˈkæʃ məˌʃiːn/ /ˌeɪ tiː ˈem/ *n* a machine in or outside a bank, from which you can get money after inserting your bank card

charge /tʃɑːrdʒ/ *v* to require payment for goods or services

circulate an agenda /ˌsɜːkjəleɪt ən əˈdʒendə/ *v* to send a list of items to be discussed at a meeting to all the people in a group

code /kəʊd/ *n* a set of moral principles or rules of behaviour that are generally accepted by society or a social group

commercial bank /kəˈmɜːʃl bæŋk/ *n* a bank that offers services to the general public but mainly deals with small companies in providing loans, etc.

compensation /ˌkɒmpenˈseɪʃn/ *n* something, especially money, that somebody gives you because they have hurt you, or damaged something that you own; the act of giving this to somebody

complaint /kəmˈpleɪnt/ *n* a statement in which somebody says that they are not satisfied with something

comply (with) /kəmˈplaɪ wɪð/ *v* to obey a rule, an order, etc.

consistency /kənˈsɪstənsi/ *n* the quality of always behaving in the same way or of having the same standards, opinions, etc.

contract /kənˈtrækt/ *v* to decrease in size

cool /kuːl/ *v* to make something less excited or enthusiastic; to reduce demand

corruption /kəˈrʌpʃn/ *n* dishonest or illegal behaviour, typically involving fraud or bribery (= the illegal act of giving a person in authority money to do something)

cost control /ˌkɒst kənˈtrəʊl/ *n* the process or method of making sure that the different parts of a company do not spend too much

cost of sales /ˈkɒst əv seɪlz/ *n* the total amount of money that a company spends on producing the goods that it sells, including the cost of **raw materials**

cover /ˈkʌvə(r)/ *n* protection that an insurance company provides against loss, damage, etc.

covering letter /ˌkʌvərɪŋ ˈletə(r)/ *n* a letter that you send with your CV when applying for a job, explaining why you are suitable for the job, etc.

crash /kræʃ/ *n* a sudden serious fall in the price of something such as shares; the occasion when a business or an economy fails: *the Wall Street Crash*

credit /ˈkredɪt/ *n* **1** an arrangement made with a shop, etc., to obtain goods before payment, based on the trust that you will pay later **2** money that you borrow from a bank

creditor /ˈkredɪtə(r)/ *n* a person or a company that somebody owes money to

current account /ˈkʌrənt əˌkaʊnt/ *n* a type of bank account that you can take money out of at any time

damage /ˈdæmɪdʒ/ *n* physical harm caused to something which makes it less attractive, useful, or valuable

deadline /ˈdedlaɪn/ *n* the latest time or date by which something must be done

deal with /ˈdiːl wɪð/ *v* **1** to do business with a particular person, company, or organization **2** to take appropriate action in a particular situation or when speaking to a client, customer, etc.

debt /det/ *n* **1** the situation of owing money **2** a sum of money that somebody owes

debtor /ˈdetə(r)/ *n* a person or a company that owes money

decline /dɪˈklaɪn/ *v* to become smaller, fewer, weaker, etc.; to decrease

decrease /dɪˈkriːs/ *v* to become smaller in size, number, etc.

delay /dɪˈleɪ/ *v* to not do something until a later time or to make something happen at a later time

delivery note /dɪˈlɪvəri nəʊt/ *n* a short form that you sign when something is delivered

demand /dɪˈmɑːnd/ *n* the desire of customers to buy or use a particular product, service, etc.

deposit account /dɪˈpɒzɪt əˌkaʊnt/ *n* a type of account at a bank that pays interest on money that is left in it

depression /dɪˈpreʃn/ *n* a period when there is little economic activity and many people are poor and without jobs: *the Great Depression*

developed economy /dɪˌveləpt ɪˈkɒnəmi/ *n* a country or region that has an advanced economic and social system with many industries

direct debit /dəˌrekt ˈdebɪt/ *n* an instruction to your bank to allow somebody else to take money from your account, especially in order to pay bills

dividend /ˈdɪvɪdend/ *n* an amount of the profits that a company pays to people who own shares in the company

division /dɪˈvɪʒn/ *n* a large and important section of a company with responsibility for a particular area of activity

downturn /ˈdaʊntɜːn/ *n* a fall in the amount of business that is done; a time when the economy becomes weaker

dramatically /drəˈmætɪkli/ *adv* suddenly, in a very great and often surprising way

earn /ɜːn/ *v* **1** to get money for work that you do
2 to get money as interest on money you lend, have in a bank, etc.

earnings /ˈɜːnɪŋz/ *n* the profit that a company makes

earthquake /ˈɜːθkweɪk/ *n* a sudden, violent shaking of the earth's surface

emerging economy /iˈmɜːdʒɪŋ ɪˌkɒnəmi/ *n* a country or region that has an economy that is growing and developing rapidly

equity trader /ˈekwəti treɪdə(r)/ *n* a person whose job is to buy and sell shares

ethical standards /ˌeθɪkl ˈstændədz/ *n* rules of behaviour that are morally acceptable

evaluate /ɪˈvæljueɪt/ *v* to form an opinion of the amount, value, or quality of something after thinking about it carefully

excess /ˈekses/ *n* the part of an insurance claim that a person has to pay while the insurance company pays the rest

exchange rate /ɪksˈtʃeɪndʒ reɪt/ *n* the relation in value between one currency and another

exclusion /ɪkˈskluːʒn/ *n* something that is not included in an insurance policy

excuse /ɪkˈskjuːs/ *n* a reason, either true or invented, that you give to explain or defend your behaviour

expenses /ɪkˈspensɪz/ *n* money that you spend as part of your job which your employer pays back to you later, for example the cost of travelling or entertaining clients

experience /ɪkˈspɪəriəns/ *v* to be affected by a particular situation

exposure /ɪkˈspəʊʒə(r)/ *n* the risk of losing money from a particular investment

external audit /ɪkˌstɜːnl ˈɔːdɪt/ *n* an examination of a company's financial accounts that is done by another company in order to check that they are true and correct

factoring /ˈfæktərɪŋ/ *n* a financial arrangement in which a company sells a debt that is owed to it at a reduced price to another company (= a factor) in order to receive cash immediately. The factor is then responsible for collecting the debt in full.

fall /fɔːl/ *v* to decrease in amount, number, etc.

file accounts /ˈfaɪl əˈkaʊnts/ *v* to present a record of a company's financial situation to a government organization so that it may be officially recorded

fill in /ˌfɪl ˈɪn/ *v* to complete a form, etc. by writing information on it

fixed costs /ˌfɪkst ˈkɒsts/ *n* the amount of money used to run a company that remains the same whatever quantity of goods is produced

flood /flʌd/ *n* a large amount of water covering an area that is usually dry

fluctuate /ˈflʌktʃueɪt/ *v* to change frequently in size, amount, etc.

forecast /ˈfɔːkɑːst/ *v* to say what you think will happen in the future based on information that you have now

fraud /frɔːd/ *n* the crime of cheating somebody in order to get money or goods illegally

gloomy /ˈgluːmi/ *adj* without much hope of success or happiness in the future

go bankrupt /ˌgəʊ ˈbæŋkrʌpt/ *v* to stop doing business because you have no money and are unable to pay your debts

go through /ˌgəʊ ˈθruː/ *v* to examine something carefully such as financial information

going concern /ˌgəʊɪŋ kənˈsɜːn/ *n* a business or an activity that is making a profit and is expected to continue to do well

graduate /ˈgrædʒuət/ *n* a person who has a university degree

grant /grɑːnt/ *n* a sum of money that is given by the government or by another organization to be used for a particular purpose

grim /grɪm/ *adj* unpleasant and depressing or worrying

gross domestic product (GDP) /ˌgrəʊs dəˌmestɪk ˈprɒdʌkt/ /ˌdʒiː diː ˈpiː/ *n* the total value of all the goods and services produced by a country in one year

grow /grəʊ/ *v* to increase in size, number, or quality over a period of time

guideline /ˈgaɪdlaɪn/ *n* a written instruction which tells you what you may or must do with a particular thing

heavy industry /ˌhevi ˈɪndəstri/ *n* industry that uses large machinery to produce metal, coal, vehicles, etc.

hedge fund /ˈhedʒ fʌnd/ *n* a type of investment company that tries to make profits by predicting market prices and using investment techniques that involve large sums of borrowed money

income statement / profit and loss account /ˈɪnkʌm ˌsteɪtmənt/ /ˌprɒfit ən ˈlɒs əkaʊnt/ *n* a list that shows the different amounts of money that a company has earned and spent during a particular period, and the total profit or loss that it has made

inconvenience /ˌɪnkənˈviːniəns/ *n* trouble or problems, which force you to do extra work or cause you difficulty

increase /ɪnˈkriːs/ *v* to become larger in amount, number, value, etc.

inflation /ɪnˈfleɪʃn/ *n* a general rise in prices, resulting in a fall in the value of money

inflow /ˈɪnfləʊ/ *n* the movement of money or **assets** into a business or a country; the amount of money or assets coming in

infrastructure /ˈɪnfrəstrʌktʃə(r)/ *n* the basic structures and facilities that are necessary for a country or an organization to operate such as buildings, transport, and power supplies

in-house /ˌɪnˈhaʊs/ *adj* existing or happening within a company or an organization

insist (on) /ɪnˈsɪst ɒn/ *v* to demand something and refuse to be persuaded to accept anything else

institutional investor /ɪnstɪˌtjuːʃənl ɪnˈvestə(r)/ *n* a company such as a pension fund, **hedge fund**, **investment bank**, or insurance company that invests large amounts of money on behalf of its clients; a person that works for such a company

insurance policy /ɪnˈʃʊərəns ˌpɒləsi/ *n* a written contract between a person and an insurance company

interest rates /ˈɪntrəst reɪts/ *n* the percentage that a bank charges in interest when you borrow money or which it pays when you save money

investigate /ɪnˈvestɪgeɪt/ *v* to find out information and facts about a subject or problem by study or research

investment bank /ɪnˈvestmənt bæŋk/ *n* a bank that deals with large businesses, especially in helping with the sale of shares and bonds

involve /ɪnˈvɒlv/ *v* to have or include something as an important or necessary part

IPO (initial public offering) /ˌaɪ piː ˈəʊ/ /ɪˈnɪʃl ˈpʌblɪk ˈɒfərɪŋ/ *n* the act of a company selling its own shares on the stock market for the first time

issue shares /ˈɪʃuː ˈʃeəs/ *v* to offer new shares for sale to the public

job application /ˈdʒɒb æplɪˌkeɪʃn/ *n* a formal request, usually in writing, for a job

leasing /ˈliːsɪŋ/ *n* the process of arranging to use another person's property for a particular period of time in exchange for payment

ledger /ˈledʒə(r)/ *n* a book or computer file in which a bank, a business, etc. records the money it has paid and received

lend /lend/ *v* to give money to a person or organization on condition that they pay it back later

level off /ˌlevl ˈɒf/ *v* to remain at a steady level after rising or falling

liability /ˌlaɪəˈbɪləti/ *n* the amount of money that a person or company owes

light industry /laɪt ˈɪndəstri/ *n* industry that produces small objects such as things used in the house

list /lɪst/ *v* to make shares in a particular company available for trading on a stock exchange

loan officer /ˈləʊn ɒfɪsə(r)/ *n* a person who works in a bank, dealing with customers who want to borrow money

loan schedule /ˈləʊn ʃedjuːl/ *n* a timetable showing the conditions for repayment of a loan and the amount of interest to be paid each month

locate /ləʊˈkeɪt/ *v* to start a business in a particular place

logistics /ləˈdʒɪstɪks/ *n* the work of planning and organizing the supply of materials, goods, and staff

loss adjustor /ˈlɒs əˌdʒʌstə(r)/ *n* an insurance agent whose job is to calculate how much money should be paid to somebody when they make a claim for loss, damage, etc.

loyalty /ˈlɔɪəlti/ *n* the quality of being faithful in your support of a particular product or company

make a claim /meɪk ə ˈkleɪm/ *v* to ask for money from an insurance company because of loss or damage to something you own or personal injury

manufacturing /ˌmænjuˈfæktʃərɪŋ/ *n* the business or industry of producing goods in large quantities in factories, etc.

market capitalization /ˈmɑːkɪt ˌkæpɪtəlaɪˈzeɪʃn/ *n* the combined value of all the shares in a company, calculated by multiplying the total number of shares by their current price

mind /maɪnd/ *v* used to ask for permission to do something, or to ask somebody in a polite way to do something

mining /ˈmaɪnɪŋ/ *n* the process of getting coal, metal, etc. from under the ground; the industry involved in this

minutes of a meeting /ˈmɪnɪts əv ə ˈmiːtɪŋ/ *n* a summary or record of what is said or decided at a formal meeting

mortgage /ˈmɔːgɪdʒ/ *n* a legal agreement in which a bank lends you money to buy a house and you pay the money back over a certain number of years

motivation /ˌməʊtɪˈveɪʃn/ *n* the reason why somebody does something or behaves in a particular way

natural resources /ˌnætʃrəl rɪˈsɔːsɪz/ /-ˈzɔːsɪz/ *n* materials or substances such as wood, gas, or oil, that exist in a country's land or sea and which it can use to increase its **wealth**

negotiate /nɪˈgəʊʃieɪt/ *v* to try to reach an agreement by formal discussion

network /ˈnetwɜːk/ *n* a closely connected group of people, companies, etc. that work together, exchange information, etc.

no-claims bonus /ˌnəʊ ˈkleɪmz bəʊnəs/ *n* a reduction in the cost of your insurance because you did not claim any money from the insurance company in the previous year

numerate /ˈnjuːmərət/ *adj* having the ability to understand and work with numbers

offshore /ˌɒfˈʃɔː(r)/ *adj* happening or located in a foreign country in order to benefit from lower labour costs or more generous tax laws

operating profit /ˈɒpəreɪtɪŋ ˌprɒfɪt/ *n* the amount of money made by a company after you deduct the **cost of sales** and the **overheads**

operational risk /ɒpəˌreɪʃənl ˈrɪsk/ *n* potential problems connected with the general running of a company such as problems caused by staff, computer systems, etc.

organigram / organization structure
/ɔːˈɡænɪɡræm/ /ˌɔːɡənaɪˈzeɪʃn
strʌktʃə(r)/ *n* a diagram that shows
the structure of an organization
and the relationship between the
departments and jobs within it

outflow /ˈaʊtfləʊ/ *n* the movement of
money or **assets** out of a business or
a country; the amount of money or
assets going out

outlook /ˈaʊtlʊk/ *n* the probable future
for somebody or something; what is
likely to happen

outperform /ˌaʊtpəˈfɔːm/ *v* to achieve
better results than somebody or
something

outsource /ˈaʊtsɔːs/ *v* to arrange for
work to be done for your company by
another company

outstanding /aʊtˈstændɪŋ/ *adj* (of
payment, work, etc.) not yet paid,
done, etc.

overdraft /ˈəʊvədrɑːft/ *n* the amount of
money that you owe to a bank when
you have spent more money than is in
your bank account; an arrangement
that allows you to do this

overheads /ˈəʊvəhedz/ *n* regular costs
involved in running a business such as
rent, electricity, wages, etc.

owe /əʊ/ *v* to have an obligation to pay
somebody for something that you
have already received

own /əʊn/ *v* to have something that
belongs to you; to possess something

petty cash /ˌpeti ˈkæʃ/ *n* a small amount
of money kept in an office for small
payments

plunge /plʌndʒ/ *v* to decrease suddenly
and quickly

portfolio /pɔːtˈfəʊliəʊ/ *n* a set of
investments owned by a person or
organization

premium /ˈpriːmiəm/ *n* an amount of
money that you pay once or regularly
for an insurance policy

press release /ˈpres rɪˌliːs/ *n* an official
statement made to journalists about
a particular subject, usually for
publicity purposes

primary sector /ˈpraɪməri ˌsektə(r)/ *n*
the part of a country's economy that

produces **raw materials**, for example
industries such as **mining** and
agriculture

private sector /ˌpraɪvət ˈsektə(r)/ *n*
the part of a national economy that
is not under the direct control of the
government

privatize /ˈpraɪvətaɪz/ *v* to sell a
business or an industry owned by
the government so that it becomes a
private company

product line /ˈprɒdʌkt laɪn/ *n* a set of
products of a particular type that are
made or sold by a company

profits warning /ˈprɒfɪts ˌwɔːnɪŋ/ *n*
a statement by a company informing
people that its profits are lower than
expected

project /prəˈdʒekt/ *v* to estimate what
the size, cost, or amount of something
will be in the future based on what is
happening now

prospects /ˈprɒspekts/ *n* the chances of
being succesful

provider /prəˈvaɪdə(r)/ *n* a person or an
organization that supplies somebody
with a service they require

prudent /ˈpruːdnt/ *n* sensible and
careful when making decisions;
avoiding unnecessary risks

purchase /ˈpɜːtʃəs/ *v* to buy something

put together /ˌpʊt təˈɡeðə(r)/ *v*
to prepare a report, presentation,
etc. by gathering together different
information

qualified opinion /ˌkwɒlɪfaɪd əˈpɪnjən/
n used to show that an audit (= an
official examination of a company's
financial records) is limited or
incomplete because of a lack of
information

quote /kwəʊt/ *v* to give the price of a
particular share on a stock exchange

raw materials /ˌrɔː məˈtɪəriəlz/ *n* basic
materials that are used to make a
product

reach a peak /ˌriːtʃ ə ˈpiːk/ *phrase* to
arrive at a point at which something is
at its highest level

rebuild /ˌriːˈbɪld/ *v* to build or put
something together again

recession /rɪˈseʃn/ *n* a period of
temporary economic decline, during
which there is less trade and industrial
activity and unemployment increases

record /rɪˈkɔːd/ *v* to keep a permanent
account of financial details such as
sales, purchases, etc. by writing them
down, storing them in a computer, etc.

recovery /rɪˈkʌvəri/ *n* a return to a
normal state of strength or economic
activity

recruit /rɪˈkruːt/ *v* to hire new people to
work at a company, an organization, etc.

regulator /ˈreɡjuleɪtə(r)/ *n* a person or
an organization that officially controls
an area of business or industry and
makes sure that it is operating fairly

reinsurance /ˌriːɪnˈʃʊərəns/ *n* an
arrangement in which an insurance
company pays another insurance
company for insurance against large
claims made by its clients

reminder /rɪˈmaɪndə(r)/ *n* a letter or
note informing somebody that they
have not paid a bill, etc.

renovate /ˈrenəveɪt/ *v* to repair and
decorate an old or damaged building
so that it is in good condition again

respond /rɪˈspɒnd/ *v* to reply to
somebody

retail bank /ˈriːteɪl bæŋk/ *n* a bank with
branches in many places that offers
services to the general public

retail investor /ˈriːteɪl ɪnˌvestə(r)/ *n*
a person who buys a small number
of shares, bonds, etc. as a personal
investment rather than for a client

retailing /ˈriːteɪlɪŋ/ *n* the business of
selling goods to the public, usually
through shops / stores

return /rɪˈtɜːn/ *n* the amount of profit
that you get from an investment

revenue /ˈrevənjuː/ *n* the total amount
of money that a company receives
from selling its products or services

rights issue /ˈraɪts ɪʃuː/ *n* an occasion
when new shares are offered at a
reduced price to existing shareholders
so that they can maintain the
proportion of shares that they
currently own

rise /raɪz/ *v* to increase in amount or number

risk audit /ˈrɪsk ˌɔːdɪt/ *n* an analysis used to identify the different kinds of risk faced by a business

rocket /ˈrɒkɪt/ *v* to increase very quickly and suddenly

sales invoice /ˈseɪlz ɪnvɔɪs/ *n* a list showing what you must pay for goods that have been sold to you

save /seɪv/ *v* to keep money instead of spending it, especially by putting it in a bank account

scope /skəʊp/ *n* the range of things that a subject, an organization, an activity, etc. deals with

secondary sector /ˈsekəndri ˌsektə(r)/ *n* the part of a country's economy that makes products from the materials supplied to it by the **primary sector**, for example the **manufacturing** industry

secure /sɪˈkjʊə(r)/ *adj* not able to be harmed or damaged; safe

secured loan /sɪˈkjʊəd ləʊn/ *n* a loan agreement which gives the bank the right to take certain property from the borrower if the loan is not paid back

security /sɪˈkjʊərəti/ *n* a valuable item, such as a house, that you agree to give to a bank if you are unable to pay back a loan

serve /sɜːv/ *v* to help a customer or to sell them something in a shop, etc.

service sector /ˈsɜːvɪs sektə(r)/ *n* the part of a country's economy that is involved in providing services to customers. Also called the **tertiary sector**.

set up /ˌset ˈʌp/ *v* **1** to arrange for something to happen: *We've set up a meeting for next Thursday.* **2** to create or start something: *I set up a £2,000 overdraft.*

settle a claim /ˌsetl ə ˈkleɪm/ *v* (of an insurance company) to pay money to somebody who has claimed money for loss, damage, etc.

share / (esp. AmE) **stock** /ʃeə(r)/ /stɒk/ *n* one of the equal parts into which a company is divided and sold to the public

sharply /ˈʃɑːpli/ *adv* suddenly and by a large amount

shipment /ˈʃɪpmənt/ *n* the process of sending goods from one place to another

shortage /ˈʃɔːtɪdʒ/ *n* a situation in which something cannot be obtained in sufficient amounts

sign off (the accounts) /saɪn ˈɒf ði əˈkaʊnts/ *v* to give your formal approval to something by signing your name

skill /skɪl/ *n* the ability to do something well

slightly /ˈslaɪtli/ *adv* a little

slow down /ˌsləʊ ˈdaʊn/ *v* to become less active due to a fall in demand

sluggish /ˈslʌgɪʃ/ *adj* (of a market, demand, etc.) happening more slowly than is usual; not very active

slump /slʌmp/ *n* a sudden fall in sales, prices, demand, etc., especially one that lasts for a long time

spread /spred/ *v* to invest in different things so that if one thing fails you do not lose all your money: *You should try to spread your risks.*

standing order /ˌstændɪŋ ˈɔːdə(r)/ *n* an instruction to your bank to pay someone a fixed amount of money from your account on the same day each month/year, etc.

steadily /ˈstedɪli/ *adv* gradually and in an even and regular way

stimulate /ˈstɪmjuleɪt/ *v* to make something develop or become more active; to encourage something

stock market index *pl.* **indices** /ˈstɒk mɑːkɪt ˌɪndeks/ /ˈɪndɪsiːz/ *n* the average value of a particular set of important shares, which can be compared with the value in the past in order to judge whether share prices are rising or falling

stockbroking /ˈstɒkbrəʊkɪŋ/ *n* the business of buying and selling shares, bonds, etc. for your clients

stocks (of materials) /ˈstɒks əv məˈtɪəriəlz/ *n* supplies of material that are available for future use in producing goods

strategic risk /strəˌtiːdʒɪk ˈrɪsk/ *n* potential problems related to choosing the best objectives for a

company such as which products to make, which markets to sell to, etc.

strength /streŋθ/ *n* a good quality or ability that gives a person or thing an advantage

suffer /ˈsʌfə(r)/ *v* to be badly affected by something unpleasant

surge /sɜːdʒ/ *v* (of prices, profits, etc.) to suddenly increase in value

tailored products /ˈteɪləd prɒdʌkts/ *n* products that are made or adapted to suit the needs of a particular person

take out /ˌteɪk ˈaʊt/ *v* to remove money from your bank account

target /ˈtɑːgɪt/ *n* a result that a business or an organization tries to achieve

tax avoidance /ˈtæks əˌvɔɪdəns/ *n* ways of paying only the smallest amount of tax that you legally have to

team player /ˈtiːm pleɪə(r)/ *n* a person who is good at working with other people as a member of a team

terms (of a loan) /ˈtɜːms əv ə ləʊn/ *n* the conditions that people offer, demand, or accept when they make an agreement to lend or borrow money

tip /tɪp/ *n* a small piece of advice about something practical

training /ˈtreɪnɪŋ/ *n* the process of learning the skills that you need to do a job

transaction /trænˈzækʃn/ *n* a piece of business that is done between two people, especially an act of buying or selling

transfer /trænsˈfɜː(r)/ *v* to move money from one bank account to another

trend /trend/ *n* a general direction in which a situation is changing or developing

true and fair view /ˈtruː ən feə vjuː/ *n* a phrase used by auditors (= people who check a company's financial records) to show that the accounts are correct and give an accurate representation of its financial state

turnover /ˈtɜːnəʊvə(r)/ *n* the total amount of goods or services sold by a company during a particular period of time

underwrite /ˌʌndəˈraɪt/ *v* to agree to buy shares that are not bought by the public when new shares are offered for sale

unemployment rate /ˌʌnɪmˈplɔɪmənt ˌreɪt/ *n* the percentage of the population that is able to work but is without a job

unlikely /ʌnˈlaɪkli/ *adj* not likely to happen; not probable

unsecured loan /ʌnsɪˈkjʊəd ləʊn/ *n* a loan agreement in which there is no **security** (= a valuable item that the bank can take if the money is not paid back)

upturn /ˈʌptɜːn/ *n* a situation in which the economy, business activity, etc. improves or increases over a period of time

virus attack /ˈvaɪrəs əˌtæk/ *n* damage caused by a hidden computer program that is designed to cause faults or destroy data; an attack by a program like this

weakness /ˈwiːknəs/ *n* a disadvantage or fault in something that makes it less attractive

wealth /welθ/ *n* a large amount of money, property, etc. that a person or country owns; how much money, etc. a person or country has

withdraw /wɪðˈdrɔː/ *v* to take money out of a bank account

work out /ˌwɜːk ˈaʊt/ *v* to calculate something

workforce /ˈwɜːkfɔːs/ *n* all the people who are engaged in work or available for work in a particular country, company, or industry

working capital /ˈwɜːkɪŋ kæpɪtl/ *n* the money, stocks of goods, etc. that a company uses for its daily business activities, calculated as current **assets** minus current **liabilities**

write-off /ˈraɪt ɒf/ *n* a vehicle, etc. that has been so badly damaged in an accident that it is not worth spending money to repair it

Abbreviations

a.m.	ante meridian (in the morning)
AGM	annual general meeting
AIG	American International Group
ATM	automated teller machine
av	average
bn	billion
CEO	chief executive officer
CFO	chief financial officer
CV	curriculum vitae
DAX	Deutscher Aktien IndeX (German stock market index)
EGM	extraordinary general meeting
EU	European Union
FSA	Financial Services Authority
FTSE	Financial Times Stock Exchange index
GDP	gross domestic product
GNP	gross national product
HBOS	Halifax Bank of Scotland
HQ	headquarters
HSBC	Hong Kong and Shanghai Banking Corporation
IFSA	International Financial Services Association
IMF	International Monetary Fund
IPO	initial public offering
IT	information technology
KPMG	Klynveld Peat Marwick Goerdeler
m	million
M&A	mergers and acquisitions
MD	managing director
MICEX	Moscow Interbank Currency Exchange
NASDAQ	National Association of Securities Dealers Automated Quotations
OPEC	Organization of the Petroleum Exporting Countries
p.a.	per annum (per year)
p.m.	post meridian (in the afternoon / evening)
plc	public limited company
RPI/CPI	retail price index / consumer price index
UK	United Kingdom
UN	United Nations
USA	United States of America
USD	United States Dollars
VIP	very important person

Currencies

Country	Currency unit	ISO code
Argentina	Peso	ARS
Australia	Dollar	AUD
Bahrain	Dinar	BHD
Bangladesh	Taka	BDT
Bolivia	Boliviano	BOB
Brazil	Brazilian Real	BRL
Bulgaria	Lev	BGN
Cambodia	Riel	KHR
Canada	Dollar	CAD
Chile	Peso	CLP
China	Yuan/Renminbi	CNY
Colombia	Peso	COP
Costa Rica	Colón	CRC
Croatia	Kuna	HRK
Czech Republic	Korun	CZK
Denmark	Krone	DKK
Egypt	Pound	EGP
Estonia	Kroon	EEK
Euro Member Countries	Euro	EUR
Guatemala	Quetzal	GTQ
Hong Kong	Dollar	HKD
Hungary	Forint	HUF
India	Rupee	INR
Indonesia	Rupiah	IDR
Japan	Yen	JPY
Kazakhstan	Tenge	KZT
Korea, South	Won	KRW

Country	Currency unit	ISO code
Latvia	Lats	LVL
Lithuania	Litas	LTL
Malaysia	Ringgit	MYR
Mexico	Peso	MXN
Morocco	Dirham	MAD
Nigeria	Naira	NGN
New Zealand	Dollar	NZD
Norway	Krone	NOK
Pakistan	Rupee	PKR
Peru	Nuevo Sol	PEN
Philippines	Peso	PHP
Poland	Zloty	PLN
Russia	Ruble	RUB
Saudi Arabia	Riyal	SAR
Serbia	Dinar	RSD
Singapore	Dollar	SGD
South Africa	Rand	ZAR
Sweden	Krona	SEK
Switzerland	Franc	CHF
Taiwan	New Taiwan Dollar	TWD
Thailand	Baht	THB
Turkey	Lira	TRY
Ukraine	Hryvnia	UAH
United Arab Emirates	Dirham	AED
United Kingdom	Pound	GBP
United States of America	Dollar	USD
Vietnam	Dong	VND

OXFORD
UNIVERSITY PRESS

Great Clarendon Street, Oxford OX2 6DP

Oxford University Press is a department of the University of Oxford.
It furthers the University's objective of excellence in research, scholarship,
and education by publishing worldwide in

Oxford New York

Auckland Cape Town Dar es Salaam Hong Kong Karachi
Kuala Lumpur Madrid Melbourne Mexico City Nairobi
New Delhi Shanghai Taipei Toronto

With offices in

Argentina Austria Brazil Chile Czech Republic France Greece
Guatemala Hungary Italy Japan Poland Portugal Singapore
South Korea Switzerland Thailand Turkey Ukraine Vietnam

OXFORD and OXFORD ENGLISH are registered trade marks of
Oxford University Press in the UK and in certain other countries

ISBN: 978 0 19 456993 4

Printed in China

This book is printed on paper from certified and well-managed sources.

ACKNOWLEDGEMENTS

*The author and publisher would like to thank the following people who assisted in the
development of this title:* Julie Butters, Paul Cooper, Jake Erlich, Andrew Frost, Dita
Galova, Jason Harman, Cindy Hauert, Melanie Johnson, Amy Jost, Peter Keevil, Jana
Kyselová.

Special thanks are also due to: Monique Carr for her long patience and ideas during the
writing, Anna Gunn (editor), Ben Francis (editor; author: Glossary, Website), and
Eileen Flannigan (author: Grammar Reference)

Illustrations by: Rob Hancock pp.4 (world map), 28 (graph), 29 (vocab exercise),
30, 36 (graph), 68 (world map), 70 (bar chart), 89, 109, 117, 143 (currencies); Bill
Ledger pp.10, 16 (Who's more in debt), 19, 29, 43, 57, 64 (Professional skills),
71 (Professional skills), 81 (Professional skills), 82, 99, 101.

We would also like to thank the following for permission to reproduce the following photographs:
Alamy Images pp.4 (Businesswoman/Andres Rodriguez), 12 (House For Sale sign/
Richard Levine), 12 (ATM machine/Michael Dwyer), 12 (Credit cards/Chris Howes/
Wild Places Photography), 14 (Bank signs/Andrew Butterton), 23 (Businesswoman/
Golden Pixels LLC), 44 (Steelworks/Jeff Morgan 04), 44 (Food processing factory/
David R. Frazier Photolibrary, Inc.), 44 (Car factory/imagebroker), 48 (Car assembly
line/Michael Dunlea), 67 (Villa with pool/PCL), 74 (Bull and bear statues/Elsen
Reiner/WoodyStock), 95 (Ernst & Young sign/Andrew Holt), 100 (Valuables on
display in car/Justin Kase z03z), 100 (Baggage reclaim/ACE STOCK LIMITED),
118 (Clothes shop/Alistair Heap); Corbis pp.4 (Businesswoman with arms crossed/
Tony Mataxas/Asia Images), 6 (New York Stock Exchange/William Manning),
13 (Businessman working in office//Comet/Helen King), 24 (Infosys's campus at
the Global Education Centre/JAGADEESH NV/epa), 25 (Businesswoman working in
office/Ivy/Helen King), 33 (The Baiterek Tower/sadat/Xinhua Press), 33 (Temirtau
and steel plant/SHAMIL ZHUMATOV/Reuters), 35 (Confident office worker/C.
Devan), 48 (Electronic book factory/Adrian Bradshaw/epa), 50 (Frankfurt,
Germany/Guenther Rossenbach), 64 (Confident businesswoman/Mark Adams),
68 (Singapore stock market/Steve Raymer), 72 (Stockbroker in New York/Ed Kashi),
79 (Serious businesswoman/Peter M. Fisher), 80 (Plastic bottles in factory/Patrice
Latron), 80 (Cheese factory/Adam Woolfitt), 84 (Business meeting/Randy Faris),
86 (Smiling businesswoman/Holger Scheibe), 91 (Hong Kong at night/Bob Sacha),
92 (Businessman sitting in waiting area/Mark Seelan), 93 (Warehouse inventory/
Chuck Savage), 97 (Gambian woman/Philippe Lissac/Godong), 102 (Currency
exchange board/Rudy Sulgan), 104 (Earthquake damage/David Alexander/epa),

107 (Lloyd's of London Offices/Robert Wallis); Getty Images pp.4 (Businessman at
company meeting/Ben Bloom/Stone), 4 (Businessman/Ron Krisel/Stone), 6 (Stock
broker/David Silverman), 9 (Manhattan, New York/Michael S. Yamashita/National
Geographic), 9 (Businesswoman smiling/Brand New Images/Stone), 12 (Bank clerk
with customers/AFP), 12 (Flooded house/AFP), 12 (Zipcar logo on vehicle/Bloomberg
via Getty Images), 20 (Supermarket shopping/Uppercut Images), 28 (Currency
rate board/AFP), 28 (Job centre queue/Oli Scarff), 33 (Construction site/Jon Spaull/
Axiom Photographic Agency), 34 (Men on horseback/Aaron Mccoy/Robert Harding
World Imagery), 34 (Rice farmer/Mark Lewis/Stone), 34 (Marrakech food stall/
Sergio Pitamitz/Photographer's Choice), 34 (The Shanghai World Financial Center/
EIGHTFISH/Stone), 36 (Construction cranes/Just One Film/The Image Bank),
36 (Padlocked gate/Bill Pierce/Time & Life Pictures), 44 (Wheat field/David Wile/
First Light), 44 (Coal mining/Christopher Herwig/Aurora), 44 (Times Square at night/
Christian Beirle González/Flickr), 46 (The Gutenberg memorial/Bloomberg via
Getty Images), 47 (Bank of China/Bloomberg via Getty Images), 50 (Businessman/
Michael Poehlman/The Image Bank), 55 (Businesswoman at laptop/Yukmin/Asia
Images), 66 (Brokers at Frankfurt's stock exchange/AFP/DDP), 76 (Warehouse/Chris
Sattlberger/The Image Bank), 80 (CBD and Esplanade Theaters/kokoroimages.
com/Flickr), 80 (Tobacco factory/Panoramic Images), 84 (Apple CEO Steve Jobs),
84 (Seehofer Visits Insolvent Rosenthal Porcelain Maker), 87 (Marks & Spencer
photocall), 87 (Speaker at podium/Bruce Ayres/Stone), 93 (Businesswoman using
computer/Hitoshi Nishimura), 93 (Delivery man with customer/Jupiterimages),
100 (Doctor with hospital patient/Jupiter Images), 100 (Family in tent/Jupiter
Images), 106 (Woman smiling at work/Brand New Images/Stone), 108 (Business
meeting/Erik Dreyer); Kobal Collection p.103 (Safety First/Hal Roach/Pathe
Exchange); Oxford University Press pp.16 (Woman shopping/Corbis), 44 (Woman
shopping/Corbis), 100 (Pick pocket/face to face Bildagentur GmbH); Photolibrary
pp.4 (Portrait of businesswoman/Cultura), 4 (Businessman/Steve Hix/Somos
Images), 8 (Woman in office at night/White), 9 (Student with books in library/
arabianEye), 14 (Business interview/Jose Inc/Blend Images), 28 (Fruit market/Michael
Sedam), 39 (Businessman/Eyecandy Images), 42 (Businesswoman/Radius Images),
42 (Businessman/Image100), 42 (Female office worker/Red Chopsticks/Glow Asia),
42 (Businessman smiling/Purestock), 42 (Businesswoman holding folders/Fancy),
44 (Garment factory/Rob Crandall), 44 (Reflection in car mirror/Chris Cheadle/
All Canada Photos), 60 (Spanish flag/White), 78 (Bills past due/Stockbroker),
97 (Senegal river/Herve Gyssels/Photononstop), 100 (Damaged car/Phillip Hayson);
Press Association Images pp.38 (Job hunters outside Newark City Hall, 1935/
AP), 84 (Electronics trade fair/Gero Breloer/AP), 100 (Flooded house/Jay Felsberg/
AP/Press Association Images/The News Herald), 106 (Coffee taster/Costa Coffee/
PA Archives); PunchStock pp.9 (Confident businessman/Digital Vision), 12 (Man
with bills and laptop/Image Source); Report Digital pp.36 (Shop window/Justin
Tallis), 36 (Chinese workers on factory line/Jess Hurd/reportdigital.co.uk); Reuters
Pictures p.40 (Bangladeshi women stitch bed cover/Rafiquar Rhaman); Rex Features
pp.71 (Warren Buffett/Norm Betts), 73 (Nick Leeson/Action Press); Science Photo
Library p.44 (Oil platform/Richard Folwell).

Cover: Getty Images (Blend Images/Klaus Tledge).

*The author and publisher are grateful to those who have given permission to reproduce the
following extracts and adaptations of copyright material:* p.31 Information taken from
'Family Spending: 2007 Edition', a National Statistics Publication, Ed Dunn (Editor).
Reproduced under the terms of the Click-Use Licence; p.38 From 'Factsheet: The IMF
at a Glance', 23 March 2010. Reproduced by kind permission of the International
Monetary Fund; p.39 Fictitious interview based on information taken from 'Who
is the IMF? The faces behind IMF functions'. Reproduced by kind permission of
the International Monetary Fund; p.53 Adapted extracts from 'Future Banking:
Profitable Growth Again' by Dr Patrick Dixon from www.globalchange.com.
Reproduced by kind permission; p.54 Adapted extracts from 'HBOS merger talk
crowns historic week' by Nick Louth, 17 September 2008. Reproduced by kind
permission; p.56 Adapted extracts from 'Mergers and Acquisitions: Why They Can
Fail'. Copyright 2010 Forbes Media LLC. 67171-10ymo. Reproduced by permission;
p.58 Adapted extracts from 'Mutual Funds Are Awesome - Except When They're
Not'. Copyright 2010 Forbes Media LLC. 67171-10ymo. Reproduced by permission;
p.70 Graph: 'Beneficial Ownership of UK shares: end-2008' published on 27 January
2010 by Office for National Statistics UK. Reproduced under the terms of the Click-
Use Licence; p.95 Extracts from 'Two men. One vision' from 'About us – Our history'
from www.ey.com. Reproduced by kind permission of Ernst & Young LLP; p.98
Article reprinted from 'KPMG Values' from www.kpmgcareers.co.uk Copyright
© 2010 KPMG LLP, a UK limited liability partnership, is a subsidiary of KPMG
Europe LLP and a member firm of the KPMG network of independent member
firms affiliated with KPMG International Cooperative, a Swiss entity. Reprinted
with permission of KPMG LLP (UK). All Rights Reserved. For additional news and
information, please access KPMG LLP's website www.kpmg.co.uk; p.106 Text and
information from www.lloyds.com have been reproduced with the kind permission
of Lloyd's of London.

Sources: p.16 www.fawcettsociety.com; p.33 www.ft.com; p.78 www.bacs.co.uk; p.81
www.doingbusiness.org; p.87 www.marksandspencer.com; p.104 www.rms.com;
p.110 www.wikipedia.com

*Although every effort has been made to trace and contact copyright holders before publication,
this has not been possible in some cases. We apologize for any apparent infringement of
copyright and if notified, the publisher will be pleased to rectify any errors or omissions at the
earliest opportunity.*